WAGE DETERMINATION
UNDER TRADE UNIONS

John T. Dunlop

HARVARD UNIVERSITY

REPRINTS OF ECONOMIC CLASSICS

AUGUSTUS M. KELLEY · PUBLISHERS
NEW YORK · 1966

Original edition 1944

Reprinted 1966 by arrangement with
John T. Dunlop

LIBRARY OF CONGRESS CATALOGUE CARD NUMBER
50-58147

PRINTED IN THE UNITED STATES OF AMERICA
by SENTRY PRESS, NEW YORK, N. Y. 10019

PREFACE TO 1950 EDITION

In recent years it has become popular, almost a fad, to declare that wage determination under collective bargaining is essentially a political process. Labor unions are political institutions and wage rates reflect internal political necessities rather than "sound economic principles."[1] It is futile in this view to attempt to explain union wage policy in economically rational terms.[2]

The systematic study of the decision-making process affecting wage rates in labor unions as well as managements is certainly to be encouraged. It is not to be denied that the institutions of the collective bargaining process have some independent effect on wage rates. Indeed, this volume emphasizes that the wage policies of labor unions may be used for a variety of purposes other than the maximization of the income of their members. (pp. 46-50.) But the thesis must be rejected that wage determination under collective bargaining is to be explained most fundamentally or fruitfully in terms of a political process.

(a) The emphasis upon political wage setting tends to reflect the experience of those newer unions in which there have been major factional struggles. But these situations are not characteristic of more mature collective bargaining relations. There is a full spectrum of union experience ranging from stable monolithic organizations to those on the verge of collapse or fission as a consequence of intense internal struggle. While explanations of wage determination need to encompass the full range of experience, the political emphasis in wage setting has relied unduly upon one end of the spectrum.

(b) The tendency to see political elements as dominant in wage determination represents a preoccupation with the very short run to the exclusion of more persistent factors. There can only be commendation for serious efforts to analyze the internal day-to-day workings of labor and management organizations. Every skilled

---

[1]Arthur M. Ross, *Trade Union Wage Policy*, (Berkeley, University of California Press, 1948), pp. 21-74; Charles E. Lindblom, *Unions and Capitalism*, (New Haven, Yale University Press, 1949); Peter F. Drucker, *The New Society, The Anatomy of Industrial Order*, (New York, Harper and Brothers, 1949), pp. 75-145. See, however, G. P. Schultz and C. A. Myers, "Union Wage Decisions and Employment," *American Economic Review*, June 1950, pp. 362-80.

[2]Peter F. Drucker, *Loc. cit.*, p. 80, n. 1.

mediator and arbitrator has insights into the decision-making processes of both which need to be systematized. But the more pervasive and enduring patterns of wage movement have been the customary subject matter of wage theory. The longer the view taken
of wage setting the less appropriate the emphasis upon internal
political considerations.

(c) The view that wage fixing under collective bargaining is
fundamentally to be examined in a political context reveals considerable ignorance of the habits of mind of labor leaders and the
intimacy of their knowledge of the technology and economic facts
of an industry. On the level of the national union, labor leaders
in my experience are generally as well informed as business executives on the basic characteristics and tendencies in an industry
and the economy. Frequently they are better informed, since they
must have the perspective of the national union as a whole representing the employees of a great many different companies. While
labor leaders are in part politicians with a constituency, wage setting involves very much more than union politics.

(d) The fundamental objection to the recent emphasis on political wage setting is that it has so concentrated attention upon one
aspect of the processes of decision-making inside unions and managements that it has neglected the stubborn facts of the external
world. Changes in prices, profits and employment in related
markets do tend to affect wage rates. While every encouragement
should be given to efforts to trace the relations between such ex-
terior developments and the decisions within unions and managements, the political slant has created the impression that political
considerations substantially determine wages, to the extent that
there can be no "economically rational" wage policy under collective bargaining.

There is no denying that wage determination under collective
bargaining is different from wage fixing under non-union conditions. But the difference is not as great on the record to date as has
been assumed.[3] Most of the same wage making forces operate
through the institutions of collective bargaining. The critical
question is how much difference do unions make? If this question
could be answered in precise quantitative terms, it still would be
necessary to separate the effect of collective bargaining on such
fundamental wage making forces as productivity and labor supply

---

[3]John T. Dunlop, Review of Lindblom's *Unions and Capitalism, American Economic
Review*, June 1950, pp. 463-68.

from its impact on wage rates directly as a consequence of independent political pressures. It is my strong conviction that in
the normal case of collective bargaining the independent effect
on wage rates of internal political considerations is not large.
There are no doubt cases, at one end of the spectrum, particularly
in the short run in new unions where rivalry and factionalism are
rampant, where the independent effect of political considerations
is even dominant. But the perspective of the full range of collective bargaining relations, in my judgment, reduces this factor to
relatively minor significance. It should not be used in any event
as the cornerstone of a theory of wage determination.

The present volume represented for the author the beginnings
of an approach to a theory of wages under collective bargaining
built upon more general and realistic views of wage bargaining.
From this start the following developments are suggested:

(1) Every theory of wages is under the obligation of making
explicit the questions it seeks to answer and to identify those features of observed behavior it seeks to explain. A beginning may be
made with two questions: What determines the general level of
wage rates and the structure of wages? What are the consequences
of a change in the general level and the structure of wage rates?
Both these questions make a distinction between the general level
and the structure of wage rates corresponding roughly to the distinction between the problems of a firm or single market and the
total economy. While the inter-relations between the two need to
be developed, the distinction is a fruitful line of demarcation in
the organization of factors influencing wage rates or the consequences flowing from wage changes.

(2) Perhaps the single most significant problem in the field of
wage theory today is whether two separate questions are posed —
one on the determination of wages and the other on the consequences of wage movements — or whether there can be developed
a single theoretical system which encompasses both problems. The
classical theory of the firm and the total system combined both.
But there has been a growing tendency in economic literature to
separate these questions, to treat the money wage rate structure
and level as somehow determined outside the economic system and
to consider within the framework of economic analysis only the
consequences of various given wage levels and wage structures.
Thus marginal productivity is said to measure but not to determine particular wage rates, and the Keynesian system operated

with rigid money wage rates.[4] Despite these developments, a theory of wages is to be preferred which permits both an explanation of wage setting and an analysis of the consequences of wage movements within one framework.

(3) All wage structures—intra-plant, inter-plant, or inter-industry—contain a limited number of "key" rates on which wage making forces tend to concentrate. Around any key rate will be others which are related by technology or work relations, in the case of intra-plant wage relations, or related by product market competition or locality ties in the case of inter-firm wage relations. These clusters of wage rates tend to move together. Thus, factors determining changes in the general level of wage rates tend to be channeled through a limited number of nationally significant bargains to which a large proportion of other rates are more or less directly tied.

(4) The determination of particular wages under collective bargaining can be fruitfully approached, for the limited number of key bargains, in terms of maximizing behavior on the part of unions and companies. On the side of the union it is important to designate the "members" whose income the union seeks to maximize. (pp. 34-44).

(5) Any analysis of the consequences of wage rate changes in the individual firm must extend the number of variables beyond the classic wage-employment relation. A more generalized view would permit wage rate changes to be reflected in price, the type of product, technology, as well as in employment. Wage changes may be reflected in any one of these directions depending upon type of competitive conditions and the effects of wage changes on technological processes. A more generalized theory of the individual firm is required to analyze the consequences of particular wage changes just as a general theory was required to reappraise the consequences of a general wage change on the total system.

John T. Dunlop

Cambridge, Mass.
July 15, 1950.

---

[4] See, Wassily Leontief, "Postulates: Keynes' *General Theory* and the Classicists" in *The New Economics* (New York, Alfred A. Knopf, 1947), Seymour E. Harris, Ed., pp. 232-42.

PREFACE

Professor Slichter has suggested that collective bargaining has two principal aspects; it is both a system of "industrial jurisprudence" and a method of setting the price of labor services. *Union Policies and Industrial Management* constitutes a landmark, largely focused toward the first range of problems. The present study is to be approached as a tentative reconnaissance of some of the more prominent and obvious features of the pricing terrain. Despite the tremendous expansion in collective bargaining in recent years, systematic inquiry has scarcely begun to explore in analytical terms or through detailed empirical investigation the luxuriant field of wage determination under collective bargaining.

The future may be reasonably expected to require careful study of this area by economists, formulators of public policy under any guise, trade unionists and business executives alike. A deep-seated aspiration behind the following pages is to call attention to some of the more intriguing problems that warrant intensive work; the study is presented in the hope that both the possibilities and responsibilities for serious inquiry may be widely accepted.

Many friends and colleagues have assisted in the formulation of the argument and in the presentation of the findings. It is a pleasure to express sincere gratitude to Mr. James Healy for careful work on the empirical aspects of trade-union wage policy (Chapters IV and VI). Mr. Herbert Woolley initially formulated the argument of Chapter VIII on labor's share in national income and directed the tedious and extensive statistical work that lies behind the summary of findings. His keen interest in the analytical problems provided many hours of stimulating and fruitful discussion. Mr. Paul Baran's wide experience and penetrating criticism helped to formulate the position advanced in the final chapter. The Harvard University Committee on Research in the Social Sciences graciously provided a grant for statistical computation and the assembly and analysis of data. Miss Virginia Caughlin efficiently typed the manuscript.

The pages which follow have materially profited from a careful and critical reading by Professor Sumner H. Slichter. It is a sincere regret that the full implications of all his suggestions could not have been developed. Naturally, his generosity cannot be used to incriminate him. The analysis of Chapter V was developed with Professor Benjamin Higgins and originally appeared in the *Journal of Political Economy*. Some modification has been introduced; the argument is presented here with the permission of both Professor Higgins and the editors of the journal. Professor Wassily Leontief and Mr. John Lintner have kindly read several chapters of the manuscript.

The deepest sense of gratitude must go to two groups, too large to enumerate individually: (1) the distinguished staffs and stimulating students of five universities in this country and England in whose intellectual atmosphere the following ideas took form, and (2) the numerous trade-union leaders, business executives, and government officials who have provided a constant brake to unwarranted and untested generality and a constant reminder of the complexity of human behavior. Special mention must be made of the Harvard Trade Union Fellows who have cut across both these groups.

These pages are dedicated to F. S. N. who insisted that Economics presented both intriguing puzzles and compelling problems.

CONTENTS

LIST OF TABLES

LIST OF CHARTS

WAGE DETERMINATION UNDER TRADE UNIONS

All the world over and at all times there have been practical men, absorbed in ":irreducible and stubborn facts:" all the world over and at all times there have been men of philosophic temperament who have been absorbed in the weaving of general principles. It is the union of passionate interest in the detailed facts with equal devotion to abstract generalization which forms the novelty in our present society. — Alfred North Whitehead, *Science and the Modern World*, pages 3–4.

CHAPTER I. INTRODUCTION

The catastrophe of underemployment in the thirties provided endless copy for model builders and scapegoat labelers alike. These talents are never entirely divorced. In his provocative funeral oration [1] on Mr. Hansen's *Fiscal Policy*,[2] Mr. Simons points the accusing finger at labor policy of government and at wage policies of trade unions.

Government, long hostile to other monopolies, suddenly sponsored and promoted widespread organization of labor monopolies, which democracy cannot endure, cannot control without destroying, and perhaps cannot destroy without destroying itself. There is evidently no means of disciplining such minorities, once strongly organized, in conformity with the public interest or even of disciplining particular organized groups in conformity with their own common interests.[3]

He interprets the past decade largely in terms of a contest between "monetary authority seeking to raise employment and trade unions seeking to raise wage rates"; he foresees in "voluntary association" a specter of "syndicalism whose norm is chaos."

The present study is not primarily concerned with appraising the importance of wage rates in the unemployment of the thirties; rather is the central emphasis the examination of the wage policies of trade unions. Mr. Simons' judgments of the past and his fears for the future hinge on the premise that trade unions behave in a particular way. But how does one know that trade unions have exacted every advantage to increase rates at the expense of employment? How have they endeavored to behave? Has one considered whether the wage movements of the thirties were a phase of organizing activity or the product of mature voluntary associations in collective bargaining? Is not the immaturity of American enter-

[1] Henry C. Simons, "Hansen 'on Fiscal Policy," *Journal of Political Economy*, April, 1942, L, p. 162.
[2] Alvin H. Hansen, *Fiscal Policy and Business Cycles*, W. W. Norton & Company, Inc., New York, 1941.
[3] *Op. cit.*, p. 171.

3

prises in industrial relations of real importance when one contemplates many of the wage increases of 1936–1937 and the "Weir cycle" of 1941? While these questions are not formulated for systematic enquiry, they do suggest the need for study of the pricing activities of trade unions in the labor market. The process of wage determination under trade unionism thus constitutes the main focus of the following pages.

Any such field of investigation not only emerges from particular intellectual and emotional perspectives but also develops others. The present chapter is devoted to these orientations. It is not intended as an exercise in introspection so much as a framework that may both illuminate the main stream of thought and indicate some of the wider applications and inferences of this study.

(1) Trade unions have been too easily relegated by economists to a part of the profession often referred to without affection as "labor economists." The main stream of economic thought has consequently suffered from presuming free and "automatic" markets and then regarding trade unions as unfortunate intrusions which complicate the models! One of the basic perspectives from which this study proceeds is that economists would have much more penetrating insight into the functioning of economic processes today, and any we are likely to have for some time, if they were more familiar with the operation of trade unions as organizations. This subject matter cannot be left any longer merely to institutional and historical methods. Just as the process of product-price formation has been illuminated by theoretical analysis of discrimination, small numbers, price leadership, and flexible plant, so organized labor markets represent a field of important theoretical enquiry. A systematic knowledge of the wage-fixing features of collective bargaining is indispensable if this analytical work is to be more than gymnastics.

(2) The trade union is clearly a decision-making unit. Since analytical models have been devised to explain the pricing and output decisions of business enterprises, Chap. III attempts to construct corresponding models of trade unions which may assist in understanding wage-rate determinations. An economic theory of a trade union requires that the organization be assumed to maximize (or minimize) something. Although not the only pos-

sible objective, maximization of the wage bill may be regarded as the standard case. But the model is not so easily constructed since the crucial question *Whose wage bill?* remains. Now, this type of approach to the problems of a trade union is strewn with pitfalls. The fallacy of misplaced concreteness which would treat the model as the real world must be avoided. Chapter IV will treat some of the many other considerations in collective bargaining that impinge on wage determination. Another pitfall would regard any economic models of trade unions as excessive rationalism. But this observer is persuaded that models of trade unions abstract no further from the richness and complexity of behavior than does the ordinary analysis of the enterprise. Regardless of subject matter, economic models in terms of the variables of economic theory can only be one approximation.

(3) One of the more dangerous habits of mind that economic theory may create is an imperialism that insists that all aspects of behavior, particularly any activity related to markets, can be explained by models with the usual economic variables. When a lack of correspondence between model and behavior is observed, the temptation arises to dismiss these discrepancies with such terms as "friction," "monopoly elements," "immobility," and "irrationality." In a certain sense, the procedure is unobjectionable; delimitation of a field of enquiry and the number of variables considered is quite proper. But the pile of discarded problems is not only large but yields high dividends to careful analysis.

A fundamental tenet of the following pages is that modes of behavior that are broader than economic theory contribute materially to the understanding of wage determination. While this is no place to develop a theory of social action, the complex ends of rational activity as well as symbolic conduct cannot be overlooked. In particular, wage rates may be a tool to achieve other ends than the maximum wage bill, and many features of the wage structure are only to be interpreted symbolically. To appraise wage policy of a trade union merely from the framework of analytical economics may be to misunderstand behavior completely. A basic perspective of these pages, therefore, is that wider analytical models than economic theory must be constructed for successful explanation of even market-oriented behavior.

(4) Another prejudice of this study is that within the market process much more attention must be directed toward speeds of reaction. Economics has examined the allocation of resources by the pricing mechanism without much concern with timing problems. Discussion must go beyond perfect and instantaneous adjustments in markets with large costs of movement, uncertainty, limited resources of most households, and aspects of behavior ordinarily excluded from economic models. Some of the "obstructions" to perfect markets may be removed but most are likely to persist; we must discover which difficulties are strategic in the sense of amenable to particular controls. When markets have been appraised from the standpoint of "frictions" that will likely persist (regardless of strategic policy), economists may be more interested in the relative effectiveness of administrative processes and the pricing mechanism in allocating resources. From this perspective, Chap. II makes a simple suggestion of technique that would direct more thinking toward the time configuration of responses to a change in the system. Chapter VII considers both the diverse media through which wage-rate changes are diffused and the typical patterns of variation in the cycle among sectors of the system.

(5) Another basic idea that underlies the following pages is that particular equilibrium techniques have created habits of mind in economists that have led them to overlook and misinterpret many aspects of market behavior. This is not to deny the usefulness of the method which looks at parts of the system rather than the whole; in fact, an attempt is made to extend the usefulness of this technique. Partial analysis has almost always meant a single market; the buyers and sellers that exchange a commodity or service (or cluster of each) are abstracted from the rest of the community. There are many problems, including the effects of a wage change, that involve a group of related markets. Impacts extend beyond the single labor market to related product and even to other factor markets. In a set of highly sensitive markets a local impact might be diffused through the system. The method of aggregates or simultaneous equations would be theoretically useful then. But in many cases there is only need for tracing the impacts of any change through several related markets; the change

exhausts its significant effects. Chapter V argues the importance of spotlighting a *cluster* of markets and provides a generalized technique of showing the relation of one market change upon another under varying types of competition in each market. Chapter VI reveals the importance of this theoretical position in interpreting phases of wage policy that have largely been neglected. Particular equilibrium techniques will be more useful when applied to a cluster of related markets rather than to a single market entirely isolated from any context in the system.

(6) A final conviction pervades the study, that the economic system we have in the next several generations will be critically influenced by the way in which collective bargaining operates, particularly as the prices of labor services are determined. This judgment may be discounted as understandable enthusiasm over the field of one's research. But contemplate some of the possible directions of movement: trade unions so strong as to translate each change in technology into higher wage rates rather than into employment; continuous warfare over rates only resolved by use of political power; syndicalist combinations of enterprises and unions by sectors where each combination attempts to secure a relatively more favorable price; bargaining over a wide area of problems between associations so matched in economic and political power in sufficiently wide units to be concerned with higher levels of national income. Through influences on wage rates and employment (for prices never respond instantaneously), collective bargaining will affect materially the rate and type of governmental participation in resource allocation. For governmental activities politically have depended largely upon the employment level the "private sector" has been able to maintain.

CHAPTER II. MARKET ORGANIZATION AND WAGE STRUCTURE

An exchange economy operates through a complex network of markets in which buyers and sellers come together to specify the terms upon which goods and services flow through the system. Resources are said to be allocated between enterprises by the market medium and directed within firms by administrative fiat. Mr. D. H. Robertson has suggested the phrase: "islands of conscious power in this ocean of unconscious cooperation, like lumps of butter coagulating in a pail of buttermilk."[1] But other organizations than the enterprise command the disposal of resources—households, nonprofit institutions, and governmental units. In household agrarian economies, for instance, little allocation is left to the market. The area of "milk surface" varies not merely, therefore, with the extent of integration but also with the importance of these other directive "lumps."

Economists have concentrated a good deal of attention on the operation of a single market; a single "synapse" in the total market network has been magnified for analysis. Market results in terms of prices, outputs, and products are to be explained. Under conditions of specified tastes and technology, three factors are determining: (a) the number of buyers and sellers clustered together, (b) the ease of entry and exit on the part of market participants,[2] and (c) the similarity between the "product" or group of "products" sold in one market and those in all other markets, as viewed by the parties to a transaction. The "character of competition" can be used to refer to these three conditions in a single market. The sample market is depicted as similar in form to a bourse. Approximately equal numbers of buyers and sellers circulate

[1] D. H. Robertson, *The Control of Industry*, Harcourt, Brace and Company, New York, 1923, p. 84.

[2] Fritz Machlup, "Competition, Pliopoly, and Profit, Part I," *Economica*, New Series, February, 1942, IX, pp. 1–23.

8

among each other; every market participant [3] knows each bid and offer or the terms of each settled transaction and may alter his proposals in the light of this information. The numbers of buyers and sellers, the entry conditions, and the degree of product standardization (perhaps, the extent of information concerning other participants should be added) will impinge on price,[4] but the technical organization of the market is impotent. All markets in the system are presumed to be bourselike.

1. *The Technical Organization of Markets*

The caption to this section refers to the procedure through which buyers and sellers are brought into contact with each other. Would the same buyers and sellers reach identical results if the market were constituted differently? The ordinary view must be that the market (itself), its technical organization, is neutral with respect to the price, product, and output results. But would not a bourse, for instance, be expected to yield different results than a closed-bid mechanism? Consider this problem in some detail.

A system of closed bids is characterized by: (*a*) only one bid may be submitted by each participant, (*b*) individual bidders are presumed to be ignorant of the prices submitted by others, and (*c*) the amount and character of the products to be exchanged is usually specified. The customary principles on which individual enterprises make pricing decisions on a bourse do not seem to apply. In particular, no revenue or demand relationship can be drawn. A knowledge of the individual cost function and the amount to be sold will set a lower limit to the bid; a price lower than the present value of variable costs will not be offered. But what bid above this amount is to be submitted?

If the lowest bid of all other sellers could be known, it might pay an enterprise to reduce its price further and secure the order. For the group of sellers as a whole, this would tend to result in the lowest bid approximating the variable costs,[5] except

---

[3] A problem of major proportions is involved in drawing the boundary lines among markets and giving precise meaning to the phrase "participating in a market." See Robert Triffin, *Monopolistic Competition and General Equilibrium Theory*, Harvard University Press, Cambridge, Mass., 1940.

[4] The price will vary with the variables considered by buyers and sellers; the considerations of the sellers are of particular importance as in Marshallian "time" analysis.

[5] For at least the marginal enterprise.

as long-run reservation prices entered into all bids. It is thus evident that a system of closed bids (*a*) puts a great premium on knowledge of the probable bids to be submitted by other enterprises, and (*b*) exerts a downward pressure on bids to values below average costs. The successful bidder may have made a mistake in the estimation of costs. The difficulty of enforcing specification standards may cushion the effect of low estimates.

There are several ways in which a bidder may be able to formulate more or less accurate information about the probable bids of others. (1) The probable cost conditions of all other enterprises may be known to each bidder in a general way. But even if the lowest variable costs are known, only lower limits to the various bids can be designated. The problem of translating these costs into bids remains. (2) There may be generally accepted formulas among the group for calculating bids which are more or less rigorously followed. It may be customary to use rule-of-thumb costs per square foot or per cubic yard, adding a fixed amount or percentage of variable costs for "overhead." These conventions are a manifestation of a common interest in setting reservation prices above the variable costs bids inherent in the system. (3) When the "product" to be supplied is selling in more regularly established markets, the price prevailing in such markets can be expected to set an upper limit to bids. While these factors do not directly determine a bid, they narrow the range of possible choices. That markets characterized by closed bids should develop quota systems and other devices to allocate business among "competitors" is scarcely surprising.

The discussion of the closed-bid market form suggests that such results vary from a bourse largely because of differences in the number of buyers and the degree of knowledge concerning the other market participants. The "technical organization" of a market as an independent factor in pricing turns out to be another name for influences identified under the "character of competition." While such a conclusion is unassailable, the market machinery and arrangements are typically institutionalized and must be regarded as given for most problems. Buyers and sellers are brought together within the framework of many markets that are technically organized quite differently from a bourse. Alternatively, deviations from a bourse or "imperfections" are built into market forms.

An auction may be thought of as the converse of the closed-bid mechanism, typically one seller instead of the single buyer. But other dimensions are relevant to the comparison. The auction permits revision of the offer which is precluded in the closed bid. The two mechanisms can also be compared on the basis of whether the highest auction or lowest closed bid can be rejected, that is, whether the market requires a transaction at these prices.

A much more frequently occurring form of a market is that with quoted prices, a "take-it-or-leave-it" situation. Either buyers or sellers, but not both, may simply announce the terms upon which they stand prepared to complete transactions; the other party typically only has the alternative of accepting or rejecting. A bourse was observed to involve approximate equality in numbers of buyers and sellers for effective bidding and diffusion of information. As the relative numbers of buyers are increased to a seller, or vice versa, a mechanical problem in bidding arises. One seller, for instance, does not have the time to engage in separate dealing with each one of a large number of buyers. The clustering of many buyers around one seller not only would tend to break up a larger market into separate parts but would require a great deal of simultaneous action on the part of the seller. The technical arrangement of a quoted price emerges from this context.[6]

The market for many types of labor services clearly falls into this form of technical organization; labor markets do not resemble bourses, auctions, nor closed-bid arrangements. A great many wage earners sell their services to a relatively much smaller number of enterprises. In the nonunionized market, enterprises typically set a wage rate, that is, the terms upon which they will hire services, if and when wage earners are required. Various enterprises in the same market may set somewhat different rates initially, and over time these quotations may be altered in the light of other offers and responses. The technical organization of the labor market

---

[6] A quoted price may arise from other circumstances. A discriminating seller may use a nominal price as a base from which to make "secret" discounts.

accounts for the fact that offers which would be effective in a bourse may not have any impact on price in a quoted-price market.

Normally it is impossible for an individual to offer to work for less than the quoted price and secure the position of anyone already at work. This crucial observation may be relegated to that convenient miscellaneous file: "imperfections in the labor market." But the quoted-price market is inherently different from a bourse in construction. The price fixer may eventually change his price in the light of many inquiries for work. But no offer below the quoted price can typically secure employment for an individual, as would be the case were the labor market a bourse. A trade union may influence the level of wage rates, but these quoted price features of the labor market arise independently of a union.

The basic discrepancy in numbers and inconvenience of transaction that is institutionalized in the quoted-price market places an advantage in the hands of the price fixer. At any one time, those that name the price can be expected to propose terms that are particularly in their favor. The price fixer has the strategic advantage of the initiative. More than one quoted price may persist in a single market with varying degrees of product differentiation. Call this advantage monopoly power or superior knowledge, the important point is that the technical organization of a market cannot be a bourse but becomes a quoted-price market under the pressure of differences in number and inconvenience of transaction. The theory of the operation of a bourse cannot be expected to apply directly to other institutionalized forms of markets such as the auction, the closed-bid, and the quoted price.

A final form of market organization tends to develop when the number of effective buyers and sellers is reduced toward one: the "negotiated-price" market. This market form may not always be sharply distinguished from the quoted-price situation, although the ideal types are clearly identifiable. The parties agree upon a negotiated price in conference; both parties customarily make concessions. Trade unions seek to alter the labor market so as to transfer the pricing of services from an employer take-it-or-leave-it situation to a negotiated-price market or a quoted-price market of their own.

2. *Time Responses of Price Variations*

A pervasive problem confronts all price fixers: the period of time between price variations or the magnitude of market impacts sufficient to induce a new price. Rules of thumb frequently develop specifying the frequency with which those making pricing decisions will ordinarily *reconsider* prices. General observations suggest, for instance, that retail egg prices may be reconsidered once a week, clothing and shoes once a six-month season,

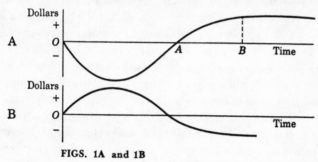

FIGS. 1A and 1B

and automobiles or agricultural implements once a year. Violent changes in market data may, of course, compel more frequent decisions.

Any determination of quoted prices or negotiated prices requires an appraisal of the time patterns of adjustment expected in response to contemplated changes in prices. Two sets of expectations will be important: the impact period, or the length of time required for the effects of any change to work themselves out through the market system, and the interval before further basic changes in the market data may be expected. The decision to change a price must clearly be influenced by the length of time required for the impacts of the decision to work themselves out and the interval before a reinforcing or counteracting change in data (other prices, incomes) may be expected. A simple diagrammatic representation of these ideas was graciously suggested by Mr. Scitovsky growing out of his own analysis of markets.

In Fig. 1A deviations from the x axis (time) depict the pattern of change in profits of an enterprise growing out of a price reduction that would ultimately improve the position of the firm. The x axis does not refer to zero profits but deviations from those profits that would be forthcoming through a continuation of present prices. A great variety of possible time configurations are immediately discerned; Fig. 1B suggests the pattern of price increase that ultimately decreases profits. In Fig. 1A, *OB* indicates the total length of time required to work out completely the effects of the price change, *OA* the time required to restore profits to their former level. The area below the x axis represents the short-run loss (reduced profits) required to achieve the higher rate of profit fully achieved at time *B*. Similarly, the area above the x axis in Fig. 1B indicates short-run profits achieved through an increase in prices that eventually results in a lower rate of profits. The magnitude of these *impact* changes on profits may be quite substantial when adjustment periods are long. The influence of these impact variations in profits will be particularly important when enterprises have short time-horizons, that is, high internal rates of discount. In the absence of perfect capital markets,[7] enterprises may be under strong pressure to avoid short-term reductions in profits or take advantage of short-term increases in profits despite longer run effects. Under imperfect credit markets, Fig. 1 suggests that the impact effects of price changes may result in price fixers showing an asymmetry in pattern. Increases tend to result in immediate gains while decreases lead to immediate losses.

Price fixers will also be interested in the interval between successive changes in the market data, particularly when the impact period is long. If opposing changes in data are expected frequently within the impact period, the enterprise will probably forego any adjustments. Graphically, curves for each change in data could be superimposed on the same diagram. Only a series of changes in one direction, expected to persist beyond the impact period, can be seriously expected to raise the issue of price revision in the quoted-price markets.

The graphic technique is intended primarily for application to the decisions of trade unions concerning wage rates. Deviations from the x axis measure the pattern of variation in the wage bill. The impact period can be expected to be generally quite long in

[7] Albert G. Hart, *Anticipations, Uncertainty and Dynamic Planning*, Studies in Business Administration, University of Chicago Press, Chicago, 1940, XI, No. 1.

the labor market, depending on such factors as the extent of non-union competition, the proportion of labor to total costs, the size of the bargaining unit, the rapidity of substitution of other factors, and entry and exit conditions.[8] Day-to-day changes in market conditions affecting the demand for services are a common feature of the labor market. The analysis of this section suggests, however, that no changes in wage rates would be forthcoming until pronounced changes in demand had taken place that could be expected to persist beyond the normal impact period. Considerable rigidity in the labor market is thus to be expected, regardless of the presence of a trade union. The technical organization of the market with a *quoted price* and the *prolonged impact period* operate in this direction. These tools of analysis readily explains why wheat prices change daily and wage rates typically remain unchanged for considerable periods.

3. *The Wage Structure* [9]

The preceding sections have oriented labor markets to the larger perspective of market organization. The final two sections of this chapter are directed toward the understanding of the terms of sale that emerge from the market. Such contracts are typically complex, specifying or implying a great many conditions requisite to the completion of the transaction. Some of these terms directly influence the price, defined as the amount of money or the present value of the credit instrument exchanged between the buyer and seller per unit of goods or services. This group of terms, designated the *price structure*, ordinarily contains a list or nominal price which may be modified by discounts, allowances, and credit terms. The remaining terms to an agreement of sale, many of which may be implicit or conventional, specify the precise character of the product, the time and place of delivery, and a host of similar conditions which may be labeled the *nonpecuniary* structure of the transaction.

This latter group of stipulations is not to be regarded as less essential to the total sales agreement than the price structure.

[8] Chapter IV considers the effect of these and other factors upon trade-union policies.

[9] See National Bureau of Economic Research, *Cost Behavior and Price Policy*, A Study Prepared by the Committee on Price Determination for the Conference on Price Research, New York, 1943, Chaps. 3, 6.

The contract is made in view of all the conditions of the exchange. At times, specific clauses of the nonpecuniary structure can be identified with distinct elements in the price structure. For instance, a cash discount may be agreed upon for accepting delivery before a particular date. But more frequently, the dimensions of the price and nonpecuniary structures bear no unique correspondence. Bargaining over the total agreement will usually include some substitution between these two groups of terms.

Economic analysis has usually reduced all these dimensions of a sales agreement to the single variable "price" (average revenue) by presuming either that the nonpecuniary structure typically remains constant or that changes in these terms do not matter. More recently, changes in a product have been incorporated into formal theory by reducing all the stipulations of a sales agreement to the two variables: price and product.[10] This construction is to be commended, for attention has been forced upon neglected phases of sales agreements. However, the simplification of all nonpecuniary structures to the single term "product" cannot be so satisfactory as the substitution of price (average revenue) for a great many clauses in the price structure. Discounts and allowances are readily combined with list prices to yield an average revenue. But dates of delivery, types of packages, and special services do not present a convenient common denominator. The device of defining a product so narrowly as to permit only a single nonpecuniary dimension may be useful diagrammatically in dealing with product adjustment, but no real simplification is involved. The sales stipulation still consists of a price structure, reducible to price (average revenue) and many diverse nonpecuniary dimensions. Any final transaction will have included bargaining over the terms of every dimension and the rates of substitution among all the clauses.

This multidimensional view of a sales agreement raises questions about price indexes and demand schedules, two common tools of economists, that must be noted in passing on to the pricing of labor services. Not only are nonpecuniary terms beyond the range of index numbers, but frequently indexes only reflect

[10] E. H. Chamberlin, *The Theory of Monopolistic Competition*, Harvard University Press, 1933, Cambridge, Mass., Chap. V.

changes in the list or nominal price, that is, only a part of the variation in price structure. The concept of price as average revenue is not adopted explicitly in most wholesale price indexes, although it would seem possible to develop just as readily available indexes through voluntary reports of "total sales" by specific commodities and "numbers of units sold." [11] A demand schedule indicating the quantity that may be expected to be sold at each price, presumes incomes, all other prices, and nonpecuniary structures unchanged. The amount taken is fundamentally regarded as uniquely determined by the price. This construction betrays the bias of preoccupation with a formalized price mechanism. It may very well be that the quantity demanded is much more influenced by nonpecuniary structures. These remarks cannot question the logical validity of demand schedules but merely refer to their usefulness in interpreting market behavior.

The distinction that has been drawn between price and nonpecuniary structures of a sales stipulation becomes even more important when labor market transactions are considered and *a fortiori* when trade unions are involved. Labor organizations have always been vitally concerned with "industrial jurisprudence," [12] that is, with the nonpecuniary aspects of the labor bargain. Some indication of the complexities in the terms of sale of labor services can be conveyed by a brief examination of a relatively simple and well-known trade-union agreement, that between the General Motors Corporation and the International Union United Automobile Workers of America—CIO which was signed on June 24, 1940. The agreement contains 16 main subdivisions and almost 150 separately numbered paragraphs. The clauses of the contract readily identifiable as directly determining the wage-rate structure [13] are those covering: overtime rates by day and week, Sunday and holiday rates, night-shift rates, basic wage adjustment, vacations with pay, and minimum hours of work possible in a day if a

---

[11] The additional information would permit indexes of the physical volume of sales which could be utilized with production data as a check on inventories. Some price indexes have been constructed from total sales data as reported to the Bureau of the Census.

[12] Sumner H. Slichter, *Union Policies and Industrial Management*, Brookings Institution, Washington, 1941, p. 1.

[13] Since the price of labor services is designated a "wage rate," the term "wage-rate structure" is used instead of "price structure."

wage earner is required to report for work. The nonpecuniary structure of the agreement is composed of clauses specifying: the form and character of union recognition, the grievance procedure, the seniority of union representatives and committeemen, seniority status of the rest of the workers, discharge and layoffs, working hours, bulletin boards, leaves of absence, strikes and stoppages, and the duration of the agreement. Mention should also be made of the implied agreement that existing measures for health, sanitation, recreation, and safety will be maintained; existing conditions of work will not arbitrarily be made less favorable.

Even such a simple agreement [14] reveals that the dichotomy between wage-rate structure and nonpecuniary terms is not entirely unequivocal. A clause on the principles to be used in setting piece rates for new operations or an agreement to maintain a reasonable speed of operations will certainly influence the earnings of workers and costs of an enterprise. The classification of such terms is thus in part arbitrary. In fact, every provision of an agreement can be regarded as influencing the price of labor in some fashion, at least through the impact on the bargaining power of the parties in reaching future agreements. For instance, to take an obvious example, a checkoff [15] clause may enable a union to be in a much stronger financial position and thus obtain a higher base rate when a renewal of the agreement is to be negotiated. Despite these difficulties of classification, the distinction between wage-rate structure and nonpecuniary clauses has seemed useful. The practical test in any specific case can be based on the directness and immediacy of the impact of the stipulation upon the amount of money received by the wage earner per unit of service rendered.

The complex character of the labor bargain renders difficult statistical measurement of changes in the price of labor.[16] Indexes of *basic rates* can only provide a valid picture of the wage struc-

[14] Many trade-union agreements are much longer and more specific. For instance, "The Rates of Pay and National Conditions of Service of Locomotivemen and Electric Trainmen" negotiated by the Associated Society of Locomotive Engineers and Trainmen (England), including older interpretations, runs into several hundred pages.

[15] A checkoff provides that the enterprise pay the union dues of individual employees directly to the union as a deduction from pay rolls. This practice may or may not require specific authorization from the individual employee.

[16] The impact of the multidimensional character of the wage structure on demand and supply schedules is discussed in later chapters.

ture if changes in base rates are not accompanied by significant variations in other terms of the structure. Overtime rates and Sunday rates, for instance, must be presumed to remain reasonably fixed while the base rate varies. But trade unions, and even unorganized wage earners, are frequently more concerned with maintaining the basic rate than with other terms in the wage structure. Concessions made in other terms are probably easier to regain and more easily "sold" to the membership. The basic rate stands as a symbol of the strength and achievements of the union; furthermore, changes in other terms than the base rate can be more easily restricted in their effects on total earnings. Business executives follow analogous policies when special discounts and concessions are made more readily than any revision in the basic list prices. It is little wonder, therefore, that no indexes of wage rates are generally available for the United States [17] and that there should develop a tendency to designate average hourly earnings as the "price" of labor.

4. *Average Hourly Earnings and Wage Rates*

The average hourly earnings of a wage earner over a specified period would appear to correspond to the definition of a price as the amount of money exchanged between a buyer and a seller per unit of product or service. In this case the amount of labor services is measured in man-hour units. However, variations in these earnings for an individual, and particularly for groups of wage earners, do take place which cannot be regarded as changes in the price of labor.

(1) Under piece rate or bonus arrangements,[18] the average hourly earnings of a wage earner may be varied for a great many reasons unrelated to a change in the wage structure. The rate of individual output can be influenced by the coordination between different operations, the wage earner's own rate of effort, and the

[17] Indexes of wage rates for England have ordinarily paid inadequate attention to these problems of wage structure. There can be little doubt that discussions of wage-rate flexibility have paid too little attention to other terms of labor agreements than the basic rates.

[18] Approximately one-third of manufacturing employees work under piece-rate arrangements, one-half under the straight-time method of payment, and the remaining one-sixth under complex bonus arrangements. See Sumner H. Slichter, *op. cit.*, p. 282, n. 1.

technical qualities of the machine and material with which he works. Gradual changes in technique and organization of a plant that are not accompanied by variations in rates may have significant effects upon average hourly earnings over a period of years. Discrepancies may arise under piece rates both because of changes in individual application and variations in the condition of equipment and material.

(2) When wage earners are grouped together, for instance, by establishment or industry, variation in average hourly earnings for the group can arise solely because of changes in the proportion of wage earners at each level of earnings. As output is expanded, the proportion of workers at starting rates may be so increased as to result in a fall in the average hourly earnings of the group. Or, after a prolonged period of high output, promotions and upgradings within each bracket may raise the average. This point is particularly relevant to the interpretation of an over-all average for manufacturing industries. Earnings are typically higher, for instance, in the durable consumer and producer's goods industries which also show the most violent fluctuations in employment. As employment contracts in the higher wage section of the economy with the start of a depression, over-all average hourly earnings will tend to fall, while as employment rapidly expands in this sector in an upswing the average hourly earnings for the system will tend to rise quite apart from other influences typically at work.

An over-all average of hourly earnings is thus influenced by the shifts in the proportion of wage earners between earnings brackets within an enterprise, by changes in the relative importance of high- and low-wage enterprises, by the relative distribution of man-hours of employment between high- and low-paid industries, by the proportion of wage earners in each occupation, and by the distribution of employment through the occupational rate range. These influences certainly do not all work in the same direction during the course of the cycle. The effects of "industry" and "firm" weights, however, are probably so important that average hourly earnings increase with the expansion of employment and decrease with its contraction by a greater amplitude than the price of labor of individual wage earners. That is, without any change in individual wage structures the shifts in "weights" are such as to magnify the fluctuations in earnings.

An illustration of the magnitude of the effect of changes in industry weights is evident from an analysis of the Bureau of Labor Statistics series.[19] The index for all manufacturing industry or any grouping of industries is obtained by dividing the appropriate total pay rolls by the corresponding man-hours.[20] The influence of overtime payments and inter-industry shifts in employment on average hourly earnings is summarized in Table I for selected dates in the period January 1941–February 1943.

TABLE I. THE INFLUENCE OF OVERTIME PAYMENTS AND INTER-INDUSTRY SHIFTS ON AVERAGE HOURLY EARNINGS IN MANUFAC-TURING

	AVERAGE HOURLY EARNINGS		STRAIGHT TIME AVERAGE HOURLY EARNINGS, ELIMINATING OVERTIME		STRAIGHT TIME AVERAGE HOURLY EARNINGS, ELIMINATING OVERTIME, AND INTER-INDUSTRY SHIFTS IN EMPLOYMENT	
	Cents	*Index*	*Cents*	*Index*	*Cents*	*Index*
January 1941	68.3	100.0	66.4	100.0	66.4	100.0
December 1941	78.3	114.6	75.0	113.0	74.1	111.6
July 1942	85.6	125.3	80.9	121.8	78.4	118.1
September 1942	89.2	130.6	84.4	127.1	80.0	120.5
January 1943	91.9	134.5	85.9	129.4	80.4	121.1
February 1943	92.4	135.3	86.3	130.0	81.9	123.4

The influence of shifts in employment among industries was measured by dividing all manufacturing industries into twenty groups and calculating average hourly earnings on the basis of the relative importance of industries in January 1941. The above data

[19] For a description of the methods of construction of these series see Bureau of Labor Statistics, *Hours and Earnings in the United States, 1932–40, with Supplement for 1941*, Washington, 1942.

[20] This index number may be written $\frac{\Sigma(P_L \cdot L)}{\Sigma L}$ or $P_L \cdot \frac{L_i}{\Sigma L}$ where L is man-hours and P_L is average hourly earnings of industries $1^P L \cdots n^P L \cdot \frac{L_i}{\Sigma L}$ is the "weight" of any particular industry in the total index. See Witt Bowden, "Wages, Hours and Productivity of Industrial Labor, 1909 to 1939," *Monthly Labor Review* September, 1940, 51, p. 525, n. 6.

cannot, of course, measure the influence of shifts in employment among firms, occupations, and within occupational rate ranges that take place within an industrial grouping.

In addition to divergences between average hourly earnings and the price of labor, there are others between the movements of these earnings and variation in the wage structure wh ch must be noted. (a) Any change in the proportion of overtime, night work, Sunday work, or other work performed at a differential from the basic rate will alter average hourly earnings. (For the influence of overtime payments,[21] see Table I.) (b) Without any change in the wage structure, average hourly earnings may vary simply because of a change in the period of time itself over which earnings are averaged. The way in which vacations with pay and pensions enter into average hourly earnings, if at all, will influence the comparative movements of earnings, the wage structure, or basic wage rates. If pay rolls per year in one case and lifetime earnings in another were divided by hours worked, average hourly earnings would reflect both vacations with pay and pensions. Since earnings indexes are calculated over the pay-roll period (usually one or two weeks), they may vary from period to period simply because vacation earnings may not be spread evenly over the whole period in which they were earned. (c) Average hourly earnings patterns can be influenced by changes in the method of counting hours at work, particularly when compensation is computed by the day or the week. For instance, earnings of coal miners per hour will be considerably different depending on whether hours at work are counted at the mine face or as hours spent on the company property. On the average, almost an hour a day is spent in getting to and from the point of actual operations. A consistent policy will not change average hourly earnings although the level will be influenced by the alternative adopted. (d) Average hourly earnings may be changed as a result of some nonpecuniary item in the labor bargain without any change in the wage structure. Illustrative of such instances are a change in the calculation of the earnings of late workers, under piece rates a variation in the standards of inspection and tolerance, any alteration in the fre-

[21] See "Elimination of Overtime Payments from Gross Hourly Earnings," *Monthly Labor Review*, November 1942, 55, pp. 1053–56.

quency and proportion of promotions, and working rules respecting assistants and helpers.

It should now be evident, particularly for groups of wage earners, that variations in average hourly earnings cannot be identified with changes in the price of labor. Neither may these earnings be an accurate measure of variations in the wage structure, and *a fortiori* of the basic wage rates. These points have been emphasized, despite their essential simplicity because of widespread confusion which fails to distinguish among average hourly earnings, basic wage rates, and total wage structure. A classic instance of such confusion is illustrated by the following quotation:

Between 1929 and 1938 the average hourly earnings of American workers (according to the figures of the National Industrial Conference Board) increased by 23 per cent in the same period. To place two figures in juxtaposition is not to prove that the one is the cause of the other. But it is at least suggestive that, while wage rates in Great Britain rose over the same period by less than a third the American increase, British payrolls . . . increased by 20 per cent.[22]

While the central argument is not relevant to the present discussion, an instance is provided of the unqualified comparison of wage rates and average hourly earnings.[23]

Granting the logic of the above distinctions, the question may be asked whether any important statistical differences are actually observed between variations of average hourly earnings and basic wage rates. The criteria of significance of any difference will, of course, vary with the problem and purpose at hand. While there is little systematic evidence on the magnitude of the differential movement of average hourly earnings and basic wage rates, the following isolated data may be typical. (a) Six studies of particular firms undertaken by the Bureau of Labor Statistics in four

[22] "Laggard Recovery in America," *The Economist*, July 1, 1939, CXXXVI, p. 2. This quotation was reprinted and endorsed editorially by *The New York Times*. Also see Waldo E. Fisher, "Union Wage-Hour Policies and Employment," *American Economic Review*, June, 1940, XXX, pp. 298–99.

[23] That the difference between the movement of average hourly earnings and wage rates for Great Britain during this period may have been appreciable is indicated by the fact that after correcting for some of the differences between these series, Professor A. L. Bowley found an increase to an index of 197 instead of 190 in 1936 from 191 in 1930 (1914 = 100). *Wages and Income in the United Kingdom Since 1860*, Cambridge University Press, London, 1937, pp. 18, 30, Appendix B.

industries showed little consistency in pattern. The comparative variations in twelve plants of the International Harvester Company for the period 1930–1937 are shown in Table II. There can be little doubt that these data show rather marked and significant variations. However, the studies of firms in the paper, boot and shoe, and cotton textile industries showed progressively less variations; in the cotton textile case average hourly earnings and basic wage rates indicated an almost identical pattern.[24]

TABLE II. RELATIVE MOVEMENTS OF "WAGE RATES" AND AVERAGE HOURLY EARNINGS [25]

Agricultural Implement Industry

PLANT	PER CENT CHANGE 1930–1933		PER CENT CHANGE 1933–1937		PER CENT CHANGE 1930–1937	
	Wage Rates	Average Hourly Earnings	Wage Rates	Average Hourly Earnings	Wage Rates	Average Hourly Earnings
1	− 18.1	− 15.9	+ 48.4	+ 50.3	+ 21.5	+ 26.4
2	− 18.1	− 19.2	+ 41.3	+ 47.5	+ 15.7	+ 19.2
3	− 18.1	− 13.3	+ 43.8	+ 72.3	+ 17.8	+ 49.4
4	− 18.1	− 13.5	+ 42.6	+ 52.6	+ 16.8	+ 32.0
5	− 18.1	− 18.2	+ 48.4	+ 68.6	+ 21.5	+ 37.9
6	− 15.6	− 20.8	+ 50.8	+ 77.8	+ 27.0	+ 40.8
7	− 18.1	− 16.5	+ 49.0	+ 52.2	+ 22.0	+ 27.1
8	− 18.1	− 25.6	+ 53.0	+ 61.3	+ 25.3	+ 20.0
9	− 18.1	− 11.9	+ 46.8	+ 43.4	+ 20.2	+ 26.3
10	− 18.1	− 19.3	+ 40.7	+ 57.9	+ 15.2	+ 27.4
11	− 18.1	− 12.1	+ 51.3	+ 68.3	+ 27.4	+ 47.9
12	− 15.8	− 23.6	+ 46.5	+ 68.1	+ 20.0	+ 28.4

(b) An unpublished study of two plants of a full-fashioned hosiery enterprise [26] shows the following comparative movements of rates and average hourly earnings for leggers and footers in the years 1937 to 1940 inclusive. Wage earners in these departments are paid entirely by piece rates. Consequently their average hourly earnings vary somewhat from month to month due to the style of hosiery knitted and the general rate of output. Table III presents

[24] Temporary National Economic Committee, *Industrial Wage Rates, Labor Costs and Price Policies*, Monograph No. 5, Government Printing Office, Washington, 1940, pp. 4–59.

[25] *Ibid.*, pp. 107–114.

[26] Melvin Jay Gordon, *A Case in the Women's Full-Fashioned Hosiery Industry*, thesis presented for undergraduate honors, Harvard University, March, 1941.

the comparative movements of rates and earnings for these two plants.[27]

(c) The study of English cotton-spinning rates and earnings reveals interesting disparities of movement. "For sixty years before 1920 it was true to say that earnings were rising more rapidly or falling more slowly than wage rates."[28] During the period 1914–1918 this pattern was accentuated by a shortage of piecers, reducing the relative importance of low-paid employees and increasing average hourly earnings. In the decade of falling rates

TABLE III. WAGE RATES AND AVERAGE HOURLY EARNINGS INDEXES IN TWO HOSIERY PLANTS

| | LEGGERS | | FOOTERS | |
	Wage Rates	Average Hourly Earnings	Wage Rates	Average Hourly Earnings
PLANT I				
January 1937	100.0	100.0	100.0	100.0
August 1937	108.2	126.6	109.3	115.4
June 1938	110.8	132.8	111.6	116.6
January 1940	110.8	128.0	111.6	134.9
September 1940	106.6	114.5	108.4	127.2
PLANT II				
January 1937	100.0	100.0	100.0	100.0
February 1937	103.0	103.1	103.0	104.5
April 1937	106.1	106.5	106.1	113.5
January 1940	106.1	112.2	106.1	119.7
September 1940	106.1	109.2	106.1	109.8

after 1922, however, average hourly earnings fell by a greater proportion.

(d) The stabilization formula of the National War Labor Board led to the tabulation of considerable data comparing straight-time average hourly earnings with (full-time) hourly earnings. Among the numerous factors enumerated in this section which may influence average hourly earnings, only the influence of overtime is removed in the "straight-time" concept. Between January 1941 and November 1942 the straight-time figure for all factory workers increased 25 per cent while the full-time earnings

[27] The results do not depend on erratic monthly movements.

[28] John Jewkes and E. M. Gray, *Wages and Labour in the Lancashire Cotton Spinning Industry*, Manchester University Press, Manchester, 1935, p. 24. See Charts II and III, pp. 21, 25.

rose 30 per cent.[29] The comparative patterns of increase in sample industries during the same period are tabulated as follows:

Industry	Straight-time Average Hourly Earnings, Per Cent	Full-time Average Hourly Earnings, Per Cent
Aircraft	26.8	28.6
Aluminum	19.8	24.8
Boots and shoes	28.5	28.9
Blast furnaces, etc.	20.3	23.7
Chemicals	22.3	25.2
Cotton goods	34.9	37.7
Electrical equipment	24.2	28.0
Machinery and machine shops	22.0	26.9
Rubber tires and tubes	9.6	13.6
Shipbuilding	34.9	41.6

In the absence of a comprehensive comparison, these scattered data, appraised in the context of the influences that may affect earnings, certainly support the inferences that (a) average hourly earnings show variations that are significantly different from rates, (b) over a long period average hourly earnings probably show an upward bias relative to base rate, and (c) without specific evidence to the contrary an error is made in regarding the two as equivalent. The importance of this last caution is illustrated in the common statement that since average hourly earnings have increased 25 per cent or 50 per cent, wage costs per unit of output (aside from technical changes and variations in rates of output) have increased by the same amount. This would be true only if rates and earnings had shown identical amplitudes of movement.

The *raison d'être* then of a discussion of the labor market and the price of labor services at the outset of a study on wage determination has been to point to the role of the technical organization of a market in pricing, to suggest the importance of the time patterns of reaction to price or wage rate variations, to emphasize the multidimensional character of the labor bargain, to distinguish between the wage structure and the nonpecuniary terms of the bargain, to show the possibility of substitution be-

[29] National War Labor Board, *Opinion*, In the Matter of Swift and Company, Armour and Company, Cudahy and Company, Wilson and Company, and Packinghouse Workers Organizing Committee (CIO), Case Nos. 186, 181, 189, 188, February 8, 1943. Also see Table I above.

tween these two main groups of terms, to indicate the difficulty of reducing even the wage structure to a single base rate, to identify the separate factors which may affect average hourly earnings, and finally to demonstrate the importance of differentiating wage rates from hourly earnings.

CHAPTER III. ECONOMIC MODEL
OF A TRADE UNION

The price of labor services, like any price, is determined in economics by supply and demand functions. The schedule of "amounts" of services offered for sale at varying real prices in any particular market is derived from the relative preferences of individuals for real income from the sale of their services and leisure.[1] These preferences indicate the amount of services forthcoming from an individual at each indicated real wage rate. It has sometimes been thought[2] that this short-run supply curve of an individual must always be backward rising (a lesser amount offered at higher prices) ; but the quantity supplied may equally well increase with higher wage rates. The net effect will depend upon whether the substitution of work for leisure at the higher relative price for effort expended is offset by the tendency to work less at the higher level of income. Should the substitution effect be the larger magnitude, the individual will supply larger amounts at higher prices;[3] the function will be backward rising when the second effect predominates.

A market supply function is usually derived from a summation of these individual choices between leisure and real income. The shape of this market function is ordinarily presumed to be the same as that of the individuals composing the market. The group curve will be similar if all the individual functions are forward rising, but the summation of backward rising curves may result in either a backward or forward rising market-supply function. This observation has been obscured by the assumption that all wage earners in a market are identical; the assumption has been removed only to deal with issues of wage differentials between in-

[1] J. R. Hicks, *Value and Capital*, Oxford University Press, London, 1939, pp. 36–37.
[2] F. H. Knight, *Risk, Uncertainty and Profit*, London School Reprint, 1933, No. 16, p. 17.
[3] The term "forward rising" will be used in contrast to "backward rising."

dividuals. Thus the shape of the market-supply function of any type of labor cannot be generalized from individual choices; furthermore, the presence of a trade union can be expected to displace these individual decisions, rendering the supply conditions of customary theory even more obscure. The present chapter attempts to resolve these difficulties by examining economic models of a trade union as a market enterprise.[4] Attention is directed first toward the locus of supply decisions.

1. The Decision Making Unit

Economic theory betrays its philosophical inspiration by presuming a community of sovereign individuals, each person registering his tastes in the market. "It was as hard for the last century to think of a group or association as it was for antiquity to think of a single individual."[5] The first and most apparent difficulty with summing individual supply functions is that the household is frequently the relevant unit of decision formation. At any real wage rate, more or less labor services will be offered by the household as a whole depending on conditions within the unit.[6,7] The amount of labor services offered for sale, measured in total man-hours or by work performed, is thus not a unique function of the real price of these services received by the *individual* wage earner. The income of the family unit, which may depend largely upon the employment status of other household members, will frequently be crucial in deciding whether a particular individual will enter the labor market. The order of magnitude of this factor is evident from the fact that "approximately one-third of the families in the United States have two or more 'worker' mem-

---

[4] Chapter IV takes a less formalized perspective of wage-rate determination in unionized labor markets.

[5] Roscoe Pound, *Social Control through Law*, Yale University Press, New Haven, 1942, p. 12.

[6] This is the problem of "additional workers." As the term has been used, no distinction is made between those labor services forced to *seek work* as a result of a decline in the household income and the smaller group that would actually simultaneously take work to supplement the family income. Only the latter group are relevant to the supply function, although the former would meet any usual statistical measure of the labor supply.

[7] Economic analysis has been much concerned recently with the problem of drawing indifference maps for a whole community. But similar methodological problems are involved in treating the household as a unit.

bers and, as a consequence, more than half of the workers are in multi-worker units." [8] The income of the family unit (which is not necessarily closely related to wage rates) can be as important a determinant of the quantity of labor offered for sale [9] as the real price.

The informal organization and social pressure of a group of wage earners, even in the absence of a trade union, substantially influences the amount of labor supplied under piece rates. Customary standards of the number of pieces that constitute a day's work develop and are typically enforced by informal and spontaneous pressures. The significant fact is that a working force is composed of much more than isolated and discrete individuals. A social community in miniature develops its own leadership, mores, and standards of proficiency and output. The individual's choice between income and leisure must be placed in this social context.

The now classic study of the Western Electric Company indicated that "the official 'bogey' meant nothing to the operators. In its stead they had an informal standard of a day's work which functioned for the group as a norm of conduct, as a social code. They felt that it was wrong to exceed this standard." [10] It should not be implied, however, that all workers accepted the group standard or that individual outputs were identical. Rather does it appear that the standard provided a maximum below which most of the wage earners ranged; persistent output above or far below the standard met with strong social disapproval, the chief weapon of the work community in enforcing its mores. The effectiveness of this pressure is indicated in the case of wage earners who refrained from reporting all the work they produced, taking a reduced income in order to adhere to the group's norm. A study of several departments in Macy's store [11] corroborates the notion

[8] Don D. Humphrey, *Family Unemployment, An Analysis of Unemployment in Terms of Family Units*, Work Projects Administration, Washington, 1940, p. xiv. See W. S. Woytinsky, *Three Aspects of Labor Dynamics*, Committee on Social Security, Social Science Research Council, Washington, 1942, Part III.

[9] The phrase "offered for sale" must not obscure the emphasis of the previous chapter that the labor market is not a bourse.

[10] F. J. Roethlisberger and William J. Dickson, *Management and the Worker*, Harvard University Press, Cambridge, Mass., 1940, p. 517.

[11] Unpublished study.

that unusually high or low outputs are frequently a reaction to social pressure and ostracism. "We are witnessing a vicious circle in which A works hard because the group derides and attempts to frustrate him; but the harder he works the more intense becomes the antagonism." [12]

Whatever the origin of such informal group standards—be it the fear of rate reductions, the concern over loss of work, a desire to increase group bargaining power by concealing knowledge of potential output from the enterprise, or simply the fact that every community sets its norms for social approval—the essential fact remains that these norms of output are not only very common [13] but arise quite independently of trade unionism. In fact, some of the most difficult problems that confront a union consist in changing mores that may have outlived any social usefulness and persist solely through inertia. Decisions respecting the amount of labor supplied in a market under piece rates are thus materially conditioned by these group standards of output. Even if the amount of labor is measured by hours worked, the community mores, although restricted in scope, may significantly affect the regular hours of work and overtime.

Finally the choices of individuals between leisure and income become even less relevant to the actual amounts of labor that will be sold at specific real prices with the introduction of a trade union. The union appears in the market as a seller in the place of a large number of isolated and independent wage earners. In analytical terms, a supply function under these monopolistic conditions is inconceivable. The amount offered for sale cannot be a unique function of the real price since the union may be able to affect the price by altering the quantity offered. The situation is analogous to the notion that a marginal cost function is a supply function of an enterprise under perfect competition. But when some control over product price is possible, the amount offered is not simply a function of price but also of elasticity of demand.

[12] *Loc. cit.*, p. 383. An instance of reduced output as a reaction to social pressure is provided by the members of clique B who instead of increasing their output under personal criticism from other workers "kept it low, thus 'getting back' at those who were displaying their superiority," p. 521.

[13] See Stanley B. Mathewson, *Restriction of Output among Unorganized Workers*, The Viking Press, New York, 1931.

No singular function can relate price and quantity offered here. Furthermore, the theory of monopoly cannot be unambiguously applied to a trade union for an appropriate cost function is not immediately evident. Apart from these theoretical difficulties, the amount of labor offered for sale at any price may deviate from that dictated by summing individual preferences because the group acting collectively through the union may have quite different preferences. The institutionalized form of collective action may introduce new preferences in the same way the household modifies the individual preferences. Thus a large gap may exist between the relative preferences of individuals for real income and leisure and the amount of labor sold at any specific price because the locus of decision formation may lie outside the individual. Preferences are both rejected and refashioned by the discretion of households and trade unions as well as by the informal standards of the work community.

2. *What May Trade Unions Maximize?*

Fruitful discussion of the "supply curve" of labor under contemporary conditions apparently must examine the principles and conditions upon which trade unions "offer" labor services. It will be useful to regard buyers of labor services as confronted by a "business enterprise" (trade union) just as when raw materials or money capital is purchased. But the crucial question arises as to the objective of this enterprise. What does it attempt to maximize? From this perspective, logical models of the trade union are as indispensable to analytical economics as the theory of the conditions under which an enterprise maximizes profits.

For the purposes of a model, a trade union is composed of wage earners in a particular market,[14] either actually employed or willing to work under some conditions, who have formed an enterprise with leadership to act as their collective agent. The enterprise does not purchase labor services for resale to other business firms at a profit. This formulation is intended to exclude an enterprise manipulated for the exclusive profit of the organizer. When a trade union is a racket, the ordinary model of the business firm

[14] The following chapter considers the bargaining unit and its impact on wage-rate determination.

suffices. A kind of demand relationship would show expected gross receipts from dues and racketeering at various prices. A cost function would show the outlays required for varying levels of activity. The level of dues and racket prices that would maximize profits thus would be formally determined. The following models do not apply to the privateer.

The trade union can be regarded as having a wage-membership function, showing the total amount of labor that will be attached to the labor organization at each wage rate. The concept envisages complete organization or a given degree of unionization. Such a function is not an average relationship; the increment in the amount of labor affiliated with the union is specified for each increment in the wage rate. The membership function must be regarded as the appraisal by the leadership of the amount of labor that will be allied to the union at each wage rate. The curve can be viewed as an array of minimum affiliation offers as viewed from the trade union. This subjective feature places the function on the same logical plane as the demand curve for the product of an enterprise or the demand curve for labor. It follows from this definition that the membership function cannot be derived solely from individual income-leisure preferences.

The customary market-supply curve may be one possible membership function. The latter will probably be thought of as to the left of the market-supply function. A trade union is in a position to affect both the shape and the position of the membership function by apprenticeship regulation, seniority, the character of working conditions, and other nonpecuniary features of the labor bargain, previous wage policy which has affected the regularity and amount of employment, as well as forcible limitation on entry through specific restriction, informal rulings, rituals (as those which bar Negroes), or prohibitive initiation fees and dues. But the membership function may be to the right of the market-supply function as the union exerts pressure for systematic attendance at work and longer hours or as increased knowledge of job opportunities and the training of members may result in a larger number of workers in any market at a specified wage. Those who are unwilling to start with a membership function in comparative static terms are reminded that the function can be logically built up from these specific policies of the union, just as the market supply curve is alleged to be built up from individual preferences.

The membership function is a reflection of the leadership's view of the willingness of individuals to become affiliated as a consequence of wage rates alone. It will reflect, in part, the attractiveness of the particular labor market as compared to other markets or nonemployment. The relationship between the individual wage earner and the union which has been described as affiliation or membership must not be interpreted too narrowly.[15] Dues payments may be in arrears or a wage earner may be unemployed. The crucial notion is that the trade union through the leadership at each wage rate regards a certain amount of labor as a part of, or belonging to, the union. The function is particularly difficult to identify conceptually when a union is in the midst of an organizing drive, for the "members" may then include those it hopes to affiliate.

Two cases involving differences in the shape of this membership function are usefully distinguished. The amount of labor may either be invariate to changes in the wage rate or forward rising. The first instance would be particularly applicable to a union which prevented admissions to the membership. More generally the case may portray the typical short-run situation for changes in wage rates within "practicable limits." That is, the union may regard the amount of labor available in the "membership" as fixed in making decisions of wage policy. The case of the upward rising membership function may be particularly applicable to very low wage rates or to rather large changes in rates.

For the purpose of the present chapter, the trade union will be envisaged as dealing with a number of different enterprises. They need not constitute a perfectly competitive product market; the important consideration is that they act in the labor market differently from a monopolist.[16] The leadership of the trade union is presumed to know not only the membership function but also the wage-bill-employment function, that is, the way in which the

---

[15] The necessity of relating the concept of "membership" to the problem at hand has not always been recognized. For instance, the success of a strike or a labor election campaign will ordinarily depend on many wage earners in the "market" or "jurisdiction" who are not strictly members.

[16] Chapters V and VI consider more complex product and factor market situations.

total wage bill in this segment of the economy will vary with the amount of labor services employed. This function is derived by summing the same function for individual enterprises. The total function for the group of firms yields both the average receipts or demand curve for labor and a marginal curve.

All of these functions will vary with the period of time required for exit or entry of business enterprises from the particular market; in particular the time pattern of shifts to lower cost (non-union) firms will be crucial. The amount of labor hired at any wage will depend upon whether the firms are envisaged as tied to the market or whether adjustments by transfer, migration, exit, and entry are contemplated. Hence the demand function for labor will be viewed as having a time dimension. In general, as wage rates are increased longer run functions will lie below those of the shorter run, decreases will find the longer run functions above those of the short run in accordance with specific impact patterns (see Fig. 1).

The shape of the demand function for labor services is ordinarily said to depend upon the technical conditions of production, the relative prices of other resources, the price of finished products, and the more dynamic factors mentioned in the preceding paragraph. In addition to these considerations, the role of corporate income taxes deserves special attention. At high surtax levels, the demand for labor by an enterprise is made particularly inelastic since changes in wage rates yield much smaller changes in profits after taxes than they would in the absence of the tax. The influence of wage-rate changes is damped by variations in tax payments. The logic of market calculations probably becomes ambiguous when high tax rates apply to a considerable range of output. While the argument that follows utilizes the conventional idea of a demand function for labor services, the precision of the concept is not so great as ordinarily supposed.

The analytical task remains of indicating the wage level that will be established with given membership and demand functions as well as with shifts in these basic relationships. Clearly, these results will depend upon the basic objectives of the union, that is, what the union is attempting to maximize. The following alternatives are discernible.

(1) The wage policy of a trade union may be directed at achieving the *largest possible wage bill* from the particular segment of the economy, quite regardless of whether all wage earners —as specified by the membership function—are employed. Figure 2A illustrates that the wage TM will be determined where the increment to the wage bill is zero; an amount of labor, MP, will be unemployed. If the membership function cuts the demand function above the wage at which the bill would be a maximum,[17]

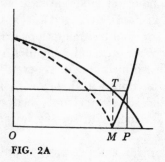

FIG. 2A

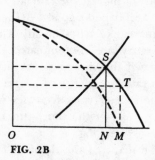

FIG. 2B

the amount of labor demanded at this wage will be greater than the union can supply. Such an instance is indicated in Fig. 2B. Under these condititons, the intersection of the membership and demand functions will maximize the wage bill for an amount of labor that can be supplied. The objective of maximizing the wage bill will thus result in a wage at least as high as that critical rate where the increment to the wage bill is zero. Higher wage rates will be specified by the demand and membership functions when they intersect above the critical rate.

(2) When a wage has been determined that leaves some amount of labor unemployed, problems are forced upon a union which may lead to another basic objective. The group without work may create difficulty for the reason that a downward pressure on the union wage scale may arise as enterprises reconsider their quoted wage rates and as existing nonunion or new establishments have their competitive position in the product market improved. There frequently may be internal struggle over the locus of unemployment. The older workers will attempt to protect

[17] The elasticity of the demand curve is unity at point T in Fig. 2.

themselves by seniority,[18] employees in favorably situated firms, departments, or occupations may attempt to pass the burden on. Furthermore, the union must make some attempt to care for these "brothers" if their loyalty and political support is to be retained. Two logical possibilities can be envisaged for the care of unemployed members. The union may organize its own unemployment fund, assessing each employed member some deduction from pay roll and paying unemployed members a minimum allowance. The payment of out-of-work benefits has historically been the function of many trade unions; [19] the photoengravers have had one of the strongest funds in this country.[20] The second alternative, of course, is a public unemployment or relief program. Thus the trade-union objective may be the largest possible wage bill from the segment of the economy *including funds from the public support of the unemployed.* A third objective may be the largest private pay roll to employed members, deducting from their wage income an amount to pay *out-of-work benefits to unemployed members.*[21] The wage rates determined under these

[18] Twentieth Century Fund, *How Collective Bargaining Works,* New York, 1942, pp. 355–356.

[19] Sidney and Beatrice Webb, *Industrial Democracy,* Longmans, Green and Company, London, 1914, pp. 152–172.

[20] The amount of unemployment benefits paid by national and international trade unions in the American Federation of Labor from 1929 through 1939 is tabulated below. These data do not include payments under local or Federal labor-union plans nor do they summarize data for international unions that do not report to the A.F. of L. executive officers.

1929	$ 276,718	1935	$ 3,356,276
1930	3,311,280	1936	10,990,104
1931	9,146,724	1937	1,671,139
1932	19,970,557	1938	2,582,543
1933	13,784,043	1939	1,815,784
1934	4,467,802		

Some indication of the magnitude of payments by some local unions may be gained from the report that locals of the photoengravers averaged over a million dollars a year in benefits in the period 1929–1939. (*President's Report to the 40th Annual Convention, International Photo-Engravers' Union,* August 21–26, 1939, pp. 54–55.) The locals of the typographical union expended $559,225.29 in the twelve months ending April 30, 1940. (*Report of Officers to the 84th Session of the International Typographical Union,* August 17, 23, 1940, p. 56.)

[21] A great many other objectives are conceivable which consist in modification of the largest wage bill for individual savings, loans from friends or family, etc. A wage rate would be set which maximized the private-pay roll plus these items. The cases of public support and union out-of-work benefits would appear to be much more important.

two objectives will modify the results of Figs. 2A and 2B in opposite directions.

The existence of public insurance or relief may permit a higher
wage rate, under the objective of maximizing the combined wage
bill, because the increase in wage income arising from the higher
rates plus the increase from the public unemployment fund may
more than offset the decrease attributable to the contraction of
private employment at the higher rates. The union will endeavor
to push the wage rate up until
these influences exactly counterbalance each other.

Figure 3 shows the impact of
these separate factors.

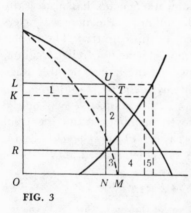

FIG. 3

In Fig. 3, OR represents the unemployment insurance rate. As in
Fig. 2A, the initial wage rate maximizing the wage bill is TM. The
total labor income with unemployment insurance will be $OKTM$ plus
rectangle 4. But the wage UN will
yield a higher total income if
rectangle 1 plus rectangle 5 is greater than rectangle 2. Rectangle 2
plus rectangle 3 represents the decline in the private wage bill due to
the higher rates, while rectangles 3 and 5 indicate the increase in receipts to the wage earners from the unemployment insurance fund.

The same discussion may be put in algebraic formulation if w is
the wage rate and r the relief or unemployment compensation rate.
The demand and the employment functions respectively may be represented as follows:

$$D(w) = x_1$$
$$S(w) = x_1 + x_2$$

where x_1 and x_2 are the amount of labor employed in private industry
and in receipt of public assistance. Then the total labor revenue is:

$$TR = w \cdot D(w) + r[S(w) - D(w)] \tag{1}$$

For the maximum total labor revenue, the wage rate must be set so
that:

$$\frac{dTR}{dw} = 0 = \frac{d(w \cdot D)}{dw} + r\left(\frac{dS}{dw} - \frac{dD}{dw}\right) \tag{2}$$

These notations may be directly related to the geometry in Fig. 3. The first term is equivalent to rectangles $1 - (2 + 3)$; $r \cdot dS/dw$ is rectangle 5 and the final term, $r \cdot \dfrac{}{} dD/dw$ is rectangle 3.

An interesting case is presented when the middle term drops out, that is, when the membership function is a vertical line within the relevant range. Then, clearly, the wage rate will be pushed up until the loss in income from private employment is balanced by the increase in unemployment assistance. More generally, the wage rate will be relatively higher with the public unemployment insurance [22] (a) the more inelastic the demand for labor services, (b) the more elastic the wage membership function, and (c) the higher the rate of public unemployment compensation.

(3) If the union seeks to maximize the private wage bill of those attached to the union, as indicated by the membership function, plus the out-of-work benefits to unemployed members financed by pay-roll deductions, the same wage will be fixed as will yield the largest private wage bill (Figs. 2A and 2B) since the out-of-work benefits are paid from this private wage bill. However, the union may wish to maximize the *wage bill of those employed*, allowing an out-of-work benefit to those remaining unemployed. Some rate lower than that which would maximize the wage bill to the group as a whole is likely to be fixed because less benefits will have to be paid out, both because more members are employed and fewer are likely to be attached to the union. The rate will be lowered until the loss to those employed due to the lower rate is exactly matched by the increase in income from those additional workers hired plus the smaller amount of out-of-work benefit paid.

In Fig. 3, *OR* may now represent the out-of-work benefit rate. The income to employed members may be initially regarded as *OLUN* minus rectangles 3, 4, and 5. Some lower rate will maximize the net income to employed members if rectangle 2 plus rectangle 3 plus rectangle 5 are greater than rectangle 1.

The algebraic notation and condition for maximization of total labor revenue developed for the case of public care of the unemployed is equally applicable to the present case with a single change in sign.

[22] The manner in which the public unemployment fund is raised may have some impact on the wage rate determined. For the present context this influence may be neglected.

The plus sign in equation (2) must be altered to the negative. Then the maximum labor revenue to those employed, after deducting out-of-work benefits, will be attained at a wage rate where the increment to the wage bill is just offset by the decrements to the out-of-work benefits. The wage rate will be lower (a) the more elastic the demand for labor, (b) the more elastic the membership function, and (c) the higher the rate of out-of-work benefits.

(4) An obvious goal of a trade union might be to secure the largest possible amount of employment, given its membership function. The wage rate that will yield the maximum employment level is designated by the intersection of the employment and demand functions. This rate is identical to that permitting the largest wage bill when the employment function cuts the demand function above the critical wage rate at which the increment to the wage bill is zero (Fig. 2B). At lower wage rates the amount of employment may be increased only at the cost of a decline in the total wage bill. The membership function may lie so far to the right of the demand function that only a zero wage, or one close to it, would secure maximum employment with the given functions. The point must be reiterated that the membership function is not the classical supply function and the intersection of the demand and membership functions does not constitute "full employment."

(5) Another conceivable objective of a union, and one which on a priori grounds might be regarded as fairly typical, is the attainment of the highest average wage income for each unit of labor affiliated with the union. If the membership functions is invariate, the goal resolves into that of securing the maximum wage bill since the total and average would then vary in precisely the same way. Should the membership function be upward sloping and intersect the demand function below the critical wage at which the wage bill is an absolute maximum, however, a lower wage rate may yield the highest average wage income. Every decrease in the wage rate from that at which the wage bill is a maximum will decrease the total wage bill, but the decrease in the amount of labor attached to the union may be even more rapid, depending on the shape of the membership function. The average wage receipts will rise as long as the denominator falls faster than the numerator.

The condition for the maximization of the average wage bill of those attached to the union can be indicated as follows. If $\begin{aligned} TR &= w \cdot D(w) \\ S &= S(w) \end{aligned}$, the maximization of the average or per capita wage bill of the membership will require that $\dfrac{dTR/S}{dw} = O$. Hence, $TR/S = dTR/S$, that is the condition must be fulfilled that the rate of change of the total wage bill must be equal to that of the amount of labor affiliated with the union.

(6) A union could attempt to maximize the *collective wage "rents"* of those employed. This objective is of analytical interest but without any readily discernible counterpart in trade-union policies.

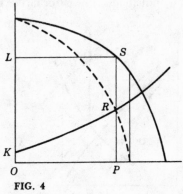

FIG. 4

In Fig. 4 the wage SP is determined by the intersection of the employment function and the marginal demand function. The return to the group of wage earners employed is the largest possible over their minimum offer prices as viewed by the trade union; the figure $KLSR$ is a maximum; no lower or higher wage rate can yield such a large collective "surplus."

(7) The preceding cases have designated objectives of a trade union with given employment and demand functions. But the wage may also be affected by the choice among alternative functions. One such instance has already been pointed out in noting that a union may regard itself as confronted by longer or shorter run demand functions, or by a demand function that specifies more detailed types and timing of adjustments. For each of the six objectives that have been suggested, a different wage rate would be determined depending on the time patterns of adjustment that are presumed to be involved in the demand function.[23]

---

[23] The diagrams of this chapter are not intended to deal with changes in wage rates arising from shifts in the demand or membership functions. This is in contrast to usual demand and supply analysis. It might have been inferred from Figs. 2–4 that every change in "demand" for labor will affect the wage rate, but the impact periods associated with the demand shift (see Fig. 1) are required to show the effect of the change in demand for labor upon wage rates.

In similar fashion, the membership function may be given several formulations. The union may envisage the amount of labor attached to the union in the absence of explicit exclusions or formal restrictions on affiliation, or a second function may include the impact of these regulations. The difference in the wage determined with these two employment functions is especially important for the problem of union policies in secularly expanding or contracting industries. The alternative functions, 1 and 2, are shown in

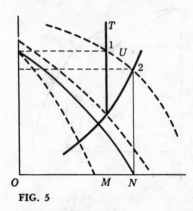

FIG. 5

Fig. 5. As demand for labor increases, the union may be confronted with the prospect of specifically limiting employment and increasing the wage rate to *TM* or accepting *UN* on the basis of an employment function that omits formal exclusion. The choice between these alternatives depends on whether the union is interested only in maximizing the position of an existing membership or considers the interests of those that might affiliate with an increase in demand for labor. In secularly expanding industries, the choice of employment function 1 (Fig. 5) tends to restrict the growth of employment. By the adoption of measures less stringent than complete limitation of entry, an employment function intermediate to 1 and 2 can be achieved.

The view that contends the amount of labor attached to the union at one time is regarded as invariate makes for lower wage rate than a forward rising employment function in a contracting sector of the economy. The wage rate would be higher at any given level of demand were the union operating on a membership function which required forcible exit or exclusion of wage earners from the union as employment declined secularly.

A number of conceivable objectives of a trade union have now been surveyed; the models proposed stressed the importance of determining a cross section of union views on (*a*) the shape of the membership function, (*b*) the relative influence of demand curves for labor with different time subscripts, (c) the influence of unemployment compensation on wage decisions of trade unions, and (d) the objectives that are most frequently maximized, that is, whose wage bill is maximized. Naturally, empirical evidence does not neatly fit into these categories, and trade-union practice varies from union to union and from time to time. Extreme caution must guide any quest for this type of material; not only is conduct seldom overt and reflective, but union activity is frequently symbolic.[24] No extensive empirical study was specifically made of these problems.

But the most critical of these issues can be pushed further: What range of wage earners are taken into specific account by trade unions when formulating wage decisions? This problem cannot even be approached until the decision-making unit has been specified. The wage earners from one department in a firm (a chapel in the printing trades), a local union, an international union, or some joint unit with other unions are all possibilities.[25] With respect to a particular wage-making jurisdiction, the problem splits into two: (a) What are union policies on entry to the union? (b) What methods of decision formation are used within the union with specified membership? Is the union organized to allow long-run interests to receive attention?

(a) Trade unions have probably learned to favor the entry of all "qualified workers." The term "qualified" is to be interpreted by the enterprise or industry primarily, rather than by the union. Consider, for instance, the statement of the President of the Musicians.

In our profession, everybody must be eligible to become a member as long as he satisfies the public and receives pay for his musical services and in an examination this fact should be established as being decisive as to whether the applicant should be accepted as a member.[26]

[24] These difficulties are further elaborated in Chap. IV.

[25] The impact of the choice of the decision-making unit upon the resulting wage is considered in the next chapter. The importance of the locus of decision formation is not peculiar to trade unions. A firm is ordinarily defined in terms of entrepreneurial decisions in economic theory. But only a little observation is necessary to show that many central decisions in modern corporations may be made by trade associations, by banking interests, and by other parties outside the firm.

[26] American Federation of Musicians of the United States and Canada, *Official Proceedings of the Forty-Second Annual Convention*, 1937, p. 74.

The decision to take in all qualified workers arises from the practical necessity of increasing the bargaining power of the union, reducing the number of potential strikebreakers. The generalization does not mean that trade unions, or at least some of them, do not succeed in restricting supply. Rather, the strategy calls for taking in all qualified workers and then affecting new entry by such diverse means as decasualized hiring halls with closed membership, licensing laws, apprenticeship periods, preferential hiring or layoffs with restricted membership by fees, rituals, or informal prohibitions.[27] But these practices probably apply only to a minority of trade unions (by membership). There are hardly any bars to entry in the large industrial-type unions. The familiar cliché that a trade union is simply a monopoly on the supply side thus retards analytical study of problems summarized by the "membership function."

(b) Wage decisions may be formulated by means that vary from those maximizing the position of the membership as a whole to those that border on maximizing the income of a single "organizer." The shape and position of the membership function relevant to wage determination will vary with the orientation of political control within the union. Reference is not made here primarily to the relative rates among occupational subgroups in the union (see Chap. IV), so much as to the people who have a voice in decision formation. Numerous devices have been used to restrict narrowly the focus of decision-making; among the more important are depriving unemployed members of votes, giving Class B members limited voting privileges, and using the usual committee and convention manipulations.

The most suitable generalized model of the trade union for analytical purposes is probably that which depicts the maximization of the wage bill for the total membership. Several variants must be kept in mind as the position of the membership function appropriate to decision formation may be altered depending upon (a) the formal bargaining unit, (b) the degree of unionization of the wage earners, (c) membership restrictions, and (d) locus of political power within a trade union concerning wage rates.

[27] These restrictions are not necessarily harmful from the standpoint of the national dividend. For a discussion of union hiring policies, see Sumner H. Slichter, *Union Policies and Industrial Management*, Brookings Institution, Washington, 1941, Chap. III.

CHAPTER IV. WAGE POLICIES
OF TRADE UNIONS [1]

The use of the term "policy" has become a fad in recent years, particularly as applied to industrial prices.[2] Such popularity breeds ambiguity. The phrase is here used simply to imply that (a) trade unions have some discretion and alternatives in the bargaining process through which a complex wage structure is determined, (b) some types of wage strategy and pattern will be found superior to others by a trade union given its objectives and specific problems, and (c) the mechanism whereby a trade union experiments with tactics and chooses among them need not connote an entirely self-conscious process. The difference between discussing "pricing policy" and "price determination", in economics really involves dissimilar levels of abstraction and degrees of generality. The main stream of the study is now shifted from the more formal models of the last chapter to wage-policy considerations.

An investigation of trade-union wage policy may be thought to be an elucidation of the obvious since the only objectives are more favorable wage structures. "I guess really what I mean when I say fair wages is more wages." [3] At times, "more wages" may be construed as only higher wage rates. All wage policy by this view is epitomized by the slogan "push 'em up." The following discussion will show not only that this view is in error, but that a great deal is to be learned from a study of the manipulation of wage structures for specific objectives. Just as the statement that an enterprise attempts to maximize profits does not preclude

---

[1] Some of the argument of the chapter was presented in a paper before the American Economic Association: *American Economic Review*, Supplement, March, 1942, XXXII, pp. 290–301.

[2] E. G. Nourse, "The Meaning of 'Price Policy,' " *Quarterly Journal of Economics*, February, 1941, LV, pp. 175–209.

[3] E. Wight Bakke, *The Unemployed Worker*, Yale University Press, New Haven, 1940, p. 66.

fruitful investigation of price policy, so the maximization of the wage bill by a trade union does not automatically dismiss all further study of the determination of wage structures.

1. *Nonincome Objectives of Wage Policy*

Aside from the obvious goal of affecting the income of a specified group of wage earners, wage policy may be directed towards a great many other objectives. Both the multidimensional feature of the wage structure and the directness of impact of changes in this structure on costs and incomes renders wage changes a highly effective tool. Unless the nonincome objectives are isolated, the wage policy of many unions will appear incomprehensible and incompetent when appraised from the criterion of maximizing the wage bill. The point is that the specific goal of a policy may have been something entirely different.

(1) Many changes in wage structure have been intended to promote membership in a trade union. An organizing drive will be more apt to succeed if prospective members can be convinced that they will immediately benefit from affiliation. And there can be no more convincing demonstration of this benefit than a wage increase. Consequently, whether the organizing drive precedes a labor board election or is part of a strike, promises of an "increase" will be made. If the union is then to hold its recruits, the goods must be delivered. In this context, the long-run effects on employment or the future of any specific enterprise are small matters; the principal objective is organization.

The trade union is not alone in recognizing the efficacy of changes in wage structure as a means for other objectives than primary effects on incomes and costs. Many enterprises have attempted to prevent or forestall organization by granting a wage increase.[4] The wage spurt of 1936–1937 was essentially of this character. Typically, these increases were not successful in their primary objective and a further increase was necessary to the union that had won an election or gone out on strike. In most

---

[4] ". . . I have yet to see (an employer) who would willingly concede to the employees better wage and working conditions unless it was . . . for the purpose of pacifying employees so that they would not organize." *President's Report, Official Proceedings of the Fortieth Convention, American Federation of Musicians,* 1935, p. 67.

cases a single wage increase (usually of 5 cents an hour or 5 per cent) would have been sufficient had not the attempt been made to buy off organization. Some industrial management has not yet understood this essential relationship between organization and wage policy. The Ford Motor Company and the International Harvester Company granted wage increases in the spring of 1941 before Labor Board elections, only to have to give further increases in subsequent negotiations. The relation between wage structure and organization extends to the form of union recognition.

(2) One of the most complex problems that faces every union is the way in which the available work shall be allocated among prospective wage earners. Wage policy may be used to effectuate this division. The payment of overtime after a standard day is an effective device to encourage the enterprise to hire additional workers rather than incur penalty rates.[5] This feature of overtime rates is most clearly seen in periods of large unemployment when strong pressure is exerted to reduce, if not eliminate, overtime. In seasonal industries, restrictions on overtime rates may be relaxed only at the peak of activity.[6]

(3) An exceedingly rapid change in wage structure has been made in the last five years with the extension of vacations with pay. Over 25 per cent of all organized wage earners received annual vacations with pay under collective bargaining agreements in 1940. Two years later the percentage of coverage had risen to sixty, representing almost eight million workers.[7] This spectacular development indicates a wage policy that is directed toward specific elements of the labor bargain: the relative preference for vacations with pay is high as compared to other terms in the wage structure. That vacations with pay should rank so high in wage-earners' preference is not unrelated to the experience with "leisure" during the period of prolonged unemployment in the early thirties. For most wage earners leisure had become

[5] Overtime is to be regarded also as a form of price discrimination.
[6] *The Hosiery Worker*, December 2, 1938, and the *Eastern Headwear Agreement of the Hat, Cap and Millinery Workers*, p. 10.
[7] "Vacations with Pay in Union Agreements, 1940," *Monthly Labor Review*, November, 1940, 51, p. 1070 and Bureau of Labor Statistics, *Vacations and Holidays Provided under Union Agreements, January 1943, Memorandum No. 6*, Washington, 1943, p. 1.

synonymous with the anxiety of job hunting. Under vacations with pay, "a workingman may have a period of leisure when he is not harassed by unemployment."[8] Furthermore, his vacation is enjoyed "not as a gratuity of the employer, but as a legally recognized right in return for employment services rendered."[9] Wage policy has been used to achieve in the vacation with pay a social status that had been reserved to other groups. "A layoff without pay is not a vacation."[10] An additional circumstance increasing the relative preference of vacations with pay to a straight wage increase is the automatic character of the saving. The psychic costs of saving may be thought lower since the funds do not pass through the wage-earner's hands week by week.[11] For these reasons, then, vacations with pay have been adopted; wage policy has been directed toward achieving a particular type of wage structure.

(4) Wage policy has also been used as an effective means of controlling the rate of introduction of technical innovations. The relative wage rates on the new and the old machine or process will significantly influence the rate at which an enterprise will find it profitable to adopt a change. Wage policy may thus be directed toward increasing costs on the new or reducing costs on the old to reduce the rate of introduction. For instance, the flint-glass workers apparently attempted to "discourage the use of lamp chimney machines by demanding rates that would equalize the cost of chimneys produced by machinery and by hand."[12] In 1908 the Glass Bottle Blowers took a reduction of 20 per cent on beer bottles to "protect the manufacturer who was unable to secure one of those machines . . . and to protect ourselves."[13] The international officials of the Glass Bottle Blowers apparently were convinced in 1927 that a basic wage of $6.50 a day in the

---

[8] *Machinists' Monthly Journal*, September, 1937, 49, p. 589.

[9] *Loc. cit.*, p. 588.

[10] *Report of Proceedings of the Fiftieth Annual Convention of the American Federation of Labor*, 1930, p. 53.

[11] This statement has frequently been made by trade-union representatives in conversation.

[12] Sumner H. Slichter, *Union Policies and Industrial Management*, Brookings Institution, Washington, 1941, p. 209.

[13] *Report of Proceedings of the 51st Convention of the Glass Bottle Blowers*, 1929, p. 213.

blown-ware departments would lead to a rapid introduction of machinery. For this reason they voted down the proposed increase favored by many locals.[14]

(5) A further nonincome objective of wage policy is frequently the attainment of desired working conditions. A wage premium put upon especially unfavorable hours of work or circumstances of employment is intended to remove these conditions. There may be great difficulty in distinguishing between policies directed at preventing undesirable work situations and policies using such conditions simply as a means of increasing income. The more certain that an enterprise cannot avoid the unfavorable situation, the more likely the policy may be said to be directed primarily toward higher income. Furthermore, direct action in the form of specific prohibition may be resorted to rather than penalty rates. None the less, there are undoubtedly situations in which differential rates are used to discourage objectionable features of work situations. The night-shift differential,[15] in rate of pay or length of shift,[16] in some cases, is primarily intended to reduce the amount of this type of work. The same applies to double-time rates on Sundays and holidays. The provision in many agreements that a minimum daily wage must be paid to any worker required to report for work is intended to remove the inconvenience of persistent unsuccessful reporting for work.[17]

(6) Wage policy may be used to implement the control of entrance to a trade by means of the differential rates paid to apprentices and to learners. Special rates to handicapped and

[14] *Report of Proceedings of the 49th Convention of the Glass Bottle Blowers*, 1927, pp. 239–247.

[15] See "Shift Operations under Union Agreements," *Monthly Labor Review*, October, 1940, 51, pp. 860–872.

[16] The differential in hours between day and night shifts with equal pay indicates something of the relative preferences towards these types of work. Machinists in Chicago in 1920 received 5 cents an hour extra for night-shift work. This was changed to equal pay for a 40-hour (5 day) a week night shift as compared to 44 hours for day work. This provides an interesting case of substitution. *Machinists' Monthly Journal*, January, 1926, 38, p. 39.

[17] "The employee gets up in the morning in the winter time and packs his lunch and gets out there and on the clock it says 'No work today; report tomorrow.' They could have at least let one of those turns know. It didn't look good to me." *Minutes of the Conference between Ball Brothers Company of Muncie, Indiana, and the Glass Bottle Blowers Association of the United States and Canada*, September 4, 5, 6, and 8, 1941, p. 35.

aged workers are intended to affect the length of the occupational life. The way in which rates are graduated during the period of apprenticeship will undoubtedly influence the length of time many apprentices will stay with their training. Rates close to the journeyman's during the latter part of the training period will induce apprentices to complete the full period. Hence the quality of training of the labor force may be materially influenced by wage policy. In addition to these relatively minor influences, the wage policy will fundamentally affect the number of job opportunities and hence affect the number attracted to an industry by both the level of rates and the prospects of employment. But this relationship between rates and employment, as an element of wage policy, requires detailed attention in a later section.

The preceding points have indicated ways in which wage policy may be used to attain essentially nonincome objectives. The desired consequences have little relation to the total volume of employment or the level of pay rolls. The wage-rate structure is used in these instances, frequently in conjunction with more direct action, simply because it may be an effective tool to achieve specific objectives. Any appraisal of wage structures that neglects these types of goals will undoubtedly conclude that the wage policy of a union has been inept; the broadest types of objectives must be recognized if wage policy is to be understood. While difficulty besets any attempt to isolate objectives in specific instances, it will be useful to examine in every case the possibility that wage structure may be directed toward: union organization, division of work, specific means of remuneration like vacations with pay, affecting the rate of technical change, desirable working conditions, and partial control over entrance to the trade and the quality of training of recruits.

2. Wage Pronouncements of National Organizations

What trade unions say about their broad wage policies is much less important than what they do in specific contexts. Labor leaders are expert in trading,

in dramatic presentation, in *ad hominem* argument and in the subtleties of political adjustment. They understand much better than most of us how to handle men, whether they wear overalls or the trappings of office. And they have no desire to subordinate that great skill to the less colorful art of juggling words, rules and precedents. . . .[18]

Never must it be forgotten that a reason or argument may be adopted simply because it proves useful. Formal pronouncements may consist of apologetics that have been most effective in negotiations with companies, in influencing governmental and public agencies, and in crystallizing the support of the membership of a union. Nevertheless, a brief review of the announced wage policies of American trade unions may be revealing as to (a) the arguments leadership has found effective both internally and externally, and (b) the way in which these slogans have been adapted to changing situations.[19]

A historical survey of wage statements reveals a single negative slogan and a succession of affirmative symbols. On the defensive, "no reduction" has always been the announced motto. A classic statement of this position is found in Samuel Gompers' last appearance before an American Federation of Labor convention:

Since 1907 the American labor movement has had a slogan for itself and for the men and women of toil of our country and whoever may wish to profit thereby: "It is better to resist and lose than not to resist at all." . . . Let it be clearly understood . . . that America's workers will resist any attempt to cut wages, no matter what the result may be to industry. An industry which cannot pay a living wage, a wage according to our best standards of American civilization, had best go out of business.[20]

No slogan is an invariant rule of action, and as will be explained later, trade unions have not only taken reductions in the wage structure, but even proposed them. However, there can be no ques-

[18] Charles E. Wyzanski, Jr., "Labor Disputes during the War," *Labor Relations Reporter*, January 19, 1942, IX.

[19] Note the way in which the arguments for shorter hours of work changed. John R. Commons, *History of Labor in the United States*, The Macmillan Company, 1936, I, pp. 13–14.

[20] *Report of Proceedings of the 44th Annual Convention of the American Federation of Labor*, 1924, p. 318. Similar statements are found in the records of almost every national or international organization. For a brief survey of English material, see John T. Dunlop, "Relative Movements of Real and Money Wage Rates," *Economic Journal*, September, 1938, XLVIII.

tion that the "no reduction" slogan is a central feature of all wage pronouncements.

The fashion in affirmative slogans has changed a number of times since the start of this century, and more than one was used at a single time. However, the following succession is based upon what appears to have been the sequence of greatest popularity. (1) At the turn of the century in the atmosphere of the anti-injunction campaign and a rapidly rising membership, trade unions demanded the "fair wage." "What we seek to do is to fix a reasonably fair rate of wages for all men who work in the mining industry, so as to give them a wage that will enable them to live in a manner conformable to American standards and put something away for old age or infirmity." [21] (2) The "living wage" received most use in the period of the early advocacy of minimum wage laws and during the 1916–1920 war period of rapidly increasing cost of living. There was probably little difference in the essential idea of the "fair" and the "living" wage, as is evident in the above quotation from Mitchell. Fairness was defined in terms of a living standard. The phrase "living wage" probably first gained popularity in the English Miners' strike of 1893. [22] In the same year the House of Commons resolved: "That in the opinion of this House, no person should in Her Majesty's Naval Establishments be engaged at wages insufficient to maintain a proper maintenance. . . ." By 1909 this had been expanded to the Fair Wages Clause for all government contracts, once again revealing the similarity in content of the two symbols. This same sequence of slogans is indicated for the American labor movement by John P. Frey in the discussions on wage policy in 1925. [23] "I have recalled when we spoke of a fair day's wage for a fair day's work. . . . Only within recent years many of our representatives adopted . . . a living wage." (3) As is well known, the 1925 and 1926 conventions of the American Federation of Labor adopted

[21] John Mitchell, "The Question of a Maximum Wage," *The Outlook*, March 28, 1903, 73, p. 721.

[22] Philip Snowden, *The Living Wage*, Hodder and Stoughton, London, 1912, p. 18. Also see Henry W. Macrosty, "The Recent History of the Living Wage Movement," *Political Science Quarterly*, September, 1898, XIII, pp. 424–431.

[23] *Report of the Proceedings of the 45th Annual Convention of the American Federation of Labor*, 1925, pp. 232–233.

the slogan of the "social wage." "Social inequality, industrial instability and injustice must increase unless the workers' real wages—the purchasing power of their wages—coupled with a continuing reduction in the hours making up the working day, are progressed in proportion to man's increasing power of production." [24] This notion of wages increasing with productivity is probably the most commonly repeated statement of wage policy within the American Federation of Labor. More than one slogan, however, has been used to express the same idea. One hears of "health and efficiency wages" and even of a "cultural wage." The 1940 Executive Council's Report contends: "The cornerstone in efforts to increase national income, to sustain business, to improve health and efficiency standards of living for all families, is to increase the real wage in step with increases in productivity.[25] The musicians have urged "the payment of a cultural, and not only a living wage so (the worker) may be able to set aside a little competency to help him to overcome the misfortune of unemployment." [26] Mr. Green has maintained that "our progress is reflected by the larger ideal expressed in the successive epithets applied to our objectives—the living wage gave way to a saving wage and that to a cultural wage." [27] These slogans, summarized under the heading of the "social wage," all lay considerable stress on the importance of matching the pace of productivity. They arose, in large measure, as a protest against the cost-of-living emphasis generated by the 1916–1920 war period and as a claim upon the rapid technical changes of the twenties. (4) The Congress of Industrial Organizations has laid particular emphasis upon the objective of securing a larger share of the national income for wage earners. Statements to this effect can be found in earlier trade-union pronouncements. In testifying.before the Commission on

[24] *Ibid.*, p. 271.

[25] *Report of the Proceedings of the 60th Annual Convention of the American Federation of Labor*, 1940, p. 557.

[26] *American Federation of Musicians, Official Proceedings, 42nd Convention*, 1937, p. 67. No attempt is made in this chapter to discuss the elaborate rationale behind these slogans and formal statements. In most instances some form of the "purchasing power" argument is used. A useful study might be made of the various formulations of this argument contained in the trade-union literature.

[27] *Report of the Proceedings of the 46th Annual Convention of the American Federation of Labor*, 1926, p. 47.

Industrial Relations in 1914, Gompers said, "The A.F. of L. encourages and stimulates the workmen in their efforts to secure a constantly increasing share in the products of labor, and increasing share in the consumption and use of things produced, thereby giving employment to the unemployed, the only effective way by which that can be done." [28] But the C.I.O. has made this slogan more central to its program than Mr. Gompers ever did. "The CIO has been winning wage increases for millions of American workers. It is moving ahead to win more . . . to secure for workers a larger share of the wealth they produce." [29]

This brief survey of wage pronouncements has shown (a) that trade-union leadership itself (Gompers and Green) regards "the living wage" or "the social wage" as slogans and epithets. As such they are useful in arousing and marshaling the support of the membership, in presenting a rationale to the rest of the community, and in fulfilling all the social functions effectuated by a creed or ritual. [30] Too frequently these broad phrases are attacked as meaningless without sufficient appreciation of the role they play in the trade-union folklore. An even more grievous error is to suppose that these slogans exhaust the content of trade-union wage policy. Wage policy as practiced by trade unions must be examined in the context of actual situations; specific collective-bargaining agreements and wage conferences constitute the basic sources. (b) The preceding summary has also shown that wage slogans may be modified from time to time in the light of altered industrial conditions and standards of public judgment. Increasingly intricate and detailed statistical work is being done to justify specific wage demands in terms of these slogans. The argumentation has become more rationalistic although the essential character of the symbol remains.

3. The Bargaining Unit

Concern with wage determination on abstract or empirical levels requires specifying the locus of decision formation among

[28] Samuel Gompers, *The American Labor Movement, Its Makeup, Achievements and Aspirations*, American Federation of Labor, Washington, p. 17.

[29] Congress of Industrial Organizations, *CIO'S Tax Program, Tax Wealth — Not Wages*, June, 1941, Publication No. 55, p. 3.

[30] See Talcott Parsons, *The Structure of Social Action*, McGraw-Hill Book Company, Inc., New York, 1937, pp. 429–441.

both buyers and sellers. The boundary lines to the administrative lumps in Mr. Robertson's sea of buttermilk must first be drawn. The single enterprise is usually taken to be the buyer in the labor market, but the effective unit may also be an industry-wide association, banking or other financial interests, or even a national confederation of all employers. Under trade unionism, the opposing sellers may be a local, a group of locals, an international, or some combination of internationals. These possible units of decision-making on either side can be thought of as arranged in concentric circles. Transactions may be effectuated between circles of any size. The Electrical Workers, C.I.O., may enter into an agreement covering virtually all employees of the General Electric Company; several disassociated locals may deal with a single enterprise; a local of the motion-picture machine operators confronts local theater managements one at a time; the glaziers in Cleveland may bargain with a local employers' group; the Allied Printing Trades in St. Louis negotiate with an association of local employers; or the National Brotherhood of Operative Potters may make an agreement with a federation of pottery concerns.[31] The jurisdiction of the parties that confront each other cannot fail to influence the resulting terms of sale.

"Exclusive jurisdiction" has been the traditional policy of the American Federation of Labor. The boundary lines among internationals are drawn by the executive committee or by the convention, presumably once and for all time; each gainful occupation or a cluster of occupations is assigned to only one union. The equivalent of "property rights" has been built up in these jurisdictions. The further determination of bargaining units, that is, the relative authority between internationals and their locals, is left to the autonomous international unions. Hybrid bargaining units can be created by agreement among the sovereign affiliates who form the American Federation of Labor.[32]

[31] See Paul H. Norgren, *The Swedish Collective Bargaining System*, Harvard University Press, Cambridge, Mass., 1941, for a discussion of industry-wide bargaining.

[32] The exigencies of competing with the C.I.O. have forced serious modifications of the "exclusive jurisdiction" principle, although the symbolism is still powerful. See, John T. Dunlop, "The Changing Status of Labor" in *The Growth of the American Economy*, Prentice Hall Inc., New York, 1943.

Compare the following quotations:

"This organization has jurisdiction over all teamsters, chauffeurs and helpers, stablemen; all who are employed on horses, harness, carriages or automobiles in and

The Wagner Act, passed in pre-C.I.O. days, has come to involve a repudiation of the received tradition. The conflict was not seen in 1935 because the only conceivable controversies over units were with employers and within the Federation. The National Labor Relations Board was given power to determine the unit appropriate for the purposes of collective bargaining in cases under its jurisdiction (Section 9b).[33] In the exercise of this power, the center of attention has been focused upon the rights of minorities, charges of favoritism, the impact on union structure, and the possibilities of gerrymandering.[34] The effects of the unit upon wage-rate determination have been neglected. A unit determination under the Wagner Act is not equivalent, however, to the locus of decision formation; the significant judgments may be dependent upon larger circles. A definitive study is thus required of the relative responsibilities of internationals and locals (and participants in multiunion units) in formulating sellers' decisions respecting wage structures.

International unions vary all the way from an extremely loose-knit alliance of locals to highly integrated and centralized bodies. The locus of decisions respecting wage rates shows the same variable pattern; several types of surveillance and controls are discernible over locals. (a) An international may simply require reports and copies of negotiated scales. (b) International representatives assist in negotiations and see that contracts conform to broad policies. (c) Each contract must be approved or countersigned by the International union. (d) All negotiations are in

around stables or garages (other than mechanics); gasoline station attendants (other than mechanics); warehousemen; all classes of dairy employees, inside and outside; workers employed in ice cream plants; all other workers employed in the manufacture and distribution of milk and dairy products; all truck terminal employees." *Proceedings of the 14th Convention International Brotherhood of Teamsters, Chauffeurs, Stablemen and Helpers of America*, September 9–14, 1940, Fourth Day, p. 17.

"President Tobin: Brother Naylor, you don't think for one minute that we, who have been fighting industrial organization, could embody in our jurisdictional claims electricians, mechanics of every description, do you? *Loc. cit.*, p. 19.

[33] The power of the Board has been upheld in the courts: American Federation of Labor et al. *vs.* National Labor Relations Board, 308 U. S. 401.

[34] Leo Wolman, "The Turning Point in American Labor Policy," *Political Science Quarterly*, June, 1940, 55, pp. 161–175; E. B. McNatt, "The 'Appropriate Bargaining Unit' Problem," *Quarterly Journal of Economics*, November, 1941, LVI, pp. 93–107. Also see the "Principles Established" section of the *Annual Reports* of the National Labor Relations Board.

complete charge of the central office. International unions also differ widely in the internal processes whereby demands are formulated and negotiations selected. Some unions consciously debate alternative policies; others attack each negotiation in an *ad hoc* fashion.

The degree of centralization of decision-making on wage rates in internationals is clearly related to (*a*) the extent of potential competition among local unions, that is, among the firms whose members constitute the various locals, and (*b*) the bargaining jurisdiction of the opposing business enterprises. An international union cannot normally permit locals to bid work away from each other; in fact, the dangers of interlocal competition were an important consideration in the founding of many international unions. The extension of the jurisdiction of either trade unions or employers can force the other party to expand—by association with others—in order to offset the change in bargaining advantage. Narrow or splintery units among trade unions are apt to persist only if the union has considerable bargaining power relative to the management unit.

A small group of strategic workers in a firm, for instance, can obtain very much higher rates than they could with a larger unit covering the whole enterprise. The wider the bargaining unit on the union side, the larger the number of wage earners whose interests will be considered and, in general, the more distant the effects that will enter into decision-making. International unions are more able to resist pressures to follow policies based simply on impact effects (Fig. 1). The larger the bargaining units, the more relative rates are apt to depend upon the internal politics of trade unions. The formulation of public policy on the bargaining unit can afford to pay much more attention to the impacts of the size of the unit on the level and structure of wage rates.

4. *Elements of Wage Policy*

Since the wage policies of trade unions are not to be found in the pronouncements of leadership, the action of locals and international must be explored in the context of specific problems and bargaining units. There are common questions and issues respecting wages that face almost every trade union, although the specific course of action may vary from one policy-making unit to another. These mutual problems will be designated the *elements* of wage policy. As would be expected, the order of importance of any single element will be found to differ among unions. At least the following elements can be identified.

(1) Every union is interested in the differential wage structures among individuals, operations, and occupations: the membership because of social and financial status, the leadership because of additional concern with the prestige of the organization and personal return to the union office. Each union then will be faced with questions of differential wages. But the importance of the issue will be largely influenced by the structure of the organization. The more narrow a craft union, in general, the fewer the number of differential rates over which to squabble. The issue may thus be expected to be most critical in industrial organizations. The conflicting pressures may be briefly noted.

The firm may press in negotiations for a considerable differential between production workers and more highly skilled individuals on the grounds of ensuring a labor supply and in order to provide suitable promotion for service well done. The higher paid workers may feel entitled to a customary dollar differential.[35] The production workers frequently constitute a large majority of the union; each occupational group may attempt to secure more favorable terms by internal political means.[36] The union leadership is confronted with the problem of securing a working compromise among these differences. The course of action adopted by a trade union in such a situation constitutes an element of wage policy.

[35] It is an open question whether small differentials in wage rates are socially significant in a community of wage earners. Mr. Bakke reports that union members in New Haven were rate conscious. "Having made an issue of and bargained over relative rates, these become symbolical of status relationships. . . ." E. Wight Bakke, *op. cit.*, p. 11.

Differences would seem to matter to wage earners when they have communal recognition. An interesting study can be made of the extent to which the various types of distinction provided by a trade union with all its local committees and offices are replacing the *social* differentiation at one time given to rates.

[36] After careful preparation the seamers, for instance, took their case to the convention floor in the Hosiery Union and secured instructions requiring the union negotiators to bargain for higher rates. *Official Proceedings of the 31st Convention of the American Federation of Hosiery Workers*, 1941.

(2) All international unions and many locals are faced with issues arising from the fact that companies with which the union deals differ as to costs and efficiency on the one hand and market position and control over price on the other. Are equal rates to be charged to low- and high-cost and low- and high-profit firms alike? Or shall the rates be staggered according to ability to pay? Each alternative is beset with its own difficulties. Equal time rates may mean a very low level since high-cost enterprises may not be able to pay a higher wage. This is certain to lead to internal pressure from the membership when some companies are shown to be making high profits.

If equal piece rates are established, no firm has a great deal of inducement to make those technical changes that will reduce the wage costs per unit of output. And even more important, the earnings of wage earners in inefficient firms will be much below those in the more competent enterprises. Such a condition will certainly lead to internal dissension within the union, resulting in either demands for wage increases where they can be least afforded or raising the serious question of assigning workers to the favored positions.

Should rates be staggered among companies dealing with the union, the first issue will be whether highly efficient firms should receive lower piece rates because of the higher hourly and weekly earnings that are possible or be charged higher rates in view of their greater capacity to pay. If time rates are typically chosen, the practical question will be whether the lower cost firms should be asked to pay the same or higher rates.

Any system of staggering is certain to raise bothersome questions of the merits of individual cases. The efforts of individual enterprises to secure a favorable differential create many a headache for the union leadership. The perplexing difficulty of assigning workers to higher paid enterprises still remains. This problem may prove especially acute if the leadership is attempting to build up a stronger *esprit de corps* among its members. These differential rates are crucially important, in addition, to the relative distribution of employment among competing enterprises. When only a part of a group of closely competing firms has been organized, the differential rates between union and nonunion firms is a decisive element of wage policy.[37]

The problem may be stated in theoretical terms. A union may discriminate among buyers and attempt to secure a share of the rents of other factors or the union may charge every firm the same price. This range of problems will be less important the more similar the competing enterprises in their cost and profit situations while these issues will be intensely vital the less differentiated the product market [38] and the greater the cost differentials.

(3) A central element of wage policy is involved in formulating some judgment of the effects of alternative wage structures on employment. Trade-union leadership, in effect, must make estimates of the elasticity of demand for labor over very short periods, the cycle, and the longer run. The time pattern of employment adjustments to wage-rate changes are involved. Any appraisal must arise from insight into the specific ways in which wage changes may have impact on employment. For instance, the independent effects must be appraised of machine substitution, the shift of business through lower product prices to nonunion firms, the birth of new nonunion enterprises, the emergence of kickbacks and other arrangements altering the basic rate, the development or expansion of substitute commodities or services, and impact on the rate of business mortality. No over-all elasticity of demand is given; the magnitude and speed of these separate effects have to be appraised for alternative wage structures if any intelligent judgment is to be made of the time pattern of the impact of wage changes upon employment. A survey of wage policy of trade unions should indicate the typical judgments of the over-all relationship between employment and wage structure in various time dimensions as well as the specific channels through which these impacts are adjudged to flow. These estimates will vary with the industrial scope of the wage-bargaining unit.

(4) Every union faces issues of the method of wage payment. Shall work be compensated for by the piece, by time, or by some

---

[37] The way in which employment will be influenced by wage differentials between enterprises is more directly a part of the next element of wage policy to be indicated.

[38] Chapter VI is exclusively devoted to the relationship between trade-union wage policy and their interest and concern with the prices of goods in product markets.

combination of the two? The choice among these alternatives has been so fully treated by Mr. Slichter in his *Union Policies and Industrial Management* (1941), as to require no additional treatment.[39] Modifying his treatment slightly, two necessary conditions may be identified for the adoption of piece rates by a trade union, (a) that units of output be definable with precision and (b) that conditions of work be not altered in a manner unfavorable to the wage-earners' over time. Trade unions may be attracted to piece rates for the reasons that small technical changes or increases in effort are automatically reflected in higher earnings, competing firms have equal direct-labor costs, older workers need have no special rate, and because an individual worker is frequently permitted his own pace, particularly when this does does not interfere with the output of other workers. The use of piece rates also involves a number of possible difficulties. Differentiated earnings may be conducive to internal conflicts within a union; conflicts with management will arise over standards of inspection as well as over the condition of equipment, organization of plant, and quality of material; and disputes may arise over the numbers of workers to be attached to an enterprise. Piece rates rather than time make wage earners much more interested, and management frequently less concerned, with the technical efficiency of operations. Certainly the choice among methods of wage payments constitutes an element of the wage policy of a trade union.

5. *Specific Wage Policies*

A. NONCYCLICAL RELATION BETWEEN WAGE RATES AND EMPLOYMENT

A number of problematic situations that are common to trade unions in dealing with wages have just been noted. The task remains of illustrating the way in which these issues are resolved by particular trade unions. A convenient start will be made with the element involving the noncyclical relation between employment and wage structure. The oft-repeated cliché that a trade union is incapable of thinking in other terms than rates is denied,

---

[39] Chapters X and XI. Also see Sidney and Beatrice Webb, *Industrial Democracy*, Longmans, Green and Company, London, 1914, pp. 279–323.

for instance, by the experience of the American Federation of Musicians.

Several features of this segment of the economy combine to present an interesting theoretical case. Musicians are usually hired to work as a unit. Within rather wide limits the revenue of the employer is not appreciably affected by the precise number of musicians in the unit. No change in "plant" is required with moderate changes in the number of musicians. As a result of this unusual situation, the union can regard a sum available for wages that is relatively independent of the number of musicians hired. The union looks upon a certain "wage fund" which it may divide among a large or smaller number of musicians depending upon the rates set. This division is accomplished both by fixing the rates of pay and regulating the number of musicians per operating unit.

Should wage rates alone be fixed, the enterprise could contract employment without loss to itself. Hence the necessity for also specifying wherever possible the number of musicians in each operating unit. If the product of rates and employment exceeds the wage fund, the enterprise will lose money and may eventually go out of business. Trade-union leadership may require considerable experience and insight in pushing this fund to its limits. Judgment is complicated by the presence of an intermediate market involving an agent or commission man. Wage-rate changes may squeeze the middleman or may be passed through to the public demand for band music, affecting the volume of employment.[40] The unique feature of these markets is that revenue may be relatively indepedent of the number of variable factors hired.[41]

That the international union has clearly understood the characteristics of its industry is evidenced from agreements which provide the amount of the wage bill to be expended by the enterprise.

We have in the past insisted upon the employment of a certain number of men. In other cases we were even successful in having an

---

[40] Chapter V provides a generalized scheme of analysis for interrelated product and factor markets.

[41] Within limits the marginal revenue product of labor would appear to be indeterminate.

employer agree to the amount of money he would expend for musicians during a certain time. No other union was ever successful in having the employer agree to the sum to be expended for the employment of its members.[42]

Where the courts have ruled against regulation of the number of men at work, or in fear of such rulings, locals have followed the policy of a sliding scale to induce the enterprise to hire more musicians.[43] Thus the choice between employment and rates appears to the locals and international in very clear outline.

The relative preferences of this union between employment and higher rates is complicated by the possibility of imposing make-work rules. The requirements for stand-by crews in radio stations broadcasting transcribed music is an illustration.[44] A unique amount of labor demanded cannot be specified at each wage rate until working rules have been determined. While the union could theoretically secure higher rates for a smaller number of musicians than would be employed in the absence of the working rules, such rates might be impractically high to exhaust the wage fund referred to above. The working rules may prove more readily enforceable than the higher rates. Furthermore, some enterprises may be forced to hire musicians that would never have done so otherwise. Through these media the pay rolls going to musicians may even be higher than they could be simply by manipulation of wage rates.

An interesting form of recognition of the relationship between wage rates and employment is provided by the photoengravers, who have typically bargained for individual rates above the minimum in an agreement and who have also built up large unemployment funds by assessment of the membership. Vice-president Woll complains of relatively inexperienced journeymen who demand higher rates and then draw unemployment benefits from the union when their demands are refused.[45] The dependence between rates and employment in this case is made

[42] President's Report, Official Proceedings of the 45th Convention, 1940, p. 72.
[43] President's Report, Official Proceedings of the 34th Convention, 1929, p. 57.
[44] Official Proceedings of the 43rd Convention of the American Federation of Musicians, 1938, p. 132.
[45] Official Proceedings of the 23rd Convention of the International Photo-Engravers' Union of North America, 1922, pp. 11–12.

vivid by the depletion of the unemployment fund by what is regarded as the unwarranted wage demands of a few members.

The relation between wage rates and employment has been forcibly brought to the attention of the hosiery workers through still another medium, that of nonunion competition. This union has been keenly aware of the limitation to a cost differential between the union and nonunion sections of the seamless and full-fashioned hosiery industries and has pursued a wage policy that will receive more detailed attention below. The awareness of the impact of a wage change on employment is illustrated by the following episode.

. . . in our first agreement with this company (making a low grade of seamless hosiery), through which a 25 per cent wage increase was secured for these workers, more than 50 per cent of them, notwithstanding the increases, were exempt from dues payments on which the minimum for seamless workers is $8.50 a week. To have forced a higher increase would have put these people entirely out of work.[46]

In a similar vein, President Stevenson of the molders contended that the officers of the union are familiar with the competition in industry and hence "they know the danger of driving too hard a bargain because of the possibility of driving work from union shops to open shops. They know that a raise is no good unless we are able to keep our members working."[47]

These illustrations (also see those indicated under the non-income objectives of wage policy) point out that the relation between employment and wage rates appears to a union in terms of *specific channels* through which employment may be varied as a result of a wage-structure change. No abstract over-all elasticity of demand presents itself. Employment may be thought to be adversely influenced in specific contexts by wage increases through mechanization, nonunion competition, a high rate of business mortality, or other factors indicated in the previous section. It is these specific avenues that will influence wage policy and spotlight any impact on employment. The more direct and immediate the employment reaction to a wage change, as may

---

[46] *Official Proceedings of the 27th Convention of the American Federation of Hosiery Workers,* 1938, p. 20.

[47] *International Molders Journal,* February, 1940, 76, p. 69.

be expected in the case of nonunion competition from existing firms, the more clearly the union will perceive the relationship. The less direct and the longer the period required for the employment reaction to work out, as may be the case through the development of substitute commodities or the entry of nonunion firms, the less likely the union may be to think of any specific relationship between employment and wage rates. This is to say, the elasticity of demand for labor varies with the time period in which employment reactions are allowed to work themselves out. The slower this response, the less occasion a union may have to recognize any specific channel through which employment is being affected.

A final indication of the recognition of an employment-wage-rate relationship is found in the growing number of agreements which provide for some form of employment guarantee.[48] In the course of bargaining with an enterprise over the terms of the labor bargain, some element in the wage structure has probably been given up or been modified in order to secure the employment guarantee. P. J. Conhon, vice-president of the machinists, recommended a program in 1928 providing that all agreements "shall contain a clause guaranteeing stabilization of employment as one of the factors in determining the wage rate per hour. If this guarantee cannot be given, then a higher wage rate must prevail to care for the employee when furloughed."[49] Ten years later the union could report that "in most of the agreements negotiated on the Pacific Coast we have been successful in including a provision for a guaranteed weekly wage for 'regular' employees, and, while the guaranteed amount varies in different agreements, it is computed at 80 or 90 per cent of the possible earnings of the employee, based on the number of hours covered by a full week's work. . . ."[50] These types of clauses are usually

[48] The Fair Labor Standards Act (1938) attempted to provide some inducement for these plans, by limited exemption from penalty overtime rates to firms that guaranteed 1000 hours, work in 26 weeks or 2000 hours a year in a bona fide trade-union contract.

[49] *Machinists' Monthly Journal*, April, 1928, 40, p. 246.

[50] *Machinists' Monthly Journal*, October, 1938, 50, p. 807. A sample clause is provided in the *Agreement By and Between Auto Mechanics' Local Union No. 289 and Seattle Automobile Dealers' Association*, signed March 27, 1941. "Weekly Guarantee: Employers shall guarantee the payment of a weekly minimum wage of $45.00 for journeymen for such of these employees as are required to report for work from week to week."

found in auto mechanics' agreements to solve the problems that arise from the fact that orders are frequently intermittent in automobile repair work.[51] The movies studio craft unions, also confronted by irregular work periods, have seriously considered a plan "guaranteeing minimum annual employment at somewhat lower rates." [52]

Annual wage or guaranty employment plans are rare; the Bureau of Labor Statistics reported only fourteen in a survey of seven thousand agreements.[53] Other plans exist, however, that have been inaugurated by management rather than under the procedure of collective bargaining. In the widely publicized plan of George A. Hormel and Company, now included in a contract with the United Packing House Workers, a clause guarantees to the regular employees 2000 hours' pay at straight time. The union cooperates with the management in preparing production schedules, employee job classifications, and interdepartmental transfers of employees. Such plans tend to concentrate the wage bill in fewer hands, providing an interesting illustration of the relevant membership function. The impact on the total wage bill is complex, depending in part upon whether any concession in base rates is made and what portion of the employees are classified as "regular." [54]

B. CYCLICAL FLUCTUATIONS IN WAGE STRUCTURE

(1) Very seldom will a trade union agree to an arrangement whereby wage structures fluctuate during the course of the cycle

[51] It is interesting to follow the justifications for such agreements. Such clauses are written "because of the unchangeable belief that (regular) employees are a necessary part of the "overhead" that must be maintained by the employer if he will furnish prompt and efficient service to the customer; in fact we believe this to be just as necessary a part of the "overhead" as is the motor analyzer, or the wheel aligning machine, or the floor space on which the employer pays rental." *Machinists' Monthly Journal*, October, 1938, 50, p. 807.

[52] Murray Ross, *Stars and Strikes, Unionization of Hollywood*, Columbia University Press, New York, 1941, p. 208.

[53] "Annual Wage and Guaranty Employment Plans in Union Agreements," *Monthly Labor Review*, August, 1940, 51, pp. 283–289.

[54] The American Federation of Hosiery Workers signed an interesting agreement with the A. Erdette Hosiery Mills, which provided that when the rate of pay was increased, the number of guaranteed weeks of employment would be reduced by the same percentage. For other plans, see H. Feldman, *Stabilizing Jobs and Wages*, Harper and Brothers, New York, 1940, pp. 185–186.

in accordance with some standard such as prices or employment. The cost of living principle has, no doubt, been used more frequently than any other sliding scale. The basic opposition to these proposals is not so much that there may be some tendency to freeze "real" wage rates over periods longer than the duration of the contract, but rather that sliding scales are a substitute for collective bargaining.[55] The union could not take credit for wage adjustments that were essentially automatic in character. The possibility of achieving cyclical wage flexibility by such a device neglects the political realities of collective bargaining.

(2) Just as quoted prices may distort judgment on the cyclical flexibility of the average revenue per unit of product, so wage rates may be deceiving in two respects. In the first place, periods of depression find undercutting, kickbacks, and other forms of concealed reduction of the basic rate more common. The basic rate in the building trades, for instance, has frequently been applicable only to the larger projects in big cities. In this light, the base rate has served as a standard from which wage discrimination is possible among various enterprises. In the second place, other dimensions of the wage structure have been modified in preference to the basic rate. For instance, the musicians in many locals were forced to make concessions in regard to employment guarantees and number of men employed in each orchestra in preference to modification of the basic wage rates.[56] The photoengravers modified a number of working rules and standards in cooperating with their employers in an effort to reduce costs. "This action kept many plants operating profitably and assisted an additional number to continue in business." [57]

(3) The quoted base rate is regarded by a trade union as a symbol of its achievements and except under special circumstances is defended very stubbornly against cyclical reductions. Vice-president Woll of the photoengravers has asserted that "the effectiveness of a trade union is . . . largely measured by the success experienced in maintaining standards of compensation during

[55] *Machinists' Monthly Journal*, December, 1936, 48, p. 751.
[56] *Official Proceedings of the 36th Convention of the American Federation of Musicians*, 1931, p. 44.
[57] *Official Proceedings of the 35th Convention of the International Photo-Engravers' Union of North America*, 1934, p. 16.

periods of depression and of elevating these standards in a time of prosperity." [58] This clearly enunciated policy of "no reductions" has the advantage of a general policy that still permits individual adjustments.[59] The general statement is intended to reduce as far as possible any gradual spread of reductions.

(4) The basic wage rate is regarded as a long-run price, usually set with an eye to noncyclical circumstances. Basic wage increases in the prosperity phase do not exploit every last degree of bargaining power of the union for short-run advantage. Similarly wage decreases in depression do not represent the full short-run bargaining advantage of enterprises. *Wage structures are bargained for in an essentially noncyclical time setting.* A partial explanation is thus provided for the fact that wage rates did not fall to much lower levels in company towns in 1931–1933 and did not go very much higher in occupations with acute shortages in 1942.

A more elegant way of stating this central point is suggested by the analysis (Chap. II) of the time patterns of impact responses. As employment declines with the start of a recession, the relevant decision unit will be confronted by the alternative effects on the wage bill of a reduction in rates or a continuation of existing wage structures. A reduction will result in an immediate loss in wage bill, even relative to continuing existing rates. For purposes of argument, grant that the reduction will increase the wage bill after the impact period (Fig. 1). In few cases involving an international union as a unit (that is excluding shifts in business among closely competing firms) would this period probably be very short, say less than a year. The full area of reduction, the speed of product price variation, accompanying fiscal policy, and the like, will influence the precise impact pattern. The practical problem is whether to take the cut with the uncertainties of the higher wage bill at the end of a relatively long impact period, or

[58] *Official Proceedings of the 28th Convention of the International Photo-Engravers' Union of North America*, 1927, p. 6.

[59] Although not directly related to cyclical problems, the refusal of the musicians to accept any general policy of wage reductions with the introduction of sound movie houses illustrates the policy of "each case resting on its own merits." *Official Proceedings of the 37th Convention of the American Federation of Musicians*, 1932, p. 40. Locals were advised to make such individual adjustments as the "local situation may demand, but the President's office discouraged agreements to huge cuts. . . ."

take the chance that business conditions (demand) will change for the better within the year anyway. Knowledge of future events seldom makes the latter alternative definitely the poorer risk. Hence, the unchanged wage structure is not a surprising choice. Wage-rate changes which simply transfer employment among the locals with impact period losses are particularly to be avoided by the international unit. Similarly, increases will be avoided when they indicate only a relatively short-term impact gain that promises to disappear rapidly.

A somewhat different approach to the relative stability of wage structures emphasizes the fact that wage policy is determined by the employed rather than by the unemployed. A reduction appears to be a complete loss to the fully employed worker. When considerable "short-time" is being worked, a reduction may still appear largely a loss unless the impact period is very short. In terms of the analysis of Chap. III, the relevant membership function to wage determination may be the employed members rather than all those who are "attached to the union." The composition of the employed group naturally changes over the course of the cycle, imparting stability to the wage structure.

(5) The policy of "no reduction" is also influenced by the cost of making wage-rate changes. "It is to be assumed that the lower wage, after the depression had passed, would have been considered the normal wage, and as a result we would have been obliged to again contend for many years for compensation commensurate with our services. . . ." [60] Because of the difficulties of again raising rates, a policy of antireductions is followed.

(6) The preceding points make it clear that reductions are most likely when relative shifts in employment are most probable, particularly between union and nonunion firms.[61] "In some cases we have taken reductions in our hourly rate in order to allow the fair employers to bid on work at a price which would permit consideration of their bid along with the bids of unfair employers." [62] Another instance in which a wage cut is regarded as the lesser evil is quoted from the English experience with approval

[60] *Official Proceedings of the 36th Convention of the American Federation of Musicians*, 1931, p. 60.
[61] The pattern of wage changes in recent cycles is presented in Chap. VII.
[62] *Machinists' Monthly Journal*, March, 1932, 44, p. 122.

by the photoengravers. The cut was determined "more from a desire to maintain the employers' organization intact, as we have undeniable evidence that many of the smaller firms will break away and become independent price cutters if an easier situation is not given to them. We have, therefore, come to the conclusion that the wages of our members will be affected, in the ultimate, less by an organized reduction of moderate character than if the whole situation should go to pieces and we should be thrown back on prewar conditions of individual settlements. . . ." [63]

C. WAGE DIFFERENTIALS AMONG ENTERPRISES

As has been noted in setting forth the elements of a wage policy, a trade union frequently deals with a number of separate enterprises, and the issue arises of the differential rate structure that shall be charged. It is a mistake to presume that all enterprises which deal with a trade union are close competitors. A trade union's structure may be organized along lines of a process or a material, and there may be virtually no competition among the firms in the different product markets. The machinists deal with auto repair firms, railway shops, and contract shops, the photoengravers have both newspapers and job printing, and the hosiery workers deal with both full-fashioned and seamless enterprises. The demand for equality of wage rates or labor costs may not be so strong from enterprises in widely separated product markets. In general, quite different wage rates would be expected in the several markets, and these variations are observed. Not infrequently, however, they present difficult internal problems to union leadership. The common-sense view requires that people who have had approximately equal training and do the same type of work ought to receive the same pay. Equal marginal physical productivities deserve the same rates. But typesetters consistently get higher pay in newspaper work than in book and job establishments. The view that book and job typesetters will bid down the price forgets the quoted-price characteristic of the labor market and the possibilities of wage discrimination by a trade union. These differences among workers doing exactly similar work are

[63] *Report of the Proceedings of the 23rd Convention of the International Photo-Engravers' Union of North America*, 1922, p. 159.

most likely to be found the less direct is the competition among the products.

The most difficult issues with respect to differentials arise when enterprises are in more or less close product competition. Equal piece rates were observed [Section 4 (2)] to result in equal wage costs to competing firms. However, the difficulties of serious unemployment in marginal firms are involved. Staggered rates give some firms a competitive advantage which may lead to serious bickering with local unions and management alike and may involve important shifts in employment at the time they are introduced. Neither alternative is without its problems. The shifting policies of the American Federation of Hosiery Workers is a classic example of these difficulties. It is to be borne in mind that the industry has both extremely easy conditions of entry and a significant nonunion section, particularly in the expanding south.

During the early twenties the full-fashioned hosiery industry expanded tremendously with style changes associated with shorter skirts. Union rates were much higher than nonunion wage scales in the newer firms. In 1929, with approximately 30 per cent of the industry organized, the union adopted a national labor agreement with union firms which contained a uniform labor cost schedule. While under strong competitive pressure from nonunion hosiery, union concerns had equal wage costs. By virtue of a vigorous policy of reductions between 1929 and 1931, the union was able to remain a going concern and participate in the expansion of membership with the New Deal. The competitive position of the unionized section of the industry in the north by 1938 was threatened by inferior technical installations. The failure to make changes can be attributed to (a) the peculiarities in the piece rate schedules which gave the employer no saving in direct labor costs after a certain point for longer machines, faster machines, or finer gauge operations; and (b) the failure to cover overhead as a consequence of Southern competition. The union leadership discarded the uniform labor cost policy in 1938 and negotiated individual supplementary agreements with employers which gave concessions in rates in return for the installation of new machinery or the rehabilitation of old. "The more or less standard bargain was that in return for the purchase of 10 per cent new equipment, the union would concede piece-rate reductions of about 15 per cent." [64] The improved machinery increased output so that average hourly earnings declined by only half as much as the rates on the average. The rehabilitation program also resulted in the liquidation of some enterprises, with consequent unemployment, that could not secure the required working capital to make the changes. The union returned to uniform piece rates in 1941 when individual bargaining had completed the new machine installations. [65] Differential rates had not been intended to take advantage of the rents of superior enterprises or to influence the geographical distribution of employment in a particular way.

Another illustration of the problems that confront a union in dealing with a group of closely competing enterprises is provided by the Stabilization Program of the Amalgamated Clothing Workers. Composed of a large number of firms, the industry affords easy entry and presents endless opportunities for product differentiation. Geographical differentials in labor cost tend to shift the industry fairly rapidly. The union signed a contract in July 1939 with the New York Clothing Manufacturers' Exchange, which put the national piece-rate scales into effect. Even with uniform piece rates, product changes would be sufficient to induce important shifts in employment and reduction in the wage bill through changing proportions of wage earners at the various operations. Hence, the union provided for the standardization of garments into six grades. Local unions could not exercise discretion in permitting departures from established specifications and labor costs; a Stabilization Department within the union was created. The program was first introduced in the two cheapest grades of garments. The standardized products and piece rates result in uniform labor costs on a national basis, clearly affecting the geographical distribution of employment.

[64] Sumner H. Slichter, *op. cit.*, p. 359. For a discussion of the problems of competition between union and nonunion plants, see *loc. cit.*, Chap. XII.

[65] *The Hosiery Worker*, May 16, 1941, XVII, p. 3, Col. 4, and *loc. cit.*, August 28, 1941, p. 1.

D. WAGE DIFFERENTIALS AMONG LOCAL UNIONS

The converse of the case of differential wage rates or costs to competing enterprises is presented by competition between two groups within a union for the same employment. A most characteristic instance is regional competition among the locals of an international. An interesting case is provided by the competition between local and traveling bands in the musicians' union. Some locals refused to allow traveling bands to play in their jurisdiction, a stand which could not be supported by the international union. Any such policy would prove a severe handicap to expansion of the organization. For a while an attempt was made to protect the local organization by requiring a stand-by local orchestra, both of which had to be paid. This device soon proved to be more than the traffic could bear. Consequently, a 30 per cent and finally a 10 per cent tax on the traveling band was added to the price.[66] This 10 per cent tax is distributed 4 per cent to the local organization in whose jurisdiction the engagement is played, 3 per cent to the members who play the engagement, and 3 per cent to the national organization. This differential in price would seem to correspond to some product differentiation, since most of the traveling bands have wider reputations.

Section 5 has been an illustrative sketch of four types of problem that typically confront trade unions in formulating wage decision. Those convinced of the fruitlessness of analytical models will be reinforced by these complexities. A more charitable view will recognize that the wage policy of a union will vary with: (a) the precise group of wage earners taken into account (the membership function), (b) the formal bargaining unit, (c) the expected time patterns of impact adjustment, and (d) the character of competition in the product markets. The next chapter (V) lays a theoretical foundation for the study of the influence of product market considerations on wage policy in Chapter VI.

[66] *Official Proceedings of the 40th Convention of the American Federation of Musicians*, 1935, p. 55.

CHAPTER V. "BARGAINING POWER" AND INTERMARKET RELATIONS [1]

The fact that all buyers and sellers, in either product or factor markets, do not meet on completely equal terms is recognized in the earliest economic literature. Adam Smith, for instance, observed that "in the long run the workman may be as necessary to his master as his master is to him, but the necessity is not so immediate. . . . Masters are always and everywhere in a sort of tacit, but constant and uniform combination, not to raise the wages of labour above their actual rate." [2] Such concern with inequalities in the process of price formation would be expected where individual incomes and amounts of services rendered are said to be determined by the price mechanism with a given distribution of ownership. In examining interferences with the operation of "free" and "perfect" markets, the term "bargaining power" has been commonly adopted; it is generally used to assert some lack of equality between buyers and sellers in a market.

The precise character of this inequality, a measure for different degrees of inequality, and the conditions for equality are seldom made explicit. In fact, while numerous instances of inequality of bargaining power abound in economic writings, few rigorous definitions have been located by the present study. [3] The follow-

---

[1] This chapter appeared in substantially its present form under the title " 'Bagraining Power' and Market Structures" in the *Journal of Political Economy*, February, 1942, L, pp. 1–26, written jointly with Dr. Benjamin Higgins. The argument and analysis is presented with his permission.

[2] *The Wealth of Nations*, Everyman's ed., London, 1933, I, 59 (Book I, chap. viii). Alfred Marshall, *Principles of Economics*, 8th ed., Macmillan & Company, Ltd., London, 1930, says: "The effects of the labourer's disadvantage in bargaining are therefore cumulative in two ways: It lowers his wages; . . . this lowers his efficiency as a worker, and thereby lowers the normal value of his labour. And in addition it diminishes his efficiency as a bargainer" (p. 569). See also *ibid.*, pp. 335–336.

[3] See the analysis of A. C. Pigou, *Principles and Methods of Industrial Peace*, Macmillan & Company, Ltd., London, 1905, Appendix A, and *The Economics of Welfare*, 4th ed., Macmillan & Company, Ltd., London, 1938, pp. 451–461. The only explicit definition found is that suggested by Sumner H. Slichter ("Bargaining power may be defined as

ing sections of this chapter are intended to suggest a definition and measure for bargaining power and to examine the amounts of bargaining power in different types of markets. The theoretical analysis of a cluster of product and factor markets provides a background for explaining the trade-union policies surveyed in the next chapter. Some readers may wish to proceed directly to the application of the analysis in Chap. VI.

1. *Some Examples from the Literature*

A brief survey of the literature using the term "bargaining power" discloses many factors which are held responsible for inequalities. "The . . . weaknesses of the individual bargainer, his lack of waiting power, his defenselessness against the competitive pressure on the employer, are to some degree offset through the device of the collective bargain." [4] The "power to withhold" [5] from making a transaction is probably the most general content of the term "bargaining power." The ability to refrain from sale or purchase is commonly said to be influenced by such circumstances as periods of prosperity and depression, the skill of wage earners, knowledge of markets, and the skill in bargaining and conducting negotiations.[6] But no measure is suggested whereby these factors may be reduced to a common denominator.

Even less satisfactory is the treatment of the interaction of product and factor markets. A popular text, for instance, in discussing the impact of competition in the product market on wage rates, contends:

The workers feel the full force of all this (pressure) because, where conditions of free competition exist, they possess the only commodity which is continuously and conspicuously overstocked. Conditions in the

the cost to A of imposing a loss upon B") in "Impact of Social Security Legislation upon Mobility and Enterprise," *American Economic Review*, suppl. March, 1940, XXX, 57. The difficulty with this definition is that the object of one party to a contract is usually not to impose a loss on the other party but to gain an advantage for itself. The ability to gain an advantage is not always commensurate with the ability to impose a loss with a given disadvantage to one's self.

[4] Solomon Blum, *Labor Economics*, Henry Holt and Company, New York, 1925, p. 373.

[5] John R. Commons and J. B. Andrews, *Principles of Labor Legislation*, 4th ed., Harper & Brothers, New York, 1936, p. 372.

[6] Although the term "bargaining power" is most commonly used in connection with the labor market, comparable points are made for other markets.

clothing, textile, and bituminous coal industries afford excellent examples of what happens under full and severe "higgling." *Only in monopolistic situations can wage earners be relieved of such pressure.*[7]

An equally interesting statement of relations between these markets is contained in the following:

The business enterprise which offers the best field for union activities is one which is highly competitive without being disorganized and which is reasonably prosperous.[8]

These two statements would appear to be contradictory.

It may be thought that the bargaining power of a buyer or seller pertains solely to the immediate market in which the individual is a participant. Even in a general and common-sense way, it is soon evident that the character of competition in markets in which the factors are supplied will significantly influence the bargaining power of buyers and sellers in the product market. For instance, the bargaining power of a textile firm dealing with a machinery company will depend in part upon the character of competition in the cotton and steel markets. Certainly, these competitive conditions will materially influence the price of textile machinery. If this be true under more rigorous definitions of bargaining power, then the present study must be concerned with the interrelations of product and factor markets.

Too frequently these markets are divorced in analysis, as in most of the monopolistic competition literature. The definitions and techniques developed below are intended to assist in studying the interactions between factor and product markets, and as such they are relevant to such problems as tax-shifting, international trade, wage and price policy—indeed, to any issue which involves tracing the impact of a change through contiguous markets in an economic system.

2. *Definition and Measure of Bargaining Power*

This section attempts to set up a definition and a measure of bargaining power which is more useful for economic analysis than the various concepts in the literature; the next section considers

---

[7] C. R. Daugherty, *Labor Problems in American Industry*, Houghton Mifflin Company, Boston, 1933, p. 415. Italics mine. The validity of this statement will be examined in considering various types of cases in Section 2 below.

[8] Blum, *op. cit.*, p. 379.

various models and determines bargaining power in each case. The example of the labor market is used in these two sections, but the application of the concept and the measure is general in scope, as will be shown below.

It is useful to distinguish between "determining" and "resultant" concepts and measures of bargaining power. A determining definition would state the factors which influence bargaining power in such a manner that the wage could be deduced from a knowledge of this bargaining power and other relevant variables; a determining measure would state some definite functional relationship between the magnitude of this bargaining power and the level of the resulting wage. A resultant measure would only permit a measurement of bargaining power by the resulting wage rather than in terms of the forces behind a wage. In a system of complete explanation of behavior, the two concepts are merged.

The factors influencing determining bargaining power, which may be interrelated, are the following:

1. Tastes of workers and employers, with respect to wages and manhours bought and sold—the indifference maps. Institutional factors such as property rights, and wage-hour legislation, which influence conditions of demand and supply, should also be included.

2. Market conditions, especially the degree and type of competition in the labor market, the product market, the market for complementary factors of production, and the market for competitive factors of production. In the last two markets, elasticities of substitution are important factors.

3. "Pure" bargaining power: ability to get favorable bargains, apart from market conditions. "Pure" bargaining power becomes particularly relevant in cases where there is a range of indeterminacy. It consists of two factors: (a) the extent of knowledge of tastes and market conditions influencing the behavior of the other party to the contract, and (b) intrinsic "toughness"; the ability to get the desired result with a given amount of energy and unpleasantness. The willingness to devote energy and bear unpleasantness in bargaining for increased income is part of basic tastes, influencing the shapes of the indifference curves.

The third factor, "pure" bargaining power, would seem to be the least significant of the three. The differences between representatives of employers and of employees with respect to knowledge of the tastes of their opponents, and to the state of the relevant markets, is not likely to be overwhelming in many contemporary cases.[9] The tastes and market conditions themselves will be much more important. An assumption that pure bargaining power is approximately equal for the contracting parties would not be too unrealistic under modern conditions (particularly with trade unions) and would greatly simplify the formal analysis.

Thus the concept of determining bargaining power consists of the relative ability of the two contracting parties to influence the wage, in terms of these three factors, and especially in terms of the first two. However, it seems impossible to measure determining bargaining power in terms of these factors. Accordingly a "resultant" measure in terms of the actual wage must be adopted.

The comparisons are made in terms of a general, rather than a partial, equilibrium analysis. The reason is simply that the general equilibrium approach, by taking account of whatever variations in the marginal utility of income there may be and of the importance of the path to equilibrium, makes the analysis more realistic. The bargaining advantage of a factor is defined as

$$A_f = \frac{P_f - S^c_p}{D^c_p} \qquad (1)$$

where A_f is the bargaining advantage of the factor; P_f is the actual price paid for the factor; S^c_p is the supply price of the factor that would rule under pure competition in all relevant markets, for the number of units *actually* taken; and D^c_p is the demand price of the commodity that would rule under pure competition in all relevant markets for the number of units actually taken.[10]

[9] Note the following interesting judgment: "The labor representatives . . . ordinarily are more skillful than the employer representatives in the arts which prevail in an arbitration tribunal. They know the terms better, they talk better on their feet or around the conference table, they know more of parliamentary and statutory law, they have frequently greater experience and wider contacts in the government. Also they are likely to have a program, whereas the employer representatives, if they have a program at all, are likely to have a negative one." Charles E. Wyzanski, Jr., "Labor Disputes During the War," *Labor Relations Reporter*, January 19, 1942, IX.

[10] The genesis of this definition may be of some interest. Lerner's definition of monopoly power was

$$M_p = \frac{p - C'(x)}{p},$$

where M_p is monopoly power, p is the price established, and $C'(x)$ is marginal cost in

It will be noted from this expression that if the competitive supply price falls while price remains constant, bargaining advantage rises; similarly, if competitive demand price falls and price remains constant; while if competitive demand price rises and price remains constant, bargaining advantage falls. With pure competition, bargaining advantage is zero. The argument turns now to a consideration of the factors influencing the magnitude of bargaining advantages expressed in this manner.

In Fig. 6 the curve I_E is the indifference curve through the origin for the employer (or employers). I_L is the indifference curve through the origin for the workers (who are assumed to be of one type); D_L is the total demand curve for labor, S_L is the total supply curve of labor, and CC is the contract curve. W_A is the wage rate, and OL units of labor are exchanged for wage bill OB. All these curves apply to the actual situation. The curves D'_L and S'_L are the demand and supply curves as they would be under pure competition in all relevant markets. The curves II and $I'I'$ are

equilibrium (A. P. Lerner, "The Concept of Monopoly and the Measurement of Monopoly Power," *Review of Economic Studies*, June, 1934). For present purposes, certain revisions in this formula were necessary. First, in order to make the definition symmetrical for monopsony and monopoly, substitute D_p, demand price, for p in the denominator. This alteration does not alter the magnitude of monopoly power in any specific case, under partial equilibrium analysis, since price is equal to demand price in equilibrium. Under monopsony conditions, M_p would be negative by this formula, since price is less than demand price, and demand price is equal to marginal cost. Second, to make the measure applicable under general equilibrium analysis, the measure of monopoly power must take into account the difference between the existing curves and those that would exist with pure competition in all related markets. $C'(x)$ is therefore defined as the marginal cost that would exist with pure competition all around, and D_p as the competitive demand price. A parallel definition for the bargaining advantage in the labor market would then be $A_L = (p_L - S^c_p)/(D^c_p)$, where A_L is bargaining advantage of labor, p_L is the price of labor, S^c_p is the competitive supply price of labor (that is, the supply price that would exist with pure competition in all relevant markets), and D^c_p is the competitive demand price. Equation 1 above is this formula generalized for any factor of production.

The bargaining advantage of a firm might be regarded as a combination of monopoly power and bargaining advantage in the factor markets. If there is only one factor of production, the bargaining advantage of the firm might be expressed as

$$B_f = \varphi \left[\frac{p - S^c_p}{D^c_p} \right] + \lambda \left[\frac{D - P_f}{S^c_p} \right]$$

that is, some function of the ratio of price of the commodity *minus* "competitive" supply price of the commodity to "competitive" demand price of the commodity, plus some function of the ratio of demand price of the factor *minus* the price of the factor to the "competitive" supply price of the factor. With pure competition throughout, the expression would come to zero.

other indifference curves, for employers and workers, respectively.[11]

With pure competition in all markets, the wage rate W_O will be established. The contract curve need not pass through the intersection of these competitive total demand and supply curves, since

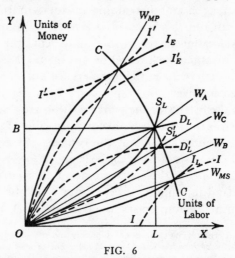

FIG. 6

I_E	Indifference curve for the employer through the origin.
I_L	Indifference curve for the workers through the origin.
II	More favorable indifference curve for the employer than I_E.
$I'I'$	More favorable indifference curve for the workers than I_L.
D_L	Total demand curve for labor.
S_L	Total supply curve for labor.
CC	Contract curve, locus of tangencies of indifference curves of workers and employers.
D'_L	Total demand curve for labor under pure competition in all relevant markets.
S'_L	Total supply curve for labor under pure competition in all relevant markets.
W	Wage rate.
W_{MS}	Monopsony wage rate.
W_{MP}	Monopoly wage rate.

[11] The diagram is an adaptation from F. Y. Edgeworth, *Mathematical Psychics*, C. Kegan Paul & Co., London, 1881, p. 28; also see Marshall, *op. cit.*, p. 844. For those readers not entirely familiar with this type of diagram the following review may be useful. The curve I_E shows sums of money which the entrepreneur can give for the corresponding amounts of labor and be just as well off as if he hired no labor at all. In most cases this curve can be identified with the curve of "total productivity of labor"; that is, the curve showing the total return to labor plus the total return to the fixed factors as a function of the amount of labor employed. There will be other indifference curves to the right of I_E, such as II, representing combinations which yield a certain balance of satisfaction, in money terms, to the employers. The slope of these curves can be defined as $(dU/dY \cdot dY/dL)/(dU/dM)$, where U is utility, Y is income derived from production, and L is amount of labor hired. The term dU/dM indicates the satisfaction gained by alternative uses of the time, energy, and capital

the actual curves may be different from those that would exist with general free competition. By the same token, the upper limit W_{MP}, and the lower limit, W_{MS}, can be called the "monopoly" and the "monopsony" wage, with reservations since they may not exist simultaneously; the shapes of the curves, and their positions, may be different with monopoly in the labor market from what they would be with monopsony in the labor market, and they depend also on conditions in other markets.

For any wage rate above W_C, such as W_A, the bargaining advantage of labor A_L is greater than zero; for any wage rate below W_C, such as W_B, the bargaining advantage of labor is less than zero.[12] No absolute values attach to the wage rates W_{MP} and W_{ms}. This result is in accordance with the situation found in reality, since all monopolistic employers (employers faced with no

which the entrepreneur must spend in employing a given amount of labor. The expression dY/dL can be written more fully: $dx/dL \cdot d/dx(px)$, where x is output and p is price of the product. The demand curve D_L is the locus of points of tangency between price lines, such as W_C, and indifference curves of entrepreneurs; that is, where the slope of the indifference curves, as defined above, is equal to the exchange ratio in the market of labor for money. These are optimum points for employers.

The curve I_L, similarly, shows amounts of labor that workers can supply in exchange for corresponding amounts of money and be just as well off as if they did not work at all. It is the "total cost" of obtaining the corresponding amounts of labor; in the long run, the amount of money that will just keep the workers "alive"; in the short run, the amount that will just keep them from striking. There will be other indifference curves, similar in shape, to the left of I_L, such as $I'I'$, showing combinations which give some balance of satisfaction to workers. The slopes of these curves can be defined as $(du/dy \cdot dy/dl)/(du/dL)$, where u is utility, y is labor income, l is amount of labor and L the amount of leisure. The total supply curve S_L is the locus of points where this ratio is equal to price (wage rate), which are optimum points for labor.

The curve CC is the locus of points where indifference curves of employers and employees are tangent to each other. That is, they are optimum points for both, for all prices between the two limiting indifference curves. Thus the curve is the locus of all possible contracts.

[12] It will be noticed that in Fig. 6 the contract curve is drawn so that wage rates and wage bills move in the same direction. As long as the general equilibrium approach is employed, where the indirect effects of a change in wage rates upon the demand for labor through the alteration in labor income involved are included, this relationship is the more likely one. Even if a rise in wage rates would reduce the wage bill, it would still represent a preferred position, however, and a relatively high bargaining advantage of labor, as long as one moves along the contract curve. Other changes in wage rates are irrelevant. Thus there is justification in measuring bargaining advantage in terms of wage rates, without taking account of the wage bill that accompanies each wage rate. The possibility will be ignored that the contract curve would move toward the origin from its upper limit; that is, the possibility is excluded that, as bargaining advantage of labor increases, the workers insist upon a lower wage rate. It follows from this exclusion that a reduction in demand for labor, other things being equal, will result in a lower wage.

close competition for the type of labor in question) do not have the same bargaining power. Bargaining power depends not merely upon the number of competitors but upon the type of resistance met from the other party or parties to the contract.

3. Types of Competition and Bargaining Power

When all relevant markets are taken into account, the number of combinations and permutations of varying degrees of competition in various markets is almost without limit. In order to make some headway toward an analysis of the effects of market structure upon bargaining power, this section is confined to three types of competition: pure competition, monopoly, and monopsony.[13] Also assume that the type of labor under consideration is the only factor of production combined with the fixed factors to turn out the commodity in question. Finally, let it be assumed that there is only one stage of production. Accordingly, the conditions of only two markets can be considered: the labor market and the product market. The following section will indicate some modifications of the results that follow from the introduction of additional complications found in reality, such as the influence of conditions in the market for complementary or competitive factors and in the markets in other stages of production.

CASE I. PURE COMPETITION IN BOTH LABOR AND PRODUCT MARKETS

In this basic case equilibrium in the labor market is established at the wage rate W_C, where the total "competitive" demand equals the total "competitive" supply. The bargaining advantage of labor is zero.

CASES 2 AND 3. PURE COMPETITION IN THE LABOR MARKET, MONOPOLY IN THE PRODUCT MARKET; AND PURE COMPETITION IN THE LABOR MARKET, MONOPSONY IN THE PRODUCT MARKET

The effect upon bargaining advantage of labor of a transition from pure competition in the product market to monopoly or monopsony is a highly complicated one. No general solution, independent of particular elasticities of demand and supply and the

---

[13] For the present purposes it is sufficient to define these cases as many buyers and sellers, many buyers and few sellers, few buyers and many sellers.

manner in which demand and supply curves shift, is possible. A sort of common-sense approximation can, however, be suggested.

For this purpose the possibility will be ignored that, with a different rate of profit, entrepreneurs may reach their optimum position (in terms of satisfaction) at levels of output and employment closer to or farther away from the maximum profits position.[14] That is, it is assumed that the demand for labor is determined solely by its marginal-value productivity. Footnote 11 defined the slope of the entrepreneurs' indifference curves (say s) as

$$\frac{dU/dY}{dU/dM}\left[\frac{dx}{dL}\cdot\frac{d}{dx}(px)\right]$$

and the demand curve for labor as the locus of $W = s$. On the basis of assumptions just made, this latter expression can be reduced to

$$k\left[\frac{dx}{dL}\cdot\frac{d}{dx}(px)\right]$$

since $(dU/dY)/(dU/dM)$ is regarded as constant, k. The use of this expression for the demand curve does not necessarily mean that the commodity is assumed to be an independent good. The "estimated average revenue curve" that is relevant for determining the demand curve for labor can just as well be assumed to take into account the reactions of other prices to a change in price of the commodity in question.

As a further simplification, assume constant returns to labor. Since industry operates at less than capacity much of the time, this assumption is not too unrealistic. The demand curve for labor then reduces to

$$k\left[K\cdot\frac{d}{dx}(px)\right]$$

Accordingly one can concentrate upon the differences between the curves of $d/dx\,(px)$, or marginal revenue to the industry, in order to deduce differences in the demand for labor in wage rates.

Under pure competition, the demand of the industry for labor is derived from the estimated average revenue curve, or demand curve for the product for the industry as a whole, each individual entrepreneur disregarding his effect upon price. If the assumption is then made that the entire output of the industry is taken over by a single entrepreneur, subject to the limitations pointed out by

[14] For a discussion of this possibility see Benjamin Higgins, "Elements of Indeterminacy in the Theory of Non-perfect Competition," *American Economic Review*, September, 1939, XXIX, pp. 468–479.

Mrs. Robinson,[15] the relevant curves can be presumed to be unchanged and the demand curve for labor is derived from the
marginal revenue curve.

Next assume that each entrepreneur in the industry finds himself faced with a single buyer. In this case the price received by
the entrepreneurs for any level of output will be the minimum
supply price for that output. The method of deriving the demand
curve for labor in each case, and the determination of the equilibrium wage rate in each case, is illustrated in Fig. 7. Since constant returns to labor are assumed, both units of labor employed
and units of output can be measured on the horizontal axis; units
of money, on the vertical axis. The curve D_P is the demand curve
for the product, MR is the marginal revenue curve corresponding
to this demand curve, AC_P is the average cost of the product, MC_P
is the marginal cost of the product. The curve D_1 is the marginal
value product of labor, when each entrepreneur disregards the
effect of his output upon price. It is drawn so that the demand
price for labor is equal to some fraction of the demand price for
the corresponding output (in this case one-half). The curve MD_1
is the corresponding marginal curve. S_L is the supply curve of
labor, and MS_L is the curve marginal to this supply curve.

Any demand curve shows the locus of equilibrium points for
varying conditions of supply. Accordingly, the demand curve for
labor can be derived in each case by varying the position of the
supply curve of labor and by tracing the locus of the consequent
equilibrium wage rates. With pure competition in the product
market, this locus will be found to be the curve D_1. With monopoly in the product market, the equilibrium wage rate for any
level of employment will lie on the supply curve of labor, vertically below the intersection of the MD_1 curve with the MS_L
curve. The locus of such points will therefore lie below the MD_1
curve, such as D_2. With monopsony in the product market, the
equilibrium wage will lie on the supply curve, vertically below
the intersection of the MS_L curve with the D_1 curve. The locus
of these points will lie between the MD_1 curve and the D_1 curve,
for example, the D_3 curve.

---

[15] Joan Robinson, *The Economics of Imperfect Competition*, Macmillan & Company,
Ltd., London, 1933, Chap. XIV.

Thus with a rising supply curve for labor, with given demand and cost curves in the product market, and with pure competition in the labor market, the wage rate will be highest under pure

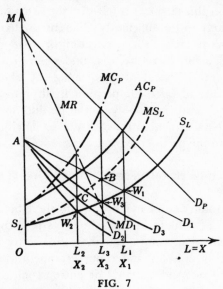

FIG. 7

D_P Demand curve for the product.
MR Marginal revenue to D_P.
AC_P Average cost of the product.
MC_P Marginal cost to AC_P.
S_L Supply curve for labor.
MS_L Marginal supply curve for labor.
D_1 Marginal value product of labor, demand curve for labor under perfect competition.
MD_1 Marginal to D_1.
D_2 Demand curve for labor with monopoly in the product market.
D_3 Demand curve for labor with monopsony in the product market.
W_1 Wage rate with pure competition in the product market.
W_2 Wage rate with monopoly in the product market.
W_3 Wage rate with monopsony in the product market.

competition in the product market (W_1), and ouput (x_1) and employment (L_1) will also be largest. The wage rate will be lowest with monopoly in the product market (W_2), output (x_2) and employment (L_2) will also be smallest. The wage rate with monopsony in the product market (W_3), and also output (x_3) and employment (L_3) will lie between those of Case 1 and those of Case 2. The advantage of restricting output and employment, and thus the pressure of competition for jobs upon the wage rate with pure competition in the labor market, is greatest in the monopoly case. While a number of simplifying assumptions have been made to get this result, it is felt that the situation in the real world is not likely to be sufficiently different in character in the majority of cases to vitiate the application of these models. This is frankly a judgment, therefore, that under pure competition in the factor market, the bargaining advantage of labor is greatest (zero) in the case of pure competition in the product market, lowest (negative) with monopoly in the product market, and is somewhere in between (negative, but not so much) in the case of monopsony in the product market.

CASE 4. PURE COMPETITION IN THE PRODUCT MARKET, MONOPOLY IN THE LABOR MARKET

With the introduction of monopoly into the labor market, say by organization of a trade union, employers may consider their work less pleasant than before, but their income for any level of employment is lower than under pure competition. While the indifference and demand curves [16] of entrepreneurs and supply curves of employees may be radically different from the basic case, let them be unchanged for the present. The "monopoly wage" for the relevant curves will be established. The bargaining power of labor, A_L, is greater than zero.

CASE 5. PURE COMPETITION IN THE PRODUCT MARKET, MONOPSONY IN THE LABOR MARKET

This case could occur only if entrepreneurs have an agreement with respect to wage rates and employment but compete openly in the product market. Since income of employers is higher for any level of employment than in Case 1, $(dU/dY)/(dU/dM)$ may fall somewhat. The income of workers for any level of employment falls, so du/dy rises, but with the costs of dealing with an employers' union, du/dL also rises; on balance let it be assumed that the supply and indifference curves for labor are substantially

[16] Chapter VI examines in specific cases the influence of a trade union on the demand curve for the output of a firm and industry.

unchanged. The monopsony wage for the relevant curves is established, A_L is less than zero, and in all probability less than in any of the previous cases.

CASE 6. MONOPOLY IN THE PRODUCT MARKET, MONOPSONY IN THE LABOR MARKET

Here the situation is the same as in Case 5, except for the same differences as exist between Case 1 and Case 2. The relevant indifference and demand curves of entrepreneurs will be below those of Case 5, and the monopsony wage established will be lower than in the previous case. A_L will be below that resulting from any of the preceding cases.

CASE 7. PURE COMPETITION IN THE LABOR MARKET, BILATERAL MONOPOLY IN THE PRODUCT MARKET

If the pure bargaining power of buyers and sellers in the product market is equal, so that the competitive price is established there, the result in this case approaches that of Case 1; A_L approaches zero. In accord with the argument above, pure bargaining advantage can be expected to be close to zero. The need for devoting time and energy to bargaining, or for hiring someone to do it, reduces $(dU/dY) / (dU/dM)$ for the entrepreneurs. There is a "cost of bargaining," subjective or objective. The demand curve for labor will be below the competitive one. Thus even with equal bargaining power in the product market, A_L is less than zero.

To the extent that the entrepreneurs are more successful than buyers in the higgling of the product market, the results approach those of Case 2; to the extent that buyers are more successful, the results of Case 3 are approached. In either of these cases the bargaining advantage of labor is less than unity, and it is likely to be less if the buyers win out than if the sellers win out in the product market. Thus while it is better for the workers to support whichever party is weaker in the product market, so as to equalize bargaining power there, if one party must have an advantage, it is better for the workers to support the buyers rather than their own employers.

CASE 8. PURE COMPETITION IN THE PRODUCT MARKET, BILATERAL
MONOPOLY IN THE FACTOR MARKET

The equilibrium position in the labor market can fall anywhere on the contract curve and depends upon pure bargaining
power. Since both employers and employees in this case are faced
with the necessity of bearing the unpleasantness of higgling, or of
devoting part of their gross income to hiring representatives to
bargain for them, $(dU/dY)/(dU/dM)$ and $(dU/dY)/(dU/dL)$
both fall, the indifference curves of employers (and the demand
curve for labor) move down, and the indifference curves of employees (and supply curve of labor) move up, so that the range
of the contract curve is less than in the purely competitive case.
Since it has been argued above that pure bargaining power is
likely to be about equal, A_L in this case will be close to zero but
may be either above it or below it.

CASE 9. MONOPOLY IN THE PRODUCT MARKET, MONOPOLY IN THE
FACTOR MARKET

In this case the entrepreneurs, while in control of the product
market, compete with other industries for a monopolized labor
supply. This case combines the conditions of Case 4 in the labor
market with those of Case 2 in the product market. The indifference curves of entrepreneurs, and the demand curve for labor, are
below their competitive position, so that the monopoly wage established is lower than in Case 4. A_L is above unity. It is worth noting that conditions in the product market influence only the
position of the contract curve, while conditions in the labor market influence both the position of the curve and the position on
the curve.

CASE 10. MONOPSONY IN THE COMMODITY MARKET, MONOPOLY IN
THE FACTOR MARKET

The entrepreneur is faced with pressure from both sides. This
case varies from Case 4 toward Case 3. The indifference curves
of the entrepreneurs fall less than in Case 9. The monopoly wage
resulting is lower than the monopoly wage with pure competition in the product market but probably above the monopoly
wage of Case 9. It would pay the workers to support their em-

ployers against the monopsonistic buyers just enough to equalize bargaining power in the product market, provided a means of doing so can be found that will not diminish the relative advantage of labor in the labor market. A_L will be above zero.

CASE 11. BILATERAL MONOPOLY IN THE PRODUCT MARKET, MONOPOLY IN THE FACTOR MARKET

Here the indifference curves of entrepreneurs fall somewhat, owing to the fall in $(dU/dY)/(dU/dM)$ associated with the cost, subjective or objective, of bargaining. As in the previous case, it would pay the workers to throw in their weight in the product market in such a way as to equalize bargaining power there, since the "monopoly price" they obtain is highest in that case, so long as their advantage in the labor market is not diminished. If an agreement can be made with the employers to split the profits of monopoly in the product market—expressed or in effect—it may pay labor to help the employer create a monopoly position for himself.

CASE 12. MONOPSONY IN THE PRODUCT MARKET, MONOPSONY IN THE LABOR MARKET

This case implies that entrepreneurs have a wage-fixing agreement but compete against each other for the business of a monopsonistic buyer of the product. The situation is analagous to Case 5 but with a smaller slope of indifference curves of entrepreneurs. The contract curve will move so that the wages bill is smaller for any level of employment, including the monopsony level. A_L will be less than in Case 5 but probably slightly higher than in Case 6.

CASE 13. BILATERAL MONOPOLY IN BOTH MARKETS

Since this case permits any of the foregoing combinations, depending upon the results of bargaining in each of the markets, the resulting wage may be anywhere between the level of Case 4, which is highest, and Case 6, which is lowest. To the extent that the "cost of bargaining" enters, the range is somewhat narrowed. The results in each market depend upon the results in the other. Given equal pure bargaining power in the labor market, for example, the wage rate is likely to be higher if the buyers win out in the product market than if the entrepreneurs win out; and it will be higher yet if the bargaining power there is equalized. Similarly, given equal pure bargaining power in the product market, the price of the product will be higher if the workers win out in the labor market than if the entrepreneurs win out. The results are mutually determined, and the *weak spot* in the whole market structure tends to determine the direction of advantage in each of the interrelated markets.

As has been indicated above, there may be an advantage to the workers in supporting the employers in the product market, if they can do so without diminishing their "pure" bargaining power and can get a "cut" of the monopoly profits by doing so. Since the establishment of monopoly in the product market reduces the upper limit of the wage they can get, and the level of the wage they could get with equal pure bargaining power, such support of the employer is advantageous only if such a share of the monopoly profits can be obtained. An agreement to share profits if the workers succeed in obtaining a monopoly position for the employer would be mutually advantageous, whenever the employer does not have a bargaining advantage in the product market without his employees' support. Accordingly, it is a sort of agreement that is quite likely to emerge whenever the workers and entrepreneurs have sufficient insight or instinct with respect to such matters. The case is analogous to duopoly in the product market, where there is a strong possibility of agreement to fix the monopoly price and share the market, whenever the entrepreneurs are "intelligent" enough. Clearly, the buyers in the product market lose by such a combination.

If a monopoly cannot be established in the product market but a monopsony can, it may pay the workers to support the buyers there, particularly if the product is a significant item in their budgets. When discussing policy for labor in general, it is perfectly clear that the prices of products are important, and a position close to the monopsony one may be optimum. The gains as consumers will offset the losses as workers, up to a certain degree of monopsony power. It becomes clear that the determination of the optimum market structure for labor is a highly complicated procedure.

SUMMARY AND CONCLUSIONS

Before proceeding to the introduction of further complications, it may be well to summarize our results so far. In Table IV the wage rate in each of the cases of product and market competition considered above is arrayed in order from highest to lowest.

TABLE IV. WAGE–RATE DETERMINATION UNDER VARIOUS PRODUCT AND FACTOR MARKET SITUATIONS

Order of Wage Rates, Highest to Lowest	Case No.	$\dfrac{P_f - S^c_p}{D^c_f}$	Situation in Product Market	Situation in Labor Market
1	4	> 0	Pure competition	Monopoly
2	10	> 0	Monopsony	Monopoly
3	9	> 0	Monopoly	Monopoly
4	11	> 0	Bilateral monopoly	Monopoly
5	1	$= 0$	Pure competition	Pure competition
6	8	$> = < 0$	Pure competition	Bilateral monopoly
7	3	< 0	Monopsony	Pure competition
8	7	< 0	Bilateral monopoly	Pure competition
9	2	< 0	Monopoly	Pure competition
10	5	< 0	Pure competition	Monopsony
11	12	< 0	Monopsony	Monopsony
12	6	< 0	Monopoly	Monopsony

Case 13, bilateral monopoly in both markets, may rank anywhere; conceivably, if monopoly power in the product market can be made high enough, it may even be the most favorable position for labor, provided a satisfactory profit-sharing agreement can be obtained.

There may be some question as to the relative rank order of Cases 1 and 8. With equal pure bargaining power, the wage rate will be about the same in Case 8 as in Case 1, but the number of employees hired will be less, since both demand and supply curves shift toward the center due to the cost of bargaining. Thus with equal pure bargaining power, the outcome is less favorable to labor as a whole than in Case 1. However, it is possible for them to get a contract more favorable than the purely competitive one, if they have a bargaining advantage. It is conceivable that the workers would prefer a situation which gave them this chance for gain, even with a greater chance for loss, to the assurance of the competitive wage.

It is perhaps worthy of mention that, without some degree of monopoly in the labor market, the bargaining power of labor is less than one. In the absence of a profit-sharing agreement, the best situation for labor in the product market, regardless of the conditions in the labor market, is pure competition. Monopsony, monopoly, and bilateral monopoly follow in that order.

There is some indication that conditions in the market for the factor with which the discussion has been directly concerned —in this example, labor—outweigh in significance the conditions in related markets. Possibly a hierarchy of markets could be worked out in more realistic cases, where more than two inter-related markets are considered. There is also a suggestion that the weak spot in the whole market structure will determine the di-rection of bargaining advantage in each of the interrelated mar-kets. Weakness may arise from a closer approach to pure competi-tion or from a lesser pure bargaining power. Given sufficient understanding, there is a strong possibility that all parties to contracts in the interrelated markets will make an agreement to take advantage of weakness wherever it lies.

4. *Further Complications of Reality*

This section will indicate, but by no means exhaust, the other analytical problems that must be solved if the analysis is to be more useful. Three new complications will be introduced: (*a*) other factors of production, (*b*) other types of nonperfect competition,[17] and (*c*) other stages of production. In no case will there be more than a suggestion of the line of attack which appears expedient.

(*a*) Limiting the argument in turn to the cases of pure com-petition and bilateral monopoly in the labor market, consider the effects of nonperfect competition in the market for other factors, either complementary or competitive. First, introduce monopoly into the market for raw materials combined with labor in the industry under consideration, assuming a low elasticity of substitution. Monopolization of the raw-materials supply will diminish the quantity used in the industry and diminish the rela-

---

[17] "Nonperfect competition" means any type of market structure other than pure competition (cf. Higgins, *loc. cit.*).

tive marginal significance of labor. With pure competition in the labor market, the wage rate, and so bargaining power of labor, falls. With a given degree of pure bargaining power in the labor market under bilateral monopoly, the wage rate will also fall. It is conceivable that the introduction of monopoly into the raw-materials market will so strengthen the resistance of employers to high wage rates that the monopsony wage will result.

The introduction of monopsony for the employer of labor into the raw-materials market will have the reverse effect. The quantity of raw materials used will tend to increase, and the relative marginal significance of labor will rise. Wages will rise with either pure competition or bilateral monopoly in the labor market. The increased desire for labor may so strengthen the workers that they may get the monopoly wage. An agreement to split the profits of exploiting the raw-materials producers is quite likely to emerge. By supporting workers in the raw-materials industry in any attempt to prevent the elimination of competition there, the workers in the industry under consideration are helping themselves and their employer as well; but there is a dichotomy of interests between the two groups of workers with respect to the maintenance of the monopsony of the raw-materials market.

Introduction of monopoly into the market for a competitive factor will raise the marginal significance of.labor in a given industry and so raise wages. Monopsony in the market for the competitive factor will lower wages, and so bargaining advantage. Elasticities of substitution are clearly of importance in determining the ultimate result.

(b) So far a definition of the terms "factor," "product," and "pure" monopoly or monopsony has been avoided. In reality, the closeness of substitutes in the product and in the factor market—the exact type and degree of nonperfect competition—will be of significance.

The analysis of nonperfect competition, and especially of oligopoly and oligopsony, is not in an altogether satisfactory state. No attempt will be made to analyze these sorts of market structures or monopolistic and monopsonistic competition. In general, however, one can say that a move away from pure monopoly in the factor market toward oligopoly or monopolistic competition will tend to lower the bargaining power of labor. The upper limit of the wage rate will be limited to the supply price of the rival factor or factors for each level of employment. Similarly, with oligopsony or monopsonistic competition in the labor market, the lower limit of wage rate becomes the demand price of the rival employer or employers at each level of employment.

An approach to monopolistic competition or oligopoly in the product market is likely to be accompanied by similar changes in the labor market. Monopsonistic competition or oligopsony in the product market will result in higher wage rates than pure monopsony in the product market, and the result will depend upon the kind of reaction entrepreneurs expect to their own price and wage policies on the part of rival entrepreneurs.

(c) A thorough study of the factors determining bargaining power would include the effects upon the wage rates in the industry of market conditions in other stages of production, above or below. The inclusion of the market for complementary factors is only one example of this sort of analysis. The bargaining power of coal miners depends upon market conditions in all stages of production following theirs, as well as in the market for complementary factors such as tools and machinery, which is at once above and below. Conditions in the coal industry influence the position both of and on the contract curve; conditions in other industries can affect the position only of the contract curve. In general, although not necessarily, the former conditions will be more significant.

It should be clear by now that bargaining advantage, interpreted as the ability to obtain the optimum price, depends upon the market structure throughout a very large sector, if not the whole, of the economy. But for many purposes of analysis it is useful to spotlight competitive conditions in a *cluster of related markets*.

CHAPTER VI. TRADE UNION INTEREST IN RELATED MARKETS

The preceding chapter constitutes a formal protest against the usual techniques of particular equilibrium as an explanation of price determination. To focus attention on the interaction between buyers and sellers in isolation from all other markets commonly neglects many of the most crucial forces in price formation. The analysis suggested a broadening of the theoretical perspective from a single market to a cluster of contiguous product and factor markets.[1] The price in any single market will depend upon the position of the buyers and sellers in the other markets in which they appear respectively as sellers and buyers. While the area of interaction reaches no limit until every single market in a total system has been included, "cluster analysis" suggests focusing attention upon a more limited range of interdependence.

The present chapter provides an opportunity to illustrate the usefulness of this larger analytical framework in an understanding of the process of wage determination; it specifies the different ways in which trade unions may actively influence wage determination by exerting pressure one way or another on price formation in contiguous markets. Some useful suggestions emerge for an understanding of the organizational scope of buyers and sellers, that is, the size and industrial jurisdiction or configuration of trade unions and firms.

Trade-union leaders, business executives, and economists alike

[1] This reorientation is crucial for fruitful empirical research. Consider, for example, the approach to price determination in the tobacco-products industry. The type of thinking characteristic of particular equilibrium (including monopolistic competition) would investigate the number of companies and how they operate in the single market. The present emphasis rather involves a simultaneous view of such markets as leaf tobacco, manufacturing labor in particular cities, wholesale and retail tobacco products. While other markets are no doubt important, such a group is a manageable cluster.

recognize that some dependence usually prevails between the demand function for a product and the demand function for the labor used to process this product, although differences arise in the mode of expressing this fact and in estimating the magnitude of this relation. A trade union's concern with either the wage rate or wage bill is likely, sooner or later, to force attention upon the price of the product. The more elastic the demand for the product and the larger the proportion of total costs that are wage

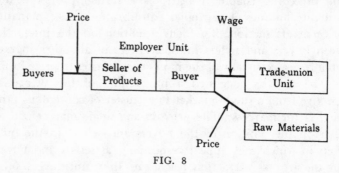

FIG. 8

costs, in general, the more difficult it will be to ignore the dependence of labor demand on product demand. This last condition is closely allied to the proportion of the total productive process included within the jurisdiction of the wage-determining unit. Negotiations or organizing activity in the day-to-day business of a trade union can be expected to require consideration of product prices. Behavior intended to influence prices in any contiguous market must be regarded as an integral part of wage policy.

A cluster of related markets is schematically presented in Fig. 8. The trade union is classically thought of as affecting the wage rate by restricting the supply of sellers in the factor market. And yet the above figure illustrates clearly that a union may equally well affect the wage by influencing the price of the product or the price of other factors. A surprising amount of trade-union activity has been directed toward these ends; that is, surprising to one reared in the dichotomy of total-system and single-market analysis. Attempts to influence the wage rate through related markets may be classified analytically into: (1) policies designed to shift product-demand functions, (2) policies affecting competitive conditions in product markets or related factor markets, and (3) policies affecting supply in the product markets through control of labor services. Successive sections will be directed toward these aspects of trade union behavior.

1. *Policies Designed to Shift Product Demand*

A trade union, logically, could attempt to alter pricing decisions under conditions of a given demand schedule for the product or it might endeavor to shift the whole function. The first alternative would involve the union in debate over the correct price structure for the industry given the objective of maximizing profits for the firms. Differences in judgment could arise over estimates of the elasticity of demand, the method of allocating overhead costs through time, and over the valuation of assets. The union would feel that if a different price policy were adopted by the industry, the wage bill or rate which could be secured would be higher. A higher or lower product-price structure might be thought desirable. A union representative in wage negotiations argued that

manufacturers of bottles today are just muffing the ball when they don't increase prices. . . . This year it is time to increase prices. Maybe the only way you will make a move to increase prices is by us stepping on the accelerator in the way of requesting increase in wage. . . . Glass is the finest, the very finest container there is on the market, and we don't think the customer would complain if you did raise the price. We know they would not go to tin, wood, or tin-foil containers for the sake of 25¢ a gross more. . . .[2]

A union might go so far as to bargain with the firms over product prices. Very few instances of this type of activity have been noted, although unions occasionally protest over the high quality of product that is being given to buyers for the price charged; a somewhat lower quality would permit a higher wage bill through higher rates.

A union can also affect prices and wage rates through influenc-

---

[2] *Minutes of the Conference between Ball Brothers Company of Muncie, Indiana, and the Glass Bottle Blowers' Association of the United States and Canada*, September 4, 5, 6, and 8, 1941, pp. 22–23.

ing demand by policies intended to shift the whole schedule or by activities which counteract decreases in demand that would otherwise take place. Such programs may be undertaken in co-operation with the firms in the industry or on the sole initiative of the union. A survey of union activities intended to increase demand for the industry as a whole (with corresponding effects on the wage bill) reveals several typical patterns. (a) The union may instigate and secure the cooperation of all parties interested in the industry in a program of mass advertising and promotion. If the product is typically purchased by the general public, a wide sales campaign may prove effective. Unions in the producers' goods area would ordinarily have to resort to other methods. (b) Political pressure may be used to exclude or restrict the introduction of competitive products, as is exemplified in the support of tariffs on foreign goods. Several important instances of these measures to influence the demand for the product merit brief review.

The International Ladies' Garment Workers' Union sponsored an extensive promotional program for the New York Dress industry [3] in negotiations for a renewal of an agreement in early 1941. The proposal was supported by a survey of the industry which examined sales, per capita expenditures, relative advertising expenditures of competing industries, as well as sample costs, earnings, and profits.[4] After ten weeks of conferences, the union's plan was adopted and the three-year agreement provided for a cooperative promotion campaign with the objective of:

. . . increasing the volume of production of the New York market, improving further the quality of its product, and offering even better values to the consumer, by publicizing the outstanding position in the field of style, fine workmanship and sound values of the New York market, by stimulating consumer demand in the United States and elsewhere, and by establishing New York as the fashion center of the

[3] While the program was intended, in part, to draw business away from other markets in the country, equal emphasis was placed upon an increased volume of business for the industry nationally.

[4] Julius Hochman, *Industry Planning through Collective Bargaining*, A Program for Modernizing the New York Dress Industry as Presented in Conference with Employers on behalf of the Joint Board of the Dressmakers' Union, New York, January, 1941.

world. Such a campaign will result in increased business to the members of the organized dress industry, and in material advantages to the members of the Union employed by them who will derive therefrom greater continuity of employment and increased annual earnings.[5]

A board was created, composed of representatives of the various employer associations and the union, to effectuate this program. A million dollars annually was to be raised from member firms by assessment on the basis of sales volume and another half million dollars by solicitation from others having an interest in the welfare of the industry—retailers, textile firms, accessory producers, real estate and banking concerns. The international union offered to contribute $100,000 toward this fund.

While any attempt to appraise the impact of this program upon the union and the industry is premature, it must be noted that the promotional proposal originated with the union and was urged upon the employers for the expressed purpose of increasing the annual earnings of the membership. Furthermore, the program was worked out in joint conferences and incorporated into collective-bargaining agreements. Concern over the wage bill forced the union into an active policy in the product market.[6]

The United Hatters, Cap, and Millinery Workers have also initiated and supported campaigns to increase the demand for the products of their industry in order to increase the wage bill. The men's hat and cap sections of the industry were seriously affected by the hatless fad of the past decade and by the alleged gangster, stigma of the cap, said to have been created by the movies. In any event, the international union, with the support of many locals, has adopted a number of measures to counteract this decrease in demand. Local No. 60 in Philadelphia sent a letter to all trade unions in the area urging that union men wear hats.

During the past few years the "hatless" fad has caused severe hardships to those engaged in the hat manufacturing industry. It has been called to our attention that many union workers fail to wear hats.

[5] The agreement is dated February 8, 1941.
[6] See Joel Seidman, *The Needle Trades*, Farrar & Rinehart, Inc., New York, 1942, Chap. 13, for reference to other activities of the same union designed to affect the product market.

. . . We feel sure that your members will not want to be among those who are helping to destroy an industry which provides a livelihood for so many workers We appeal to all organized workers to wear hats. . . . Use your head—wear a hat—and keep our members employed.[7]

The same local, with the support of the International, initiated the Philadelphia Hat Week idea and contributed $1600 to the campaign. Support was secured from the manufacturers, the chamber of commerce, the central labor union, and the newspapers. A large publicity campaign was apparently considered so successful that the device of a "hat week" has spread to other cities.

Even more importance should be attached to the Millinery Stabilization Commission, Inc., an administrative board created in 1936 by agreement between the Cap and Millinery Department of the union and several associations of millinery manufacturers in New York City.[8] The commission is composed only of public members and includes no representatives of the signatory parties who created the organization, although a joint advisory committee assists the commission. The commission provides a "Consumer's Protective Label" to be affixed to headwear manufactured and sold under conditions specified by the commission. The union supports the commission by requiring in every agreement that the firm adopt this label.

The commission was developed after the N.R.A. had been declared unconstitutional to eliminate methods of unfair competition. The union clearly recognized the dependence of the level of wage rates and earnings upon competitive conditions in the market for millinery products and took the initiative in the formation of the commission. While the specific trade-practice rulings are relevant to Section 2 of this chapter, certain other activities of the commission are intended to increase the total demand for the industry. A trade-promotion committee, made up of manufacturers, is concerned with sales expansion. Fashion shows are

[7] The letter was signed by Philip J. Thomas, president of the local.

[8] Additional employers' organizations have been brought under the jurisdiction of the Commission. Over 50 per cent of the total volume of business in the millinery industry falls under the jurisdiction of this commission. *Second Report of the Millinery Stabilization Commission, Inc.*, mimeographed, New York, November 1, 1940, p. 23 and Table B, Appendix I.

sponsored two to four times a year in New York. Four national millinery weeks for the country as a whole involve an extensive advertising program closely integrated with retail outlets. This committee under the commission also furnishes photographs, style notes, and editorial matter to newspapers and radio stations.

Few other unions have organized such elaborate programs to influence the demand for the product of an industry. However, a number of instances of sporadic interest in increasing demand may be identified. This activity is frequently semipolitical. The Glass Bottle Blowers, for instance, strongly supported a higher tariff on French perfume bottles. The union sent representatives to France to compare costs of manufacturing; others appeared before the Congressional committees to explain the position of the union. The same union has striven to maintain sales in the industry by vigorous opposition to paper substitutes.[9] An attempt was made to impose a 1-cent tax or premium on milk sold in paper containers. The support of the teamsters and other unions was solicited.[10] The photoengravers resorted to more usual business tactics in making "substantial regular monthly contributions . . . to provide greater distribution of *More Business* being published by the American Photo-Engravers' Association for the purpose of further interesting the buyer of engravings of the full possibilities of the process and thus encourage an increasing demand for our product."[11] The same union complained of the increasing share of advertising business going to radio stations and made favorable mention of European systems of radio control.[12] The market for engravings was being affected by radio competition. The typographical union also has been much interested in radio competition with printed material; it has fought against higher postal rates for second-class mail. The hosiery workers are concerned with the fashion of slacks among women. The brewery workers were opposed to prohibition. The teamsters protested

[9] *Official Proceedings of the 51st Convention of the Glass Bottle Blowers' Association*, 1929, p. 122.
[10] *Official Proceedings of the 53rd Convention of the Glass Bottle Blowers' Association*, 1936, p. 200.
[11] *Official Proceedings of the 39th Convention of the International Photo-Engravers' Union of North America*, 1938, p. 59.
[12] *Official Proceedings of the 32nd Convention of the International Photo-Engravers' Union of North America*, 1931, p. 62.

the purchase of gasoline and oil in tank-car lots by larger consumers. The carpenters have opposed legislation against bill boards. The United Mine Workers' political opposition to the St. Lawrence project is a protest, in part, against a possible decrease in the demand for coal. Virtually every trade union, with the possible exception of those constituting exceedingly narrow bargaining units, comes to be interested in factors affecting product demand of the industry. Furthermore, trade-union leaders are usually remarkably well informed as to conditions of the trade. But the extent and methods of shifting market demand vary enormously from union to union.

2. Policies Affecting Competitive Conditions in Product Markets

Trade unions may operate in the product or allied factor markets to alter consciously the competitive·conditions in order to implement wage-bill objectives. Regardless of the specific magnitude a union may attempt to maximize (Chap. III), the market product-demand function is not really given to the union independently of its own policies, much less the demand schedule for labor in a single firm. The market function may be shifted, by devices considered in Section 1, or can be altered in shape by methods still to be considered. That is, the wage bill will be influenced by the character of price and production competition among enterprises, which is in turn subject to union manipulation. Even with a specified product-demand schedule the union may take an active part in setting the particular price. More indirect methods of influence are available in control over entry to the product market and specification of subsidiary terms in the product price structure. More direct action to influence product prices by manipulation of labor supply is considered in the next section.

A. CHANGE IN MARKET DEMAND ELASTICITY

The union label is one of the oldest and most respected techniques in the trade-union kit of tools. The cultivation of this form of consumer loyalty is a type of product differentiation. The union label, first popularized by the cigar makers, was originated in 1869 by the carpenters' eight-hour league to distinguish products from planing mills running ten hours. The American Federation of Labor created a Label Department in 1909 following court decisions against the boycott. By 1940 over fifty international and national unions had adopted labels and were affiliated with this department; the unions which placed most emphasis upon the label included the typographical, cigar, garment trades, bakers, boot and shoe, brewery, and musicians. Each year the Label Department issues a directory of firms that use and display union labels. ·

B. DIFFERENTIATION BY FIRM

An instance in which unions have resorted to other devices than the label (applicable to every firm meeting union conditions) to alter elasticity of demand is provided by the hosiery workers in full-fashioned manufacture. The competitive character of the product market, it was noted in Chap. IV, has kept a great deal of pressure on union wage rates. The chief activities of the union to meet this situation have been the programs of modernization of equipment and cost reduction described earlier. The union has also encouraged, and in many cases has given active support to, firms setting up branded names for their hosiery.

I am not trying to create the impression that the solution of the hosiery problem lies in manufacturing and selling branded merchandise, but I do wish to show that the control of the secondary hosiery market by the manufacturer does allow him to obtain relatively better prices for his goods and a better margin over cost. . . .[13]

Local 38 of the union composed of employees of the Strutwear Knitting Company undertook a promotion campaign for the products of the company. They set up sales districts, contests, and quotas and enlisted the support of other unions in the community.[14] While part of this program is concerned with shifting the demand for the product, the interest here is in the support of the brand name. It is no surprise that a company would initiate a brand, but a view of the cluster of markets as a whole shows that the union actively supports the brand program.

[13] *Official Proceedings of the 28th Convention of the American Federation of Hosiery Workers,* 1939, p. 18.
[14] *Business Week,* March 22, 1941, pp. 69–70.

C. PRODUCT PRICE-FIXING AND ENTRY

The photoengravers' union presents one of the most interesting cases of concern with conditions of product market competition. The members either work in newspaper plants with other skilled crafts or in contracting shops where the sole product is some form of engraving. The contract shops are small and require relatively small outlays of investment. The consequent price and product competition is strenuous and would be expected to delimit severely the level of wage rates and the wage bill that the union can secure. The fact that the union interested itself with product prices under these conditions is not at all surprising, particularly since wages constitute a significant element in total costs.

The international union attempted to reverse the skeptical view that many locals had of cost accounting and encouraged the adoption of the standard system devised by the employers' association. The labor committee of the Philadelphia local, for instance, agreed to cooperate with the system provided it was not used as a "check-up or speed-up system." [15] There can be little doubt that the intended effect of such a system was to reduce price competition. The union also proposed clauses for agreements that prohibited sales of product below costs of production. The Seattle contract, for instance, provided that the employer:

. . . shall not sell engravings or any product upon which members of the union shall have worked . . . at a price which shall be less than the actual cost of production thereof, and that the employer shall not . . . engage in any unfair discrimination between buyers of such engravings and/or products as to price or service.[16]

In other instances, strike action has been used against firms that persist in price cutting. Employers complained to the union in Toronto, Canada, against one of their members who used such tactics.

Representatives of the union attempted to secure some assurances from this firm that they would stop the practice of which they were accused by the other employers. As no understanding could be reached

---

[15] *Official Proceedings of the 25th Convention of the International Photo-Engravers' Union of North America*, 1924, p. 35.

[16] *Official Proceedings of the 33rd Convention of the International Photo-Engravers' Union of North America*, 1932, p. 12.

with this firm, the matter was placed before our members who were employed in the shop, and it was decided to withdraw their services until such time as this employer maintained a fair competition with other employers.[17]

The most famous instance in which the union tried to affect product prices by regulating competitive conditions involved clause 10 in the New York Agreement with an employers' association, which provided:

In order that the Union may secure the adoption and carrying out by all Photo-Engraving concerns . . . of the scale of wages and working conditions herein specified . . . the Union hereby requests, and the Photo-Engravers' Board of Trade hereby agrees, that the said Board of Trade will admit to its membership all reputable Photo-Engraving concerns in New York City; and in consideration hereof . . . the union agrees that its members will work only for such Photo-Engraving concerns as are members of the said Board of Trade. . . .[18]

A similar provision was inserted in other contracts until it could be regarded as a standard feature of photoengraving agreements in large cities. The Federal Trade Commission in 1928 issued a decision against both the union and the employers' association charging conspiracy in restraint of trade.[19] The union successfully claimed that wage earners had the right to "refuse to cooperate with any employers who so conducted his business as to cause us to endanger our immediate and future well being."[20] But combination among employers to fix prices was held to be illegal. The union regarded the decision as leaving it alone in the task of preventing cut-throat competition.

The union was forced to examine entry into the industry by its concern with product prices. Frequent complaint is made of journeyman members who go into business for themselves. "This tendency has resulted in creating a more intensive competition

[17] *Official Proceedings of the 23rd Convention of the International Photo-Engravers' Union of North America*, 1922, p. 64.

[18] See, "In the Matter of American Photo-Engravers' Association, *et al.* and the International Photo-Engravers' Union of North America, *et al.*," *Federal Trade Commission Decisions*, January 30, 1928–June 11, 1929, 12, pp. 29–69.

[19] *Complaint against the American Photo-Engravers' Association, et al., and the International Photo-Engravers' Union of North America, et al.*, loc. cit.

[20] *Official Proceedings of the 29th Convention of the International Photo-Engravers' Union of North America*, 1928, p. 21.

between employers, in lessening the income to the industry and in endangering the whole structure of our industry." [21] A survey of 588 shops in 1931 (a large sample) found journeymen members financially interested in 53.1 per cent of the commercial shops tabulated. As a partial way of discouraging such entry, many agreements include clauses which give preference in overtime work to journeymen not financially interested in a shop. The 1938 convention of the union called upon the supply houses serving photoengraving establishments to "cooperate in stamping out some of the growing evils in the industry caused by the unethical business methods of furnishing equipment and granting undue and unwarranted credits to those not entitled to such consideration." [22]

No sector of the economy is more commonly associated with trade-union policies altering the competitive conditions in the product market than the building and construction fields. Strong craft organizations bargain with local associations of contractors who constitute the focal point of the regular line of distribution through manufacturers and local distributors. The possibility of using local building codes and political connections to keep out foreign contractors and materials completes the ideal case in which the union and contractors may find it profitable to combine against the unorganized buyer of construction and to split the monopolistic returns. The problem of securing conformity to the price scales from dissident firms may be achieved by a boycott enforced by manufacturers and dealers,[23] by threats of violence and dissemination of misleading statements in the community, or by the strike power of the union. Slow downs or the assignment of incompetent workmen to noncooperating contractors may be equally effective.

Sometimes a union may be led to police pricing and bidding arrangements among contractors by some union official who receives a personal return. More frequently, it would appear, the union is simply supporting a market situation in which the profits of

---

[21] *Official Proceedings of the 25th Convention of the International Photo-Engravers' Union of North America*, 1924, p. 22.

[22] *Photo-Engraver*, April, 1939, XXXI, p. 325.

[23] These practices were charged in *U. S.* v. *Southern California Marble Dealers' Association, et al.*, U. S. District Court, Southern District of California, Indictment, February 16, 1940. Also see *U. S.* v. *The Central Supply Association, et al.* U. S. District Court, Northern District of Ohio, Eastern Division, Indictment, March 29, 1940.

restriction are shared with employers. The investigations of the Antitrust Division have focused attention on a number of these union-employer combinations. The interest in these cases is not the legal question of the liability of a trade union under the antitrust laws but rather the illustrations they afford of arrangements between product and factor markets. Locals 6 and 595 of the International Brotherhood of Electrical Workers in San Francisco were indicted for depriving some contractors of union labor because they declined to file all bids with a depository, to discuss all bids at "survey meetings" of an association, and to use the resale prices of the association in figuring bids. The employers against whom the union struck were said to be willing to continue bargaining with the union, as they had in the past, over wages, hours, recognition, and working conditions.[24] The indictment made the business agents and presidents of the locals as well as several international officials parties to the case. Two locals in the building trades in Detroit were charged with refusing to handle tile manufactured or sold by firms outside the contractors' association, "without regard to whether such nonmembers were willing to abide by union rules as to wages, hours, working conditions, and collective bargaining."[25] A consent decree was secured in the tile industry in which the Tile Contractors' Association and the Bricklayers', Masons' and Plasterers' International Union of America, as well as their subsidiary organizations and officers, were enjoined from withholding labor or refusing to negotiate an agreement with nonmembers of the association, from operating a bid depository, and from penalizing or blacklisting members who dealt with nonmembers of the association.[26] The union and the Tile Association agreed to discipline violations of the decree in accordance with clauses in their constitutions. The

[24] *U. S.* v. *San Francisco Electrical Contractors' Association, Inc., et al.*, District Court of the U. S., Northern District of California, Southern Division, Indictment, March 2, 1940, p. 17.

[25] *U. S.* v. *Detroit Tile Contractors' Association, et al.*, District Court of the U. S., Eastern District of Michigan, Southern Division, Complaint and Consent Decree, July 9, 1940, p. 10. The unions involved were Bricklayers, Masons and Plasterers' International Local Union, No. 32, and Local No. 40 of the International Association of Marble, Stone and Slate Polishers, Rubbers and Sawyers, Tile and Marble Setters Helpers and Terrazzo Workers Helpers.

[26] *U. S.* v. *The Tile Contractors' Association of America, Inc., et al.*, U. S. District Court for the Northern District of Illinois, Eastern Division, Complaint and Consent Decree, June 10, 1940.

national investigation of the plumbing-supplies industry may also be mentioned; it resulted in an indictment charging the United Association of Journeymen Plumbers and Steam Fitters of the United States and Canada and nine locals with refusing to work for nonmembers of the National Association of Master Plumbers. They were also charged with combining with the employer's association and manufacturers to prohibit the installation of supplies not sold through the "restricted system of distribution." Even though contractors were willing to bargain collectively and to abide by union rules as to wages, hours, and working conditions, supplies furnished through mail-order houses, for instance, would not be handled.[27]

The examples of activities of building trade unions in product markets summarized from antitrust investigations could be multiplied many times. There can be little doubt that agreements in this field have frequently been characterized by (a) delimitation of employers for whom the union may work, and (b) specification of materials that will be handled. The first group of provisions may be enforced by the union support of uniform costing systems, strictures against bids below cost, bid depositories, extra fees from nonmembers of employers' associations, or outright strike against all but members of these groups. The second type of clause may require penalty rates for foreign material or explicit prohibition of this work. By these two devices, the union is able to secure a higher rate and probably a higher wage bill for the relevant membership group at the higher price in the product market.

The genesis of these arrangements for splitting the advantages of restriction is to be sought in the structure of the complex of markets. A relatively large number of contractors with low costs of entry confronted by a narrow bargaining unit of skilled workers would tend to make for marked price competition. The use of the closed-bid method of pricing was shown to have the tendency of shading estimates. The union is apprehensive lest contractors attempt to make up their low estimates by speed-ups, kickbacks, or overt rate reductions. The unions' support of pricing conventions and agreements is consistent with its desire

[27] U. S. v. *The Central Supply Association*, et al., *op. cit.*, pp. 35–37.

to remove all possible downward pressures on wage rates. The analysis of the preceding chapter would suggest that, since contractors are frequently confronted by an unorganized group of buyers, wage demands can more readily be granted and recovered in higher prices than can the risk be taken of a strike against a strong union. This is particularly true since the union is willing to cooperate in securing the effectiveness of the higher price. The weakest link in the chain of markets is seen to absorb the wage increase. Agreements between unions and employers' associations, such as exist in the building trades, are too frequently regarded as *ad hoc* combinations rather than the outgrowth of particular market situations. The joint control over price arises from a complex of circumstances, the most important of which include the local markets, unorganized buyers, strong craft organization of wage earners, bidding methods of price quotation, and the small proportion of total building costs involved in any one craft. The union supports the restrictive practices because it is assured of a cut in the monopolistic returns.

The teamsters have acted to influence competitive conditions in the product market and consequent product prices and the wage bill. At times, the union has taken direct action on product prices, while on other occasions the entry of firms has been its concern. The Des Moines local picketed eight service stations handling the products of major companies in July 1939 for posting prices $0.002 below the rest of the retailers. The action was probably the result of earlier agreement with important dealers. The union began to organize the retailers in the spring of 1939, partly at the instigation of large dealers. At the time of the strike about 385 of the 425 dealers were reported to be members of the teamsters' union. The union carried on an extensive program of organization among independent dealers and lessees, arguing that higher margins and price stabilization would result. The initial interest in retail prices could have arisen from concern with impacts upon truckers' wages, but the expansion of jurisdiction to include dealers greatly intensified the concern with these retail prices.[28] An interesting insight into market rela-

---

[28] The reason the union expanded its jurisdiction presents a question of the relevant membership function. The organization of the dealers would improve the position of the union in its dealings with the oil companies.

tions is presented by the protest of the jobbers who would find themselves squeezed between the oil companies and the union once organization were completed.[29]

The Journeymen Barbers' International Union of America would obviously be interested in the prices charged by the employer. A large part of the price goes directly to wages; wage income is tied closely to gross income of the enterprise. Furthermore, about 30 per cent of the union members operate one-chair or partnership shops. As in other industries with one-man or producer cooperative firms, the union is vitally concerned with the prices charged in the product market. One group of members is in a position to affect substantially the income of the rest. If wage decisions are to be centralized in the union, product prices must be agreed upon. Thus, two-thirds of fifty agreements studied in 1936 revealed price specification. Not only were prices for shaves and haircuts regulated, but in some cases the prices of other services were fixed in order to prevent intense product or service competition. Although the General Executive Board in 1912 advocated a policy of no concern with prices, a study [30] of trade-union agreements during subsequent years indicated that few locals complied, as would have been expected given the character of the intermarket relations.

The concern of the United Mine Workers with the price of coal is too well known to require details. Suffice it to recall that the union played an important role in the legislation setting up the Bituminous Coal Commission with its powers to fix prices. These illustrations can be multiplied many times; the conclusion is inescapable that intermarket relations have compelled trade unions to be vitally concerned with product market prices directly and with entry conditions when these factors are likely to have important impacts on the wage bill.[31] Union wage policy is designed in the light of the specific character of the product market.

[29] See the editorial of the Illinois Petroleum Marketers' Association in *National Petroleum News*, July 12, 1939, pp. 15–16.

[30] W. Scott Hall, *The Journeymen Barbers' International Union of America*, The Johns Hopkins Press, Baltimore, 1936, pp. 67–69.

[31] See Solomon Barkin, "Industrial Union Wage Policies," *Plan Age*, January, 1940, pp. 13–14.

D. SUBSIDIARY TERMS OF SALE

The initiative exercised by the Hatters, Cap, and Millinery Workers in the formation of the Millinery Stabilization Commission has already been noted. While no prices were apparently set, the regulation of conditions of fair competition required the determination of some elements of the price structure. The trade practice provisions prohibited discounts in excess of 7 per cent, ten days E.O.M. (except after the 25th of the month) in addition to forbidding advertising allowances and "refunds, rebates, donations, gifts, credits, excess discounts or special privileges or services unless (they) are openly extended to all on like terms and conditions." [32]

The commission's specification of uniform conditions of sale further required that all merchandise be shipped F.O.B.; open orders subject to consignment or approval are prohibited. Section II of the provisions explicitly prohibited "the practice of selling goods below the seller's cost, with the intent and with the effect of injuring a competitor and where the effect may be substantially to lessen competition or tend to create a monopoly. . . ." [33] Until a firm abided by the regulations of the commission, the Consumer's Protective Label was refused, and the union forbade its members from working under nonlabel conditions in accordance with its agreements.

The union's interest in competitive conditions in the millinery market, evidenced by its support of the commission, was predicated fundamentally on the impact of these conditions on wage rates and the wage bill. By organizing and supporting the employers in their dealings with department stores and other buyers of millinery, the union was probably enabled to secure a larger wage bill. The superior bargaining power of the millinery buyers was offset by the pressure of the union, and other sections of the market cluster, such as suppliers of raw materials, blocks, and dies

[32] Section I, No. 7 of the "Trade Practice Provisions Applying to Millinery Manufactures," reprinted in *Second Report of the Millinery Stabilization Commission, Inc.*, pp. 10–12.

[33] The section specified that "all elements recognized by good accounting practice as proper elements of such cost shall be included in determining cost under this rule."

that the union was able to mobilize.[34] The policies adopted by the union and the commission may very well have resulted in a more nearly competitive wage, considering the whole cluster, because the monopsonistic power of the syndicates and department stores has been reduced. The anomalous situation, described as a theoretical possibility in the previous chapter, may have been created in which the decrease in competition among millinery manufacturers brought about by the combined policies of the commission and the union may very well have resulted in a more competitive price level for the product and factor markets.

E. ACTION IN RELATED MARKETS

The Hosiery union has been very much concerned with the character of competitive conditions in markets which significantly influence the labor bargain with hosiery manufacturers. The leadership has shown keen recognition of the dependence of wage rates and the wage bill upon these competitive conditions. The market situation is deplored where firms are little more than commission knitters. "By this I mean that they depend upon one, two, or three volume merchandisers for an outlet for their goods. The loss of one or more of such accounts is a serious blow to any mill, and we find such mills . . . in an unfavorable position in maintaining a price level for their goods. . . ."[35] The possible impacts upon wage rates and the wage bill are not difficult to follow.

A further instance of the importance of related markets to a single price determination is seen in the demand by many manufacturers for wage reductions with sharp advances in the prices of raw silk.[36] Except under union conditions these demands were sometimes successful. Partial equilibrium analysis that is confined to a single market is apt to conclude that a rise in materials prices can only result in a rise in product prices. The broadening of analysis to include closely related markets permits different results depending upon the relative competitive conditions in each.

---

[34] See "In the Matter of Millinery Stabilization Commission, Inc., et al." *Federal Trade Commission*, September 26, 1941.

[35] *Official Proceedings of the 28th Convention of the American Federation of Hosiery Workers*, 1939, p. 18. Also see quotation from G. W. Taylor, *The Hosiery Worker*, December 2, 1938, XVI.

[36] *The Hosiery Worker*, December 29, 1939, XVII, and *loc. cit.*, April 7, 1939.

The support the Hosiery union gave the manufacturers in this case is to be interpreted as an equalization of the bargaining power in the product market.

The Cigar Makers' Union was able to organize only the relatively small enterprises which were at a competitive disadvantage in the important tobacco-leaf markets. Mr. G. W. Perkins, international president, suggested that the union manufacturers form an association for the purpose of buying and distributing leaf tobacco.[37] He also suggested that the union firms should agree on fewer sizes and brands.[38] In 1930, a Cigar Manufacturers' Cooperative was formed to establish a pool for the buying and selling of leaf tobacco. There was even some thought of using a common brand name which would make possible national advertising.[39] This case vividly illustrates the importance of intermarket relations for wage determination.

3. Policies of Direct Action in the Labor Market

The analytical view of a trade union as simply a monopoly in the labor market would emphasize the importance of apprenticeship rules, closed membership lists, initiation fees, and dues. The range of activities explored in the two preceding sections would be largely neglected. But even the restriction of labor supply may be oriented directly toward product prices. with or without the cooperation of business enterprises. The history of labor organizations in both Great Britain and the United States reveals instances where unions have quit work to reduce the stock of goods on hand with their employers. Large stocks threaten declines in product price and in turn declines in wage rates.

The first miners' union in America, the Bates Union among anthracite miners in Schuylkill County, Pennsylvania, ordered a suspension of work in July 1849 "for the purpose of reducing the stock of coal on hand, to steady the market and stave off a reduction in wages." [40] The United Mine Workers at their Potts-

---

[37] Cigar Makers' Journal, February, 1923, 47, p. 6.

[38] Ibid., September, 1925, 49, p. 12.

[39] Ibid., September, 1930, 54, p. 8.

[40] Edward A. Wieck, The American Miners' Association, Russell Sage Foundation New York, 1940, p. 63. Almost five thousand men on a Fourth of July picnic resolved to take four days off to reduce the coal stocks. Peter Roberts, The Anthracite Coal Indus, try, The Macmillan Company, New York, 1901, p. 173.

ville and Hazelton conventions at the turn of the century considered the same tactics when confronted with the possibility of a wage decrease. The English miners used identical methods. The *Articles of Regulation of the Operative Collieries of Lanark and Dumbarton* of 1825 provided that "there should never be allowed to be any stock of coals in the hands of any of the masters." Almost seventy years later, in March 1892, the Miners' Federation resolved to "take a week's holiday" with the consequence that stocks of coal were reduced and the threat of a wage reduction disappeared.[41] There can be little doubt that unions in the coal industry have resorted to enforced idleness to protect their wage-rate levels.

Among other unions that have adopted these methods, the Lancashire spinners and weavers favored short-time operations when wage reductions were proposed in order to remove the glut from the trade. "So far as the Central Committee was concerned, they should oppose tooth and nail, and dispute inch by inch every attempt to reduce wages until at least some honest attempt was made by employers to curtail production and thus try to bring about a healthier state of trade."[42] The relative infrequency of the resort to shutdowns to influence product prices and wage rates is probably explained by the specialized conditions that make this technique possible. (a) A highly competitive sector of the system seems required, otherwise employers themselves are apt to have curtailed output with reductions in demand. (b) Production for an organized market is essential in which spot prices reflect discounted expectations from day to day. Prices set over longer periods by contract or formal business decision would render the stoppage useless to affect price. (c) The commodity must be relatively standardized rather than made to order if stocks are to be accumulated. The custom tailors, for instance, could not prevent a wage reduction by the method of the min-

[41] Sidney and Beatrice Webb, *Industrial Democracy*, Longmans, Green, and Company, London, 1914, pp. 447–448.

[42] *The Cotton Factory Times*, March 20, 1885, I, p. 6, columns 1–3. The statement was made by David Holmes of Burnley at a meeting of weavers at Ashton. Many similar statements may be found in the same paper. In 1878 the Northeast Lancashire weavers offered the employers a reduction in wage rates provided short time was run. The reduction was to be restored when full-time operations were renewed. *Loc. cit.*, June 19, 1885, p. 1, column 1.

ers for they would be incapable of similarly affecting product prices.

A classic case of withdrawal of labor services, with the cooperation of at least the larger enterprises, is provided by the Window Glass Workers in the eighties and nineties of the last century [43] and the first decades of the twentieth. The union enforced a shutdown by constitutional provision: "Blowers and gathers shall not work from June 15 to September 15." The policy of restriction resulted in a break in the ranks of the union members and the formation of a new union. At the shorter work periods and higher prices, wage earners organized producers' cooperatives, attracted by the high profits in the industry. Although these small enterprises were induced to restrict output by payment of a bonus in lieu of operation, the union received wage increases in return for the shorter periods of production. But price reductions and secret wage concessions eventually broke the conspiracy.

4. *Implications for Public Policy*

The preceding sections have briefly surveyed those aspects of wage policy that involve union activities in product markets. The theoretical possibility of more competitive prices and allocation of resources as a result of a combination between a trade union and employers (against monopsonistic buyers in the product markets) was observed to be an empirically significant case. The implications for public policy, and for antitrust prosecution in particular, warrant brief elaboration. Amid the uncertainty as to the precise boundary line of conduct that violates the antitrust laws, there is relatively little question that overt agreements to suppress commercial competition, 'that is, agreements as to product price, are a violation of law.

This stricture applies equally to trade unions making agreements concerning these prices. Just as the common law, so the Sherman Act sought the "prevention of restraints to free competition in business and commercial transactions which tended to restrict production, raise prices or otherwise control the market to the detriment of purchasers or consumers of goods and serv-

[43] *Eleventh Special Report of the Commission of Labor on Regulation and Restriction of Output*, 1904, Chap. 11.

ices." [44] The *sine qua non* for the invocation of the Sherman Act is the showing of "substantial restraint of commercial competition in the market." But like the common law and most economic theory, the ideas behind the antitrust laws run in terms of the single market and monopolistic *sellers*. All price agreements can only be regarded as restricting competition.

The argument of the last two chapters would suggest, however, that the effects of attempts to influence product prices cannot be presumed. Each case must be appraised in the context of a market cluster and wide impacts on the total system. Often price agreements will worsen the allocation of resources, but there are important cases when prices may be made more nearly competitive as a result of pressures in the cluster. Excessive attention paid to the techniques of restriction may neglect the results on the structure of prices. The attempt to confine "legitimate" trade-union policies to the labor market [45] is probably unaware of the general extent of intermarket manipulations and fails to recognize that bargaining powers may be grossly unequal in closely allied markets.

(*b*) The scope of the organizational activity of a trade union as well as the boundary lines of a firm are more readily understood in the focus of a cluster of markets. The *de facto* abandonment of the principle of exclusive jurisdiction leaves a problem of the market configuration of a union. The personal factors of leadership and struggle for prestige and power no doubt are important. But why does the expansion in the "territory" of a union take one direction rather than another? The similarity of process, materials, and training of wage earners is probably of first importance, but the degree of competition among product markets and the allied materials and supply markets are not to be overlooked.

For instance, the extension of the activity of the teamsters into condensery and creamery establishments arises in part from the relations among teamsters' wages in fluid milk and wage rates and prices in condenser firms. [46] Or, Mr. Lewis's interest in organiza-

[44] *Apex Hosiery Co.* v. *Leader*, 310 U. S. 469 (1940).

[45] See the discussion of Richard M. Bissell, Jr., *American Economic Review, Supplement*, March, 1942, XXXII, pp. 481–486.

[46] *Proceedings of the 14th Convention, International Brotherhood of Teamsters, Chauffeurs, Stablemen and Helpers of America*, September 9–14, 1940, Sixth Day, pp. 25–26.

tion of workers in the steel and automobile industries was not entirely dissociated from the market interrelations between coal and steel. The precise market configuration of wage-determining units is certainly a problem of wider public ramifications than the private structure of a trade union ordinarily suggests. Wage decisions would seem more apt to take into account the full impact of their effects—with the relevant time patterns—the more clearly the product market relations were discerned. The argument is not necessarily for larger bargaining units, rather for those which follow the contours of the more significant market clusters. The wage decisions in condenser firms and fluid milk transportation can be made with a fuller recognition of effects by virtue of a unit which recognizes the product market relations.

(c) Governmental administrative agencies have not always been organized to recognize clearly these market relations. For example, wage-rate decisions may be made in the railroads by emergency boards. Yet freight rates are decided by the Interstate Commerce Commission. The separation of decision-making can result in a failure to consider larger impacts of wage changes. Similarly, wage rates are determined by the collective bargaining between coal operators and the United Mine Workers and coal prices are fixed by the Bituminous Coal Commission. Since pricing decisions are not given independently of wage decisions by perfect markets, the separation of decision making is conducive to mutual irresponsibility for the wider effects of wage and price changes. The coordination of decisions made by governmental units (railroad case) is a difficult enough administrative problem, but the coal case raises even more perplexing issues with the compartition of public and private sectors. Perhaps some contribution could be made by requiring the presence of Bituminous Coal Commission representatives at negotiations of coal wage rates or on arbitration panels.

5. Summary of Trade-union Wage Policy

The first six chapters of this study have endeavored to explore in a preliminary way some aspects of the wage policies of trade unions, providing at the same time certain analytical tools to assist in the interpretation of union activities. The following points are reiterated here *seriatim* to give perspective to the main stream of the argument, but they must not be construed outside of their context and qualifications.

(1) The labor market was found to be structurally different from a bourse; wage rates are typically quoted prices. Price setters in factor or product markets will be particularly concerned with the time patterns of adjustment and the frequency of changes in data. These considerations result in relatively stable prices in the labor market.

(2) The labor bargain, which specifies all of the conditions and terms of sale under which services are rendered, may be divided into the price structure and nonpecuniary terms. The bargaining process involves substitution between these conditions. The base rates plus all the other dimensions directly determining the money outlay of the enterprise per unit of labor services constitute the "price of labor."

(3) No existing statistical series exactly portrays changes in the price of labor, as just defined. Since average hourly earnings may diverge from wage rates because of changes in piece-rate earnings, shifts in the proportion of wage earners at each rate bracket, and because of the period of time over which earnings may be averaged, the movements of rates and earnings cannot be presumed to be identical. In fact, unless specific evidence exists to the contrary in any particular instance, the presumption on available material is that earnings would tend to increase faster than rates in periods of prosperity and over any secular period.

(4) The classical supply function of labor does not recognize that even in unorganized labor markets decisions affecting the amount of labor forthcoming are made by the household and in conformity with group standards. Under conditions of trade unionism the classical function loses almost all relevance. A membership function was substituted, indicating the amount of labor that would be attached to the union at each price. The function shows the amount of labor that the union takes into account in making its wage-rate decisions. In the short run the function may be virtually vertical in shape; over time its position can be expected to shift.

(5) If a union may be presumed to face a demand function, as a first approximation, the membership function and the demand function can be regarded as determining the wage provided the objective that the union seeks to maximize is specified. The logically conceived objectives were seen to be: the largest wage bill, the largest labor income including public unemployment compensation or out-of-work benefits, the maximum level of employment, the highest average wage income, and the maximum collective rents over the minimum price required to induce attachment to the union. Probably the most generalized assumption respecting actual aims of trade unions would be the maximization of the wage bill.

(6) Trade unions have wage policies in the same sense that companies have price policies; alternatives exist for the union with respect to the level of rates, the elements in the wage structure, and the differentials among members and among firms. Specifying the objective of maximizing the wage bill still leaves many issues unsettled.

(7) Wage policies may be directed at many objectives that have little to do with the wage bill of the union simply because control over the wage rate is a very effective device of securing other objectives. It is most important to recognize the use of wage policy for organizing purposes by unions and as a countermeasure by companies. Under these circumstances wage movements may appear incomprehensive if appraised from the sole perspective of maximizing the wage bill.

(8) Every union makes wage pronouncements that serve the very useful purpose of symbols. The mistake should be avoided of presuming that the union always follows its slogan just as the cynical remark that the statements have no meaning or serve no purpose is an error. Such slogans as "a living wage," "a cultural wage," or a "larger share of the national income" provide a rallying point for union membership and a sales campaign to the rest of the community.

(9) Almost every union must eventually face a number of problems respecting its wage structures; these were designated the *elements* of the union's wage policy. In particular, the issue of differentials among union members must be met; the relative

rates and costs to different firms within the jurisdiction of the union must be settled; some judgment must be formed on the impact of wage changes on employment; and unions must be concerned about methods of wage payments. The alternatives open to trade unions on each element were specified and the conditions under which unions prefer one alternative to another were indicated.

(10) The price in the labor market is set with cyclical variations in output in mind, that is, with cyclical time horizons. The full bargaining advantage is not utilized by trade-union units in booms nor by employer units in depressions. Negotiations do involve, however, the idea of a rising trend. The time patterns of adjustment in typical bargaining units involve such long impact periods as to preclude rapid wage adjustments.

(11) The presumption that a demand function confronts each union was seen to be not entirely valid; the union may be able to affect the position and shape of this schedule as well as the final price by its own activities in the product market. Thus the techniques of particular equilibrium analysis prove to be inadequate for they focus attention upon buyers and sellers in a market in isolation from all other markets. The alternative of using a complete system of equations for the total system would not prove feasible. Hence the device was developed of focusing analytical attention upon a cluster of contiguous product and factor markets.

(12) A wealth of material exists to show that trade unions are very much interested in product markets and other supply markets and undertake elaborate programs to affect their pricing decisions. Particular equilibrium analysis has led to the implicit notion that unions affect wages primarily by acting as a restriction upon the supply of labor. Actually, the findings would suggest that they affect the wage rate to a considerable extent by acting in the product market through one device or another.

(13) A very typical market situation exists in which unions support their employers against large buyers in the product market. They help make their employers act as monopolists in dealing with otherwise monopsonistic buyers. By this type of activity the price of the product will be raised, although not neces-

sarily above the competitive level, and the wage bill and the wage rate also increased. The union will be most well off when it supports the weaker party in the product market, unless it can make an arrangement with the employer to receive a cut in the profits of restriction.

The next three chapters are concerned with wage rates and labor income as reflected in the experience of the United States in the period between the First and Second World Wars. The objective is not to allocate the observed statistical behavior to particular policies. Rather the intention is to interpret recent patterns of wage change (Chap. VII) and variations in labor's share in costs and income (Chaps. VIII and IX) in terms of the lines of analysis that have emerged from a consideration of trade-union wage policy.

CHAPTER VII. CYCLICAL PATTERNS
OF INDUSTRIAL WAGE VARIATION

The discussion of changes in wage rates, and their impact on the economic system, has usually been in terms of general or uniform and simultaneous variations affecting every segment of the economy. This simplification has no doubt contributed to an understanding of the relation between wage rates and effective demand. But wage rate changes simply do not take place in such an orderly fashion, at least in the absence of uniform government edicts. Recent experience suggests that even governmental regulation does not result in uniform wage patterns. No bargaining unit is system wide. Variations originating in one sector of the system are diffused to others after a lapse of time, and common circumstances impelling wage changes may mature at diverse speeds in popcorn fashion. Surprisingly little attention has been paid to differential wage movements, even in business cycle literature, beyond rather vague references to unusual wage rigidities in the construction industries that may magnify the intensity of depression and delay revival.

A useful study, broader in scope than a single chapter, would establish the characteristic features of the patterns of wage variation. The investigation would constitute not only another phase of the description of cyclical fluctuations but also would be crucial for models designed to appraise the effects of wage variations. Such data would reveal the speed with which a wage reduction or an advance in the investment-goods field could be expected to spread. The impact of the initial wage change upon total employment will be critically influenced by this rate of speed.

The material on wage patterns may also reveal objective data by which to appraise expectations as to wage changes. Analytical discussions have emphasized that decisions of an enterprise will be contingent upon expectations of wage changes. An impasse often has been reached in which analysis has been seemingly left to the mercy of *ad hoc* expectations. All results depend upon what businessmen expect, and they may be assumed to expect anything. If an enterprise expects a reduction in wage rates to lead to further declines, for instance, no increase in investment follows. Opposite expectations, including an immediate fall in materials prices through related labor markets, may induce expansion. Certainly, one way out of this morass must be the discovery of typical patterns of movement which reveal an objective basis for expectations. Finally, a study of the patterns of wage variation may be expected to provide insight into the functioning of the labor market and, in particular, into the interdependencies that exist among its various sections.

The claims for the proposed field of study will appear Utopian until the specific connotation of "patterns of wage variation" is made explicit. The term will be understood to include the timing of wage changes by labor market and product classifications, the amplitudes measured in percentage and in dollar terms, the geographical pattern of changes, the relation within market clusters of wage variation to price leadership, the identification of enterprises that are regarded as wage leaders, and uniformities in nonbase rate wage changes. Defined in this fashion, the pattern of wage variation presents many fields of inquiry. The present chapter is concerned only with the first of these areas, the timing of wage changes by market classifications.[1]

1. *Mechanism of Transmitting Wage Variations*

Specific wage-variation patterns may be made more intelligible by a preliminary examination of the mechanisms through which wage changes are transmitted. Reference is made to institutional arrangements rather than simply to the general categories of shifting supply and demand. Certain of these channels will be found to be particularly adapted to transmitting decreases while others are specialized to forwarding increases.

---

[1] The whole field of "patterns of wage variation" is a neglected area of research. Wage data need to be analyzed with financial, price, and market information for the enterprises involved. See Temporary National Economic Committee, *Industrial Wage Rates, Labor Costs and Price Policies*, Monograph 5, for a small beginning with certain aspects of wage patterns. Also see *Hourly Earnings of Employees in Large and Small Enterprises*, Monograph No. 14.

(a) An important part of the mechanism by which wage changes are diffused is the way in which information is transmitted respecting rate structures and their variations. Rumor, sporadic advertisements, and informal contacts constitute the chief source of information among unorganized workers. With the advent of the trade union and the personnel department in their modern form, knowledge of wage variations to participants and observers alike in related and similar labor markets becomes much more inclusive and systematic. A wider and more accurate coverage of wage data results, and better records are compiled. However, great variation exists in the quality of this information.

Some labor organizations, such as the United Steel Workers of America, have a highly integrated system of coverage and reporting that permits a comprehensive picture of wage rates for the gamut of relevant labor markets as well as recent variations in these rates. Other unions seem to rely on the rather general knowledge of their scattered business agents. Business firms and trade associations reveal a similar diversity in the quality of wage records available. Wage-hour legislation has tended to standardize as well as improve the quality of pay-roll records, particularly among smaller enterprises. The most comprehensive and systematic wage data available for a large number of enterprises in an industry (to the author's knowledge) is compiled by the Automotive Parts and Equipment Manufacturers. Government reports have long been issued on wage levels, but only in 1929–1935 and again after 1940 did the *Monthly Labor Review* carry reports of the number and magnitude of wage-rate changes and number of wage earners affected.[2] The impression is easily formed that sources for general knowledge of wage changes have multiplied very rapidly in recent years.[3]

[2] The National Industrial Conference Board also began in 1940 to publish similar data in the Monthly Review of Labor Statistics issue of *The Conference Board Economic Record*. *The Ministry of Labor Gazette* has carried for many years more detailed material for English wage changes.

[3] The *Labor Notes*, published by the Labor Research Association, each month carries a list of important wage rate changes. The Industrial Research Section of the Massachusetts Institute of Technology began to publish in 1940 a very useful list of wage changes gathered from an extensive survey of trade papers, union agreements, and daily press reports. These reports were discontinued in 1942.

(b) Wage changes may spread by means of impacts on cost-price relationships in several different ways. A decrease in wage rates may lead to product price reductions, aimed at securing a larger share of orders. These price changes may in turn force competing enterprises to reduce prices and enforce wage reductions. Trade unions have been concerned with this pattern as reductions may arise in nonunion sections of an industry. A second variant may be initiated through the action of large buyers in the product market forcing price reductions after an initial wage cut, or more generally, after any increase in "weakness" in the markets behind the product seller. The product price decline in turn may force further wage declines. The variants differ depending on whether the initiative for the reduction arises directly from the employer or is passed on from the product buyers.

The area of eventual impact of a wage reduction through either variant of these price circuits will depend in large measure upon whether the commodity is used in other stages, the proportion of costs it constitutes in these stages, the number of points in the system at which the commodity enters as a cost, the elasticity of substitution with other factors, and the length of impact periods. Induced price changes in a basic fabricated material, such as steel, may be expected to induce many more diffused wage changes than would arise from induced price changes for a semi-finished specialized product like match wood.

A third variant of wage changes induced through the price mechanism operates through the cost of living which may alter wage rates under automatic or permissive sliding scale arrangements. Only after changes had spread quite widely would the average price of wage goods be substantially affected.

The third variant would appear to be the most common avenue for the spread of wage increases. The extent to which trade unions are aware of changes in the cost of living has not ordinarily been understood. Mr. Keynes' emphasis upon the asymmetry in wage earners' attitudes toward real and money wage-rate changes,[4] perhaps, arising from the "allusion of gold," [5] ap-

---

[4] *The General Theory of Employment, Interest, and Money*, Harcourt, Brace and Company, New York, 1936, pp. 13–15.

[5] A. C. Pigou, *Industrial Fluctuations*, 2d Ed., Macmillan & Compa., Londonny, Ltd, 1929.

pears to be exaggerated.[6] A weighted index smooths out variations that are concentrated in a few items. Even small changes in the index may be accompanied by rather large changes for particular groups of individuals who soon press for higher money wage rates. Frequently difficult situations are created by such pressure groups for union officials and business agents. The experience of the first six months of 1941 would seem consistent with the importance of even small changes in the cost of living for wage increases.[7] The other two media through which wage changes are diffused by the price system are less significant for wage increases than they are for wage-rate decreases.

(c) Wage changes may spread by the simple method of imitation and social transference. Wage increases originating in one sector may be diffused because wage earners are determined to fare just as well as their associates. The argument that "everyone is getting an increase" is not simply a superficial point advanced in all negotiations but a vital force in the labor market that deserves more detailed attention. Even in an unorganized district, the fact that some wage earners get increases creates social pressure for other increases. The community of housewives, with the inevitable "you are as good as the next fellow," is not to be underestimated. These pressures are no respecters of areas of increased demand or capacity to pay.

When trade unions are organized along lines of a process (photoengravers), a material (rubber workers) or a craft (electricians) and include workers from separate enterprises making different products, the pressure for spreading wage increases is magnified. If an increase has been granted to machinists in contract shops because of peculiarly favorable conditions, other machinists in the same union working under different conditions may also demand a raise. The fact that the demand function for the particular type of labor may not have increased is irrelevant to the members who can only see that others whose jobs are no

---

[6] See the analysis of James Tobin, "A Note on the Money Wage Problem," *Quarterly Journal of Economics*, May, 1941, LV; also John T. Dunlop, "Movement of Real and Money Wage Rates," *Economic Journal*, September, 1938, XLVIII, pp. 425–428.

[7] Many trade-union agreements included provisions for the reopening of the wage scale in the event of a "substantial" increase in the cost of living. In a number of cases the union requested increases under this clause after a 2 to 3 per cent increase in the index.

different from their own have been given increases. The leadership of a trade union under these circumstances is confronted by a difficult problem that is not ordinarily appreciated.

This type of social or trade-union pressure for increases portends the importance of inquiries into the geographical pattern of wage changes. The path of wage variation may be obscured if data by industrial classification alone are examined; [8] unfortunately, these are the only comprehensive materials available. The infectious character of wage increases in a region is attested to by the facility with which local enterprises in unrelated product markets have agreed tacitly, if not overtly, to refrain from unconventionally high rates. The protests lodged with violators of this code are further testimony to the spreading character of wage increases. If the labor requirements of a group of firms in a locality are not highly specialized, a few firms may be able to increase the going rate for the whole market by granting a raise. Under these circumstances each firm may regard itself at the mercy of more favorably situated enterprises; the development of a mores against unsanctioned wage increases is not at all surprising.

A wartime economy is likely to exhibit in extreme form the case of wage increases spreading by imitation. [9] The wage structure in the sector of the economy producing military goods is likely to be increased as a result of attempts to attract workers, the fact that enterprises may be less concerned with costs, and the willingness of governmental and arbitration bodies to grant increases to secure uninterrupted production. Quite apart from other mechanisms through which wage changes are diffused, the nondefense sectors of the system will also demand increases. Other wage earners are getting more. The problem may be posed as to how the "useful" functions of the increases may be performed without incurring the induced effects on the rest of the wage structure which may prove to be cumulative. The depres-

[8] Jacob Perlman, *Hourly Earnings of Employees in Large and Small Enterprises*, Temporary National Economic Committee, Monograph No. 14, pp. 4–7.

[9] The process of imitation no doubt plays some role in the spread of decreases; employers may use the facts to advantage in bargaining or arbitration. On the whole, however, it would appear to be of secondary importance to the market mechanisms of cost-price relations in spreading decreases.

sion counterpart is the difficulty of confining decreases to markets in which they may be expected to have the most favorable effects on employment.

(d) Wage variations are diffused through the system also as a result of wage leadership, or more appropriately, wage "repetition," chosen to emphasize that initiative lies with the follower. Imitation has been institutionalized. Wage changes adopted by strategically located enterprises may be more generally followed than would be apparent from any obvious variant of cost-price relations. Not all wage changes are equally contagious. A variation by the United States Steel Corporation, for instance, may be immediately followed not only in the industry but by many other enterprises. Within a group of firms closely related by market ties as competitors or suppliers, wage repetition may be anticipatory to the working out of competitive cost-price relations or an adjunct to customarily accepted price leadership. But equally important is the fact that many enterprises may find it cheaper to let other firms, typically large ones, bear the costs of bargaining and tacitly agree to accept the results. This policy would most likely be adopted, as with product price leadership, when fairly similar cost conditions exist among a group of competing enterprises. When a union exists in the industry, the crucial negotiations with a large enterprise may result in greater over-all decreases and smaller increases than would arise from negotiations with small enterprises.[10]

It is little wonder that the bulk of the firms in an industry may be content to follow the wage changes arising from the negotiations between the union and major producers. The union is saved many days of protracted negotiations by the acceptance of the wage change of the principal producers; the wage "leader" is glad to be a party to the informal procedure since no change in cost differentials will be risked. With particular reference to decreases, the union can hardly insist on a lesser reduction than it has already negotiated with a principal producer. There can be little doubt that one of the informal understandings of many negotiations with principal producers provides for bringing smaller

[10] With the exception that the product market positions of the two types of enterprises are seldom indentical.

competitors up to union wage standards. Thus, all parties to the wage leadership may have a stake in seeing the system function.[11]

Even firms outside the relationship of market competitors or suppliers may elect to follow the wage changes of a large enter prise, if not in amplitude, at least in timing. The example of a large concern may be more than a mere argument when considering reductions in negotiation or arbitration. There is a deep-seated notion that large enterprises are in a position to "know best" with their high-paid executives and access to economic and political information. The wage reduction imposed by Big Steel in the summer of 1931 had precisely this type of an effect on other enterprises outside the industry. Conversely, a trade union may be able to use the argument in reverse when pressing for increases.

Another medium through which wage changes may be diffused is allied to the role of repetition; wage decisions may really be made by banking interests whose orders start variations at several points simultaneously. Small financial institutions may make a decision forcing wage changes as a result of the policy of a major industrial corporation.

The current·section has pointed out three channels—cost-price relations, imitation and social transference, and repetition—through which wage variations are typically diffused throughout the system. Not all changes have the same total area nor speed of transfer. The difficulty of confining a wage change to originating labor markets helps to account for the observation, noted in Chap. VI, that both trade unions and enterprises come to regard the price of labor as determinable by relatively longer run considerations. The international union opposes reductions by a local because the decrease is certain to spread to others; the trade-union movement adopts strong symbolism against reductions because once started they are diffused. Among unorganized enterprises tacit agreement against increases is a part of the business mores. Various types of business associations formalize the pressure against violators. Surprising as it may seem, what is ordi-

[11] One of the most interesting features of trade-union wage tactics involves the issue of which firms in a market should be approached for negotiations first. Likewise, when more than one union deals with the same enterprise (as in the printing trades) tactics must decide which union is to "go in first."

narily termed "wage rigidity" may arise from the essential volatile character of wage variations. Changes in wage structure that might be regarded as "equilibrating" may always set in motion a larger number of aggravating movements. Hence, both parties to the labor bargain may find it to their interests only to make those changes that can be regarded as semipermanent.[12]

2. The Pattern from Average Hourly Earnings Series

Any attempt to establish a pattern for the order in which wage structures *by industries* have varied in major cyclical movements must realize that changes may proceed by other categories. No distinct industrial sequence may be discernible because the path of variation may have proceeded by firms unrelated to usual industrial classifications, region, imitation, union jurisdiction, or other sequences of diffusion. Since wage changes may be simultaneously taking place in all industries, the problem of what constitutes a lag must be faced. (a) If sufficiently complete data were available, the first change in each industry might be specified. But erratic variations would render the results virtually useless. (b) If the proportions of wage earners or firms affected by wage changes were available, month by month, the lag between industries could be based upon the time elapsed between months in which these ratios were a maximum. (c) An industrial pattern of wage variation can be built up from the timing of the cyclical movements of average hourly earnings indices. At least three difficulties arise in the use of these series. Average hourly earnings may vary for many other reasons than changes in wage rates, as was indicated in Chap. II; hourly earnings may have a seasonal pattern which renders lag detection not only arduous but also tenuous; the same series may show several different periods of change or may simply reveal an unbroken movement as changes spread among firms. Most of these limitations can be mitigated, in part, by taking only "substantial" changes in the indices.

A start may be made with industrial wage patterns derived from average hourly earnings indices; the next section will examine cyclical wage patterns measured by specific base-rate variations.

---

[12] A single product price variation ordinarily does not have an equal propensity to spread from the point of impact through the system because fewer points of subsequent impact are involved.

Attention will be directed first in this section to periods of wage reduction. The National Industrial Conference Board data were studied for the periods 1929–1933 and 1937–1939. Series by series, the attempt was made to designate the month in which the first substantial decrease occurred. The dating was done by inspection, but only after examination of the seasonal earnings pattern and the separate series for "female," "male unskilled," and "male, semi-skilled and skilled." In most series these breaks were readily apparent, although in a few, alternative months had to be specified. When the industries were then arrayed in the time sequence of the first identifiable gap, a most interesting pattern emerged. These results for the 1929–1933 decline are presented in Table V, where alternative datings are indicated in parenthesis. Two industries that appear to be decidedly out of line with the general pattern are starred. Printing (news and magazine) and chemicals that appear first in order had small declines in January 1930 but did not show any further break until July and August of 1932. The alternative ratings would place them at the bottom of the sequence, at which point they would appear to be consistent with the general pattern.[13]

An intriguing pattern is immediately apparent in the above sequence of wage variations. Decreases first appeared in hosiery, boot and shoe, cotton manufacturing, furniture, lumber, silk, wool, and some foundry shops. The iron and steel decline then ushered in reductions in agricultural implements, automobiles, paper and pulp and meat packing; eventually the printing industries were affected. While this order fairly radiates explanations, considerations of analytical models must await a later section when more empirical evidence has been marshaled. Mention may be made *en passant* that the sequence appears to correspond roughly to the order of price declines in the product markets; wage declines appeared first in the sectors of the economy with product markets usually regarded as most competitive; and the sequence shows some inverse correlation with the proportion of labor costs to total costs as among industrial groupings, as is evident from the second column of Table V.

The timing of industrial wage changes in the period 1937–1939

---

[13] Printing (book and job) shows a first break in the average hourly earnings series in April 1932. See Table VII for additional evidence.

TABLE V. INDUSTRIAL TIMING OF WAGE DECREASES, 1930–1933 [14]

Industry	Percentage of Wages in Value of Output (1937)	Sequence of Gap in Hourly Earnings Index
*Chemicals	11.9	January, 1930 (August, 1932)
*Printing, news and magazine	15.8	January, 1930 (July, 1932)
Hosiery	30.4	February–March, 1930
Boots and shoes	25.0	October, 1930
Cotton, North	25.4	October–December, 1930
Furniture	26.2	October, 1930
Lumber	32.4	December, 1930
Other machine products		January, 1931
Heavy equipment		February, 1931 (September, 1930)
Leather	15.5	February, 1931
Silk	22.8	February, 1931
Wool	22.2	April, 1931 (November, 1931)
Rubber	19.6	May, 1931
Hardware	29.6	June–July, 1931
Electrical	20.6	June, 1931
Paper products	14.8	July, 1931 (February, 1932)
Iron and steel	19.8	September–October, 1931
Paper and pulp	15.2	October, 1931 (January, 1932)
Foundries	39.6	October, 1931
Meat packing	6.1	November, 1931
Agricultural implements	22.4	November, 1931
Automobile	9.1 †	November, 1931
Machine shops	23.8	January, 1932
Paint and varnish	7.8	March–April, 1932
*Printing, book and job	24.1	April, 1932 (July, 1932)

* These industries appear to be out of line.
† The percentage is 24.5 in the industry defined to include body and parts.

provides a comparison with the succession just observed. Not only was the later recession materially shorter in duration but somewhat sharper in the initial stages. The attempts of the Federal government to maintain the wage structure in the summer of 1931 were perhaps more formal than the activities of the government in 1937–1938.[15] The N.I.C.B. series reveal a variation pattern for the 1937–1939 recession that is in many respects similar to the first year and a half following the 1929 collapse. Compare Table V and Table VI. While the rank order of the in-

[14] The table was compiled from National Industrial Conference Board, *Wages, Hours, and Employment in the United States, 1914–1936,* National Industrial Conference Board, New York, 1936.

[15] However, the Fair Labor Standards Act with a 25 cents minimum wage, except as otherwise determined by the industry committees and the Administrator, became effective October 24, 1938; a year later the minimum was increased to 30 cents an hour.

TABLE VI. INDUSTRIAL TIMING OF WAGE DECREASES, 1937–1939

Industry	Sequence of Gap in Hourly Earnings Index
Cotton, North	February, 1938
Boots and shoes	April, 1938
Wool	May, 1938
Leather	July, 1938
Hosiery	September–November, 1938
Silk	September–October, 1938

dustries is far from identical, the same industries are involved that reduced wages up to April 1931 with the exception of furniture, lumber, and the two foundry series which did not decline in 1937–1939. Of even more significance is the observation that not one of the industries reducing wages after April 1931 is included in the list for the later recession. It is tempting to suggest that had rubber, electrical manufacturing, and iron and steel wages been reduced in the fall of 1938, the rest of the 1930–1933 sequence might have been repeated. There was considerable pressure on the part of some corporations in the steel industry for wage reductions following the price concessions of 1938.[16] The hypothesis may now be suggested that for some periods of depression there is an industrial pattern of wage movements which involves reductions first in a group of industries typified by cotton goods, boots and shoes, leather, wool, hosiery and some foundry firms. Decreases then affect wage earners in electrical manufacturing, paper products and iron and steel industries. This latter decrease helps to precipitate a series of reductions in the rest of the manufacturing sector of the economy.[17]

[16] The Steel Workers' Organizing Committee (now the United Steel Workers of America) had a bill ready to introduce to Congress providing for the stabilization of steel prices.

[17] A check of the results for the period 1937–1939 was made against the series of the Bureau of Labor Statistics. The pattern indicated by N.I.C.B. data was confirmed. The larger number of series suggested that additions might be made to Table VI. These might possibly include radios and phonographs, brass, bronze and copper products, lighting equipment, lumber, and clocks, watches, and time-recording devices. It is to be noted that industries of this type fall next in order under the 1930–1933 pattern. The same data indicated that leather might be omitted from Table VI. Considerable difficulty was experienced in separating seasonal movements of the indices for 1938; in general, if a series returned to the same level in early 1939, the movement in 1938 was regarded as seasonal (provided it checked with earlier years as well). The timing of reductions in rates seems quite readily identifiable as can be seen by studying the movements of the textile group, and the woolen and worsted for the period 1938–1939.

It is very doubtful if the 1921–1922 recession conforms to the suggested pattern. A final judgment is not entirely possible since the National Industrial Conference Board series are not available for the first halves of 1920 and 1922. The wage reductions of late 1920 and early 1921 were so closely bunched that no distinctive pattern seems to emerge from the timing of initial declines. The reductions can be viewed as having been simultaneously initiated in many sectors of the economy rather than developing in sequence with the decline in income as in 1930–1931 and 1938. The recognition that wage levels were materially above "customary" levels contributed to this general decline with the evident collapse of the immediate postwar boom. All of the twenty N.I.C.B. series for 1920–1921 seem to have turned between October and July with almost two-thirds of the series turning in December, January, and February. The simultaneous response of virtually all sectors of the wage structure as in 1920–1921 must be regarded as a second type of wage pattern rather than some variant of the industrial configuration noted for the two following major downturns.

The industrial pattern for wage increases suggested by gaps in average hourly earnings series remains to be explored. Here again two types of situations are encountered: simultaneous movements in virtually all sectors of manufacturing and a distinct sequence pattern. The latter configuration is to be regarded as the more usual *cyclical* pattern. The N.R.A. provides an excellent illustration of the first, with isochronous increases in both the early fall and the spring of 1933–1934. The distinctive pattern includes sharp advances in August and September and then again in April and May.[18]

The next period of substantial increases in wages, 1936–1937, may be thought to involve the same kind of simultaneous changes as the N.R.A. The first impression is that few "market" regularities could be expected from the welter of labor organizing campaigns, political elections, social tension and unrest, and the expansion and subsequent contraction in output that ensued in

---

[18] Iron and steel and agricultural implements showed some tendency to rise first in July, and even more important is the failure of boots and shoes, cotton (North), and silk to participate in the spring advance.

the twelve months following July 1936.[19] The more than ninety Bureau of Labor Statistics series for the period no doubt reflect these developments. A great many show marked increases in December, 1936, after months of virtual constancy, and further advances in April, 1937. But some series increased before the general movement in December, while others only joined in the spring increase or were advancing in the summer and fall of 1937 after the leading series had attained a stable level. These diverse movements constitute the industrial pattern for the period.

The groups of series that advanced prior to the December, 1936, surge are as follows:

Petroleum refining
Rubber goods
Rubber tires and inner tubes
Cash registers, adding machines, and
    calculating machines
Printing, newspaper
Baking
Plumbing supplies

Aluminum
Brass, bronze, and copper products
Smelting and refining—copper,
    lead, and zinc
Stamped and enameled ware
Rayon
Radios and phonographs

Automobile
Agricultural implements
Shipbuilding
Bricks, tile, and terra cotta
Machinery

The first group of series rose in July–September, the second in October, and the last group in November. The first two groups of industries may be designated "light metals" and "light manufacturing." The heavy-industry increases in November, 1936, and the steel advances of December may have ignited the general December upsurge. A still better insight into the period can

[19] Chapter IV briefly discussed the characteristics of the wage changes of this period from the standpoint of trade-union and enterprise wage policy.

be had by examining the industries that escaped the first rise and only participated in the spring and summer increases of 1937. Three-fourths of the twenty-four series are from the clothing, knit goods, food, boots and shoes, and silk sectors of manufacturing,[20] as is evident from the following listing:

Aircraft	Men's furnishings
Steam railroad	Shirts and collars
Lumber	Boots and shoes
Glass	Beverages
Marble, granite, slate, and other products	Confectionary
	Flour
Pottery	Ice cream
Cotton small ware	Cottonseed oil, cake, and meal
Knit goods	Hosiery
Silk	Knitted outerwear
Men's clothing	Knitted underwear
Women's clothing	Knitted cloth
Corsets and allied garments	

Perhaps the most conclusive evidence concerning the industrial wage pattern of the period is seen with N.I.C.B. data.[21] With the exception of foundries and machine tools, only the following eight out of thirty series increased substantially after the month of July in 1937: boots and shoes, cotton (North), furniture, hosiery, leather, lumber, paper products and silk. This is almost the identical list of industries that fell first in the 1930–1933 period (Table V) and includes those that decreased in the recession of 1938–1939 (Table VI). These data suggest a thesis regarding wage patterns in periods of increase to correspond to that proposed for decreases.

If wage variations are of the type in which most industrial groupings appear to vary simultaneously, the issue of sequence is irrelevant by definition. A model is suggested for the other general type of increase; the first advance is found in light manufacturing. Later iron and steel is affected, and just as with reductions, these increases are rapidly diffused throughout the system by the mechanisms described in Section 1. Only eventually

[20] The cotton textile, wool, and leather industries which one might have suspected of falling into this group followed the general pattern of December increases.

[21] *Wages, Hours, and Employment in the United States, July 1936–December 1937*, Supplement to Conference Board Service Letter, June, 1938, XI.

do increases appear in the clothing, boots and shoe, food and similar sectors of the economy. The combined models for increases and decreases suggest that industries in which wage rates decline first are apt to be the last to secure advances. The converse is not necessarily implied; some of the series which declined last may not be among the first to receive increase. The printing industries would seem to be in this category. The proposed cyclical pattern may be modified in any particular case, of course, by wage movements of the simultaneous variety. Such has certainly been the historical pattern. But these uniform changes would appear to be associated with special [22] conditions, such as war or *ad hoc* governmental policies.

3. *The Pattern from Wage Rate-Change Data*

The patterns of industrial wage changes examined in the preceding section were developed from average hourly earnings series and as such depended upon determining an initial break in the indices. Furthermore, too little attention was devoted to subsequent changes; that is, the total pattern through the cycle was not sufficiently emphasized. A check upon the industrial configuration already suggested may be made from data summarizing the number of wage rate changes occurring in a period and the number of wage earners involved.

Starting in the fall of 1929, the *Monthly Labor Review* for the next six years carried monthly tables showing the number of establishments reporting wage rate changes and the number of wage earners affected. The data were tabulated from the voluntary reports that form the basis of the Bureau of Labor Statistics series of manufacturing "employment" and "pay rolls." Both the number of wage earners affected and the number of establishments reporting are available in a detailed industrial classification. The sample included over fifteen thousand establishments with about three million manufacturing employees in the fall of 1931. The number of reporting establishments was relatively stable through the period, although there was some tendency for the coverage to

---

[22] An interesting methodological problem is raised. The conditions referred to are regarded as "special" only because they are considered outside the usual models of cyclical behavior. A broader analysis might regard the governmental policies as directly related to the severity of the cycle, in which case the model of the sequence of wage variation would require a simultaneous upward movement.

TABLE VII. NUMBER OF ESTABLISHMENTS REPORTING WAGE RATE DECREASES, BY QUARTERS, SEPTEMBER 1929–JUNE 1933

	Number of Reporting Establishments*	1929	1930				1931				1932				1933	
		4	1	2	3	4	1	2	3	4	1	2	3	4	1	2
Slaughtering and meat packing	232	1	0	3	5	1	13	10	13	26	35	23	37	9	27	9
Confectionery	341		1	2	2	2	20	6	20	10	46	28	14	11	26	9
Flour	448		1	0	9	3	16	24	16	29	74	25	28	6	58	8
Ice cream	392	2	0	0	0	5	2	3	6	12	21	62	22	28	38	12
Baking	940		2	3	2	8	21	15	29	33	74	85	34	32	77	30
Cigars and cigarettes	222		7	0	4	3	17	6	9	8	9	6	9	4	22	9
Cotton goods	692		6	12	15	13	42	42	68	144	105	130	118	23	51	27
Hosiery and knit goods	465		5	26	27	6	34	14	21	40	38	74	43	9	47	12
Silk goods	272	2	1	15	22	12	12	5	5	21	51	36	23	3	12	6
Dyeing and finishing textiles	154		1	0	2	0	5	2	7	36	26	31	26	6	17	7
Woolen and worsted	264		3	1	2	4	25	8	13	32	38	74	44	2	31	9
Carpets and rugs	34		2	0	3	0	11	1	0	3	5	7	6	1	3	3
Shirts and collars	108				4	1	6	7	4	10	14	17	9	2	3	2
Men's clothing	376		1	7	3	2	14	8	6	15	50	23	17	5	20	9
Women's clothing	385			3	9	3	1	3	4	4	9	12	9	2	19	6
Millinery and lace	140			1	1	2	3	6	6	11	10	13	6	3	7	0
Boots and shoes	339		3	4	15	10	15	6	23	28	29	27	24	3	20	4
Leather	165	1	1	2	2	2	9	7	6	32	18	37	16	6	16	2
Furniture	496	1	3	4	15	12	44	30	41	38	90	62	49	17	65	11
Lumber, sawmills	652	6	17	58	60	33	88	69	66	61	78	112	55	16	57	21
millwork	460	2	5	7	21	12	32	29	34	35	56	68	53	23	66	18
Paper boxes	323		2	0	2	4	22	12	11	14	40	27	24	5	30	8
Paper and pulp	423				4	2	24	28	41	28	40	78	46	14	52	17
Printing, book and job	770				1	1	11	14	26	29	90	109	29	51	60	21
newspaper	450				2	2	9	6	13	10	44	49	27	27	65	33
Fertilizer	207		4	5	1	14	6	25	16	30	25	24	13	2	15	1
Chemicals	118		1	0	2	0	3	3	2	5	7	11	5	1	8	8
Pottery	124					4	6	11	10	4	9	17	20	2	9	2
Paints and varnish	363				1	4	11	11	11	26	34	50	29	13	46	6
Rubber goods other than shoes and tires	104			1	1	5	4	5	1	5	2	8	6	0	8	1
Rubber tires	42			2	2	1	6	0	1	3	7	2	3	1	3	0
Rubber boots and shoes	10			1	1	0	0	1	2	1	1	0	1	0	0	0
Petroleum refining	120				1	0	1	2	0	4	2	9	5	4	1	0
Electrical machinery	294					2	4	8	6	22	23	40	20	7	32	20
Foundry and machine shops	1101	3	2	7	24	19	47	73	66	115	160	171	104	43	123	43
Structural iron works	196		1	1	4	9	20	19	7	30	30	30	17	7	22	13
Machine tools	157		0	0	4	0	5	7	6	11	11	15	13	5	13	3
Steam fittings and hot water apparatus	112				8	1	7	5	6	4	28	14	6	5	13	2
Brick and tile	693	13	4	16	23	66	33	72	48	42	50	79	47	7	30	22
Glass	197				1	0	8	3	1	17	32	17	32	11	14	4
Agricultural implements	78			1	0	1	6	6	6	10	8	5	3	7	4	3
Automobile	236		1	0	4	3	2	5	3	9	28	30	14	26	23	5
Stoves	164			2	3	2	15	5	4	8	25	14	13	6	21	3
Iron and steel	220		5	10	10	3	14	7	34	91	11	98	28	4	13	0
Radio	45		2							2	1	6	2	1	1	2

* May 15, 1932 selected as a sample date.

increase. Table VII summarizes for over forty industrial groups the number of establishments reporting wage rate decreases by quarters for the period September, 1929, to June, 1933.

The table clearly reveals the fact, ignored in the preceding section, that wage reductions typically continued to take place in an industry once they were started. The point cannot be denied that decreases seemed to spread fairly evenly over the period in some groups, while others were characterized by marked bunching of wage cuts. The cotton goods and iron and steel series are typical of this contrast. Some differences may be attributed to the limitations of the sample.[23] But the extent of geographical concentration, the importance of wage leadership in some instances, and the scope of collective-bargaining agreements all influence the distribution of wage reductions through time. Establishments reporting a reduction (for any period save the first) include both those making an initial reduction as well as those enforcing a second. No distinction between these two types of reports is possible, although the sequence of the number of establishments reporting in certain industries suggests several waves of reductions.[24] Very few of the industrial groups [25] can be characterized by simultaneous and final reductions.

Attention may be directed, however, to the issue of the industries in which cuts first appeared. The following series showed a substantial number of decreases in 1930:

Cotton goods	Lumber, mill work
Hosiery and knit goods	Fertilizer
Silk goods	Foundry and machine shops
Boots and shoes	Brick and tile
Furniture	Iron and steel
Lumber, sawmills	

[23] No extensive attempt was made to test the selectivity of the sample. Table VIII shows the number of employees for the month ending May 15, 1932, to be compared with the number of reporting establishments for the same date in Table VII. The agricultural-implement industry with seventy-eight reporting establishments and only six thousand employees would seem to involve poor sampling.

[24] In many industries the total number of wage changes does not add up during the 1929–1933 period even to the total number of reporting establishments. The reason for this discrepancy is not clear since it would appear doubtful if many establishments existed in which no reductions took place.

[25] Perhaps printing, pottery, and rayon (not tabulated) approximate the simultaneous change closest.

This list corresponds very well with the industrial pattern indicated in Table V. No brick and tile nor fertilizer series were compiled by the Conference Board; [26] only iron and steel is out of place. This discrepancy is easily explained when the number of wage earners involved is considered (see Table VIII). The reductions in 1930 in this classification involved only a relatively few wage earners, probably in small enterprises which may very well have been more appropriately classified as foundries.[27]

Table VIII indicates the number of employees affected by reductions in a more restricted group of industries. Essentially the same pattern emerges that was suggested in the last section; the main outline of significant reductions is clearly evident, appearing first in hosiery, silk goods, cotton goods, lumber, furniture, boots and shoes, brick and tile, and foundries and machine shops. No attempt is made to assign a sequence within this group of industries. The woolen and worsted, carpets and rugs, paper and pulp, and paper boxes series seem to follow as a group. Finally, the impact of electrical machinery, iron and steel, automobiles, and agricultural implements is felt.

Table VIII suggests a qualification for any analytical explanation of these wage patterns; some few reductions do appear at an early date in industries that are characterized by late declines. Iron and steel and slaughtering are illustrative. The precise character of the labor and product markets involved would be revealing. The suggestion is made that sectors of the iron and steel and slaughtering industries as classified by conventional methods really include markets (particularly product markets) that resemble those in which wage declines first emerged.[28]

[26] The fact that chemicals showed an initial decline in Table V at a very early date can probably be explained now in terms of the fact that the series includes firms making fertilizer.

[27] Comparisons between the National Industrial Conference Board and Bureau of Labor Statistics series are particularly difficult for foundries and machine shops. The former publishes a series of "Foundries and Machine Shops" broken into five components; only these components were used in Table V. The Bureau of Labor Statistics published during the period 1929–1933 two series: "Foundries and Machine Shops" and "Machine Tools."

[28] Although the relative amplitudes of wage patterns were excluded from the scope of the present study, there is some evidence that those series which first declined most (with the clear exception of the printing series). For findings on some aspects of the amplitude problem, see John T. Dunlop, "Cyclical Variations in Wage Structure," *Review of Economic Statistics*, February, 1939, pp. 30–39.

TABLE VIII. EMPLOYEES AFFECTED BY WAGE REDUCTIONS JANUARY 1930–DECEMBER 1932 [29]

	Total Employees May 15, 1932 in Thousands	1930											
		Jan.	Feb.	Mar.	Apr.	May	June	July	Aug.	Sept.	Oct.	Nov.	Dec.
Slaughtering and meat packing	83				81	14	364	22	177	160	58		
Confectionery	30		40	40		174		64				83	
Cotton goods	194	370	5301		868	334	1498	1285	623	1051	1436	1420	1637
Hosiery and knit goods	98	167	495		2685	559	1356	684	2522	1525	401	110	1015
Silk goods	36		51		215	355	71	1327	2660	122	1083	398	10
Woolen and worsted	40		241					199		114	374	53	
Carpets and rugs	14								250	41			
Men's clothing	52				338	186	84	5	597				47
Women's clothing	26			155	78			322	387	206	31	114	185
Boots and shoes	101	25	269	31	577	70	102	1564	762	333	86	236	1232
Leather	24			92		229	289			457			
Rubber tire	46				40			2500	55			12	
Furniture	43		35	110		19	242	237	837	604	983	562	
Lumber, sawmill	61	1052	395	719	1961	2975	4108	5139	4637	2667	1427	4357	657
mill work	20	27		35	50	101	149	1104	734	157	209	336	25
Paper boxes	21	344	66										
Paper and pulp	80							285	377	59	130	775	130
Electrical machinery	132										450		18
Foundry and machine shop	112	32		148	695	115	93	1570	6008	531	176	1355	238
Brick and tile	20		85		70	123	525	165	635	190	934	361	578
Automobile	240	290						78	340		126	278	
Agricultural implements	6					70							
Iron and Steel	194	42	492	492	93	494	1600	1695	452	613	400	42	38

[29] Bureau of Labor Statistics data from *Monthly Labor Review*.

TABLE VIII. EMPLOYEES AFFECTED BY WAGE REDUCTIONS JANUARY 1930–DECEMBER 1932 (Continued)

	Total Employees May 15, 1932 in Thousands	Jan.	Feb.	Mar.	Apr.	May	June	July	Aug.	Sept.	Oct.	Nov.	Dec.
							1931						
Slaughtering and meat packing	83	406	138	97	262	305	63	373	839	508	5769	4545	889
Confectionery	30	704	109	209	107		235	350	165	656	362	134	304
Cotton goods	194	2604	6036	1789	4014	1472	1843	4817	3192	10164	19700	18281	20320
Hosiery and knit goods	98	3516	5368	2095	216	521	606	2120	176	1863	4852	2454	1287
Silk goods	36	872	532	237	159	264	120	220	18	172	1326	616	1007
Woolen and worsted	40	2597	3317	471	234	302	385	769	49	466	3930	2378	3600
Carpets and rugs	14	2931	2700	1217	30							118	
Men's clothing	52	679	448	58	170	181	460	173	34			2674	186
Women's clothing	26	430			52	302		240		83		138	20
Boots and shoes	101	1039	2147	710		61	713	4090	101	533	1171	2199	2441
Leather	24	235	793	261	854				118	428	1554	2795	1435
Rubber tire	46	176	24							255	10	279	41
Furniture	43	1484	860	1137		909	423	888	1319	1629	723	2396	1544
Lumber, sawmill	61	7487	3908	2317	2064	6243	2009	3782	3015	2236	7118	2172	1841
mill work	20	377	300	508	1396	309	1721	625	420	984	690	805	325
Paper boxes	21	119	1777	694		612	144		14	735	208	1159	89
Paper and pulp	80	2158	1288		337	5201	4880	1083	2395	4276	4685	2226	1244
Electrical machinery	132	864		1146	95	1053	960	607	102	23	1437	2038	463
Foundry and machine shops	112	1447	1293	796	2979	2932	2955	1140	1405	4182	4734	7717	2248
Brick and tile	20	562	251	1077	1102	2138	416	697	856	378	1250	558	333
Automobile	240	1277			1076	125	880			39	3658	531	15
Agricultural implements	6	1806		15	633		34	252	32	388	329	1021	60
Iron and steel	194	869	555	4503	110	1102	398	687	1245	18641	62506	46371	1000

TABLE VIII. EMPLOYEES AFFECTED BY WAGE REDUCTIONS JANUARY 1930–DECEMBER 1932 (Continued)

	Total Employees May 15, 1932 in Thousands	1932											
		Jan.	Feb.	Mar.	Apr.	May	June	July	Aug.	Sept.	Oct.	Nov.	Dec.
Slaughtering and meat packing	83	1098	1032	1504	1522	1286	8110	8612	4798	252	240	201	174
Confectionery	30	2650	1460	1505	1078	316	1306	349	297	133	135	246	23
Cotton goods	194	9876	14126	5053	6667	8339	24115	16489	20841	7037	2080	1095	2002
Hosiery and knit goods	98	1247	1778	2800	4001	6227	6177	2505	4036	197	275	331	160
Silk goods	36	2495	1485	2710	273	4004	1879	2116	293	255		112	110
Woolen and worsted	40	3086	2483	3629	2027	4101	5939	7908	5313	768	82		
Carpets and rugs	14	185		1152		3127	545	982	182				
Men's clothing	52	3089	1926	426	859	2613	2510	1176	175	758	28	613	525
Women's clothing	26	380	901	121	356	303	183	15	321	269	47		
Boots and shoes	101	1481	687	887	1193	1450	1711	2669	341	809		11	466
Leather	24	519	449	1342	759	1276	2815	209	496	658	9	194	186
Rubber tire	46	3725		11770	528	250	575		216	10198	2578	0	
Furniture	43	3637	2481	1750	1089	968	1694	2063	1451	994	169	290	344
Lumber, sawmill	61		3721	3137	7312	4209	5535	3831	2505	469	536	10	1653
mill work	20	1481	968	348	1400	785	937	1000	757	467	68	235	322
Paper boxes	21	1064	809	334	166	1561	712	708	428	153	69	26	
Paper and pulp	80	4570	280	573	3900	3861	7718	4567	3371	2455	486	582	1612
Electrical machinery	132	952	1676	4613	2342	3977	2622	2360	54	112	1439	175	49
Foundry and machine shops	112	6857	6575	2815	3762	7665	5006	2865	2152	1941	443	434	2128
Brick and tile	20	1241	624	446	578	1020	2711	1079	1419	223	260	451	259
Automobile	240	1753	3864	15530	1181	2594	1508	72	1133	1781	48806	154	493
Agricultural implements	6	173	55	209	204	0	13	38		152	65	162	121
Iron and steel	194	2257	1102	1051	4090	2200	84233	12431	5437	1595	181	1326	

4. *Analytical Inferences*

The hypotheses concerning cyclical patterns of industrial wage changes that emerged from the last two sections suggest the following model. The decline of investment expenditures and income that constitutes the onset of a recession involves, at the level of the individual firm, an initial fall in the volume of sales. Since each firm in the system is not a vertical cross section of the productive and distributive process, the relative materials, labor, and fixed costs throughout the system will vary. The proportion of labor costs to value of output for certain industries was shown in Table V; the proportions in boots and shoes and hosiery were between 25 and 30 per cent although less than 8 per cent for paint and varnish and meat packing. When the reduction in sales volume takes place, the quest for cost reduction is certain to be made. Firms having a higher proportion of labor costs will have a greater relative interest in reducing wage costs and thus wage rates. But this is only part of the picture.

Other firms in the system will be attempting to reduce costs at the same time. Some will be relatively more interested in the materials they buy than in labor costs. Among these firms will be the buyers of manufactured or processed goods, such as the wholesale buyers of shoes, hosiery, steel, and automobile and agricultural-implement dealers. Among these buyers, materials cost constitutes a very much larger proportion of total costs than labor costs; in fact, virtually the whole amount may be purchases or materials cost. Hence these buyers will be primarily interested in the price of the manufactured commodities they buy.

Just as there are wide differences in the system in the proportion of labor costs to total costs, so there are differences in the ability to influence the price of commodities purchased, or more generally, differences in the character of competitive conditions in product markets. The buyers of boots and shoes, cotton textiles, furniture, lumber, hosiery, and foundries—those industries in which wage decreases emerged first—are in relatively stronger bargaining position than the manufacturer-seller. These buyers are typically large department stores, commission houses, syndicates, larger manufacturing enterprises; they are in a position to force price concessions. Usually, price declines occur in this section of the economy first. On the other hand, the buyers confronting steel companies and meat-packing concerns may be large, but their relative bargaining power would appear to be less. Price concessions cannot be so easily secured.[30] The net result is that in the sector of the economy in which wage reductions typically take place first, two separate pressures must be identified. Not only are labor costs relatively more important, but price declines in the product market (attributed largely to the character of competitive conditions) tend to force wage decreases. The decline in product prices is the more important influence. Little wonder that under this dual pressure wage rates are cut early in recessions in sectors of the system at the top of the list in Table V in contrast to industries at the bottom of the listing.

The analysis suggests that the pattern of reductions is much more significantly influenced by the proportion of total costs that are wages and the character of competition in the product market than by the degree of unionization. The industries in which reductions took place first, the reader has no doubt noted, were not less organized than those in which reductions appeared late. Only if a union could effectively bring pressure against the product price declines could the wage decline be substantially postponed. The interest of trade unions in product prices, explored in Chap. VI, takes on added significance in this context of ability to resist wage reductions. The present argument is not intended, however, to imply that a wage pattern is unalterably fixed. A trade union without affecting product price may postpone a reduction for a short time and by acting on product prices for a much longer period.

The preceding analysis has purposely laid emphasis on the importance of the bargaining power of the buyers in the product market in setting forth the mechanism of wage reductions in the gamut of industries. The more usual formulation would be to presume that prices in the commodity markets fall first in one segment of the system because these markets are more competitive. While this procedure may be analytically satisfactory for some

[30] A complete explanation of relative price movements is not attempted at this point.

purposes, and really applicable to some of the industries, important features of the pricing process are neglected.

Even the competitive markets here involved are much less automatic and mechanical than the model bourse. Decisions are made without a general knowledge of all bid and ask prices; established lines of business prevail such that an attempt to transfer business to other purchasers may involve large temporary losses. Quoted-price markets with significant impact periods are involved. Not only does the emphasis on the buyers seem more appropriate, but a more useful explanation is provided in that an active agent appears to *force* the price down. Certainly the price could be said to be "forced down" by competition among sellers. But the present formulation has been adopted to emphasize that initiative is probably typically with the buyer.[31] The prices in the steel and agricultural implement industries do not decline earlier, in this formulation, simply because no party with sufficient bargaining power exists to force them down. Hence, in such sectors of the economy relatively less pressure is exerted on wages, not only because they constitute a relatively smaller proportion of total costs, but also owing to the lack of effective downward pressure on price. The central theme is that *declines in product prices and not unemployment constitute the effective downward pressure on wage structures*.

The explanation for the industry pattern of wage increases can be inferred from the discussion of decreases. The increases will be made first where wage costs constitute a relatively smaller proportion of total costs and where the manufacturers are in a relatively strong position to offset wage increases by price increases or cost declines either through effective pressure on other suppliers or through technological change. Even all this is incomplete. There is upward pressure. Trade unions, in fact virtually the whole community, operate on the expectations of secularly rising wage

[31] One of the important advantages of buyers in many of the markets considered is knowledge of the costs of the enterprises. Many enterprises may expand vertically just to secure this information, supplying only a part of their requirements but using their parts or suppliers plants as guides to costs of the firms from which they purchase. Much more attention could usefully be given to this matter of knowledge of the market and cost position of the other party to a sales contract. See Conference on Price Research, National Bureau of Economic Research, *Cost Behavior and Price Policy*, National Bureau of Economic Research, New York, 1943.

levels. The advent of recovery will ordinarily be greeted by rate demands that have for their immediate objective the restoration of previous reductions. Demands may frequently be made for other terms of the labor bargain which the enterprise evaluates in labor cost terms. For instance, the threats of organization in 1936 may have been just as effective a pressure for a wage increase as a specific rate demand.[82]

The preceding statistics of wage variation, the suggested patterns, and the explanation just set forth have some wider inferences that may be mentioned in concluding the chapter. (a) If simultaneous or general wage changes can be regarded as "unusual," in the sense of arising from "outside" the system as ordinarily understood, then the pattern of industrial variation is of extreme importance. It is not simply a matter of convenience of analysis whether the cycle is analyzed in terms of general wage changes or specific variations. The assumption of a general wage change becomes incompatible with the structure of the economic system. Cyclical expansion and contraction, given the various types of markets, necessitate some wage pattern. The industrial sequence suggested above will not be observed if within each grouping are included firms that may be forced to take early price declines which lead to wage reductions. In fact, the early declines in steel and meat packing that do not conform to the generalized pattern may be explained largely in these terms. The final emphasis is not so much upon the "industrial" pattern as upon the market clusters out of which wage changes develop. Cycle analysis must reckon with the fact that wage reductions spread gradually, that they will be anticipated by other sectors of the economy once introduced, and that they are typically first introduced in the sector of the system making consumers' goods where the chance of stimulating recovery by a reduction is generally admitted to be the least. Only at a later date do the wage reductions appear in the durable goods and investment sector.

(b) A cherished view among economists has been that wage rates advance in any market when unemployment has been reduced below a "critical" level and are reduced when unemployment exceeds another "critical" level. Ordinarily the proposition is stated in terms of the wage structure for a total system.[33] The industrial sequence of wage variation suggested in this chapter would render the first formulation of the proposition invalid. Wages fell last (and probably least) in the sector of the economy in which unemployment was clearly relatively greatest and rose first where it was also relatively greatest. Furthermore, these differential wage movements could not possibly be attributed to union activity, since if anything the degree of union organization was relatively greater in those industries in which declines occurred first and increased last. The proposition that is being rejected follows from the narrow particular equilibrium view that the price of labor is to be explained by dealings between a group of buyers and sellers in isolation from closely related markets. The effects of these contiguous markets is "buried" in the curves. Once more it is apparent that this technique, though useful for many purposes, has many pitfalls that have not always been avoided. A cluster of markets is to be preferred.

(c) The apparent conflict between the slogan of "no reduction" that was observed to be widely adopted by trade unions on the one hand and actual wage policy on the other (Chap. IV) can now be better understood. The extent to which the slogan may be translated into effective policy does not depend only upon the strength of the union in the factor market. No matter how strong a union might be in the labor market, reductions would be necessary if the employer were forced to make substantial price concessions. It follows that the slogan of "no reduction" must lead to action and policy in the product market to be effective. There can be little doubt that concern over wage rates and labor income in the industries specified as typically first receiving wage reductions compels unions to be concerned with product prices.

[33] Joan Robinson, *Essays in the Theory of Employment*, The Macmillan Company, New York, 1937, pp. 7–8.

CHAPTER VIII. CYCLICAL VARIATION
OF LABOR'S SHARE IN NATIONAL INCOME

A prominent strand in trade-union pronouncements and folklore on wage policy, amplified by the C.I.O. in particular, was shown to be the objective of securing a larger share of the national income for wage earners (Chap. IV). The end is to be achieved within the pricing mechanism by securing higher rates. The main stream of economic thought, on the other hand, has no doubt regarded the manipulation of the wage rate inappropriate to the objective; inheritance and income taxes are the approved media of affecting the distribution of real income.

Professor Taussig in the 1928 Wertheim Lecture Series agreed with

those who contend that the mere matter of wages is not likely to be greatly affected one way or the other by the presence or absence of unions. . . . Economists would agree (he continued), in saying that for the material prosperity of the great mass of workmen it makes no great difference in the long run whether there is closed shop or open shop, militant union or peaceful company union; while yet they would agree that there are periods of considerable length when the wages of a particular trade or group may be kept higher by union strength.[1]

While the rate could be forced above the competitive wage in sections of the system, resulting in some higher individual incomes, the inference must be that the share of wage earners as a group in the total income could not be raised. [2, 3]

---

[1] F. W. Taussig, "The Opposition of Interest Between Employer and Employee: Difficulties and Remedies," *Wertheim Lectures on Industrial Relations*, Harvard University Press, Cambridge, Mass., 1929, p. 222.

Compare this statement with views expressed by Justice Holmes in dissenting in *Plant* v. *Wood* 176 Mass. 492 (1900): "Organization and strikes may get a larger share for the members of an organization, but, if they do, they get it at the expense of the less organized and less powerful portion of the laboring mass. They do not create something out of nothing."

[2] A. C. Pigou, *The Economics of Welfare*, 4th ed., Macmillan & Company, Ltd., London, 1938, pp. 690–693, takes essentially the same view. "It follows that the estab-

But what of the possibility of increasing the share in income of the wage earners of a single enterprise or segment of the system by raising wage rates? The relative share will rise, by definition, provided the increase in wage payments is greater than any rise in revenue, *a fortiori* if there is a decline in revenue with the increase in wage disbursements. It is apparent at once that the elasticity of substitution among factors will significantly influence the change in the rate of participation of wage earners with any change in rates. If a wage increase induces considerable substitution, the rate of participation of wage earners can be expected to fall, while their relative position may improve if substitution be virtually impossible. In these general terms, the final reaction on labor's share will vary with the period of time in which adjustments are envisaged.[4] The judgment of economists, then, has been that increases in wage rates cannot improve the share of all labor in national income, at least out of a given income;[5] small groups may better their relative position more readily in short periods than in long, and only if the labor services cannot readily be displaced will the share ultimately be higher.

In addition to the conflict between the verbal and symbolic objectives of trade-union policy and the verdict of economists, the

lishment of an uneconomically high wage rate for a particular group of workpeople is much less likely to involve a real increase in the earnings of workpeople as a whole than it appears to be when the distinction between money earnings and real earnings is ignored. So far, however, the possibility that it may involve remains." Emphasis upon the long-run adjustments in the supply of capital (p. 691) removes this possibility. Also see Alfred Marshall, *Principles of Economics*, 8th ed., Macmillan & Company, Ltd., London, p. 700.

[3] A recent textbook, Richard A. Lester, *Economics of Labor*, The Macmillan Company, New York, 1941, p. 233, criticizes this classical view but concludes with the statement: "Consequently, increased money wage rates would tend to increase the share of the nation's income received by workers, unless such higher rates caused employment to decrease by an offsetting amount."

[4] The rate of participation under conditions of perfect competition with first-order homogeneous production functions will depend solely upon the elasticity of substitution. A rise in wage rates will lower the share if the elasticity of substitution is greater than unity and increase the share if less than unity. The conclusion may be derived analogously to the argument by which Mr. Hicks demonstrates that "An increase in the supply of any factor will increase its relative share . . . if its 'elasticity of substitution' is greater than unity." J. R. Hicks, *The Theory of Wages*, Macmillan & Company, Ltd., London, 1935, p. 117; also see pp. 241–246. When more general assumptions are made, with the enterprise possessing a negatively inclined demand curve for the production and a production function of higher orders, the rigorous determination of the share is highly complex.

[5] The possibility of a larger share at lower absolute incomes is not precluded.

present chapter must be placed in the general context of recent technical discussions. Much attention has been directed to the surprising constancy of the share of national income received by wage earners.[6] Standard textbooks, on the other hand, have more commonly stressed the view that the share of labor declines in periods of depression.[7] It is not always clear whether these differences reflect variations in the "propensity to be surprised," definitions of the group designated as wage earners, concepts of national income, or still other difficulties. Even more serious ambiguities have arisen, the following pages will endeavor to show, from the failure to go behind the over-all share of the national income to the component picture in small segments of the system. The chapter will treat in turn the relevant concepts, the statistical picture, and the explanations that are suggested by the empirical investigations.

1. *The Meaning of Labor's Share*

Since neither "income" nor payments to "labor" are unequivocal, alternative meanings of these concepts must be explored.[8] A later section will be more directly concerned with the appropriateness of various definitions to specific problems of inquiry. Three concepts may be introduced immediately that refer to the value of the national product, secured by summing the magnitudes appropriate to individual enterprises: (*a*) gross sales, (*b*) gross income, and (*c*) net income. (*d*) From the opposite pole of the expenditures-receipt flow, income may also be regarded as "income paid out" or "income payments." But payments by a firm may be made out of surplus or may themselves involve capital consump-

[6] Michal Kalecki, *Essays in the Theory of Economic Fluctuations*, Farrar & Rinehart, Inc., New York, 1939, pp. 13–41, and "A Theory of Long-Run Distribution of the Product of Industry," *Oxford Economic Papers*, June, 1941, 5, pp. 31–41; J. M. Keynes, "Relative Movements of Real Wages and Output," *Economic Journal*, March, 1939, XLIX, pp. 47–50; Alvin H. Hansen, *Fiscal Policy and Business Cycles*, W. W. Norton & Company, Inc., New York, 1941, pp. 244–247; Simon Kuznets, *National Income and Capital Formation, 1919–35*, National Bureau of Economic Research, New York, 1937, pp. 27–33; and *National Income and Its Composition, 1919–1938*, National Bureau of Economic Research, New York, 1941, I, pp. 215–265.

[7] Harry A. Millis and Royal E. Montgomery, *Labor's Progress and Some Basic Labor Problems*, McGraw-Hill Book Company, Inc., New York, 1938, pp. 166–167; Richard A. Lester, *Economics of Labor*, The Macmillan Company, New York, 1941, pp. 221–222.

[8] No attempt is made to enter into the numerous refinements growing out of the problems of statistical approximation. See Simon Kuznets, *loc. cit.*

tion. Net savings (positive or negative) of corporations and governmental units must be added to income payments to individuals to equal the value of net output. The share of labor in aggregate income payments may be expected to differ, therefore, from that in the value of net product. An indication of the magnitude of this difference is suggested by the fact that net savings of enterprises fluctuated from a positive 10 per cent of income payments in 1926 to a negative 20 per cent in 1932 and 1933.

Each one of these four concepts of income may have variants depending on how additional complications are handled. (a) A "real" and money variant is possible. The real national output for a period may be viewed as a heap of goods and services. One part is set aside for capital maintenance and the remainder divided among the factors. Statistical investigations measuring "real income" over time involve deflating money estimates of both total income and labor's return by "appropriate" price indices. (b) Other variants of the income concepts arise from the way in which income generated by government units is handled. For purposes of examining labor's share in income produced by the private sector of the system, government-produced income and payments to labor would be excluded. An interest in the share of "real income," for instance, would certainly require the larger concepts. The method of valuation of government-produced income results in other variants of labor's share; public services may be included at their tax cost to the system or at the full value of expenditures. Net savings (positive or negative) of governments is represented by the difference in valuation by the two methods. (c) Another set of variants of the four concepts of "national income" may be mentioned which arise from alternative definitions of business savings and profits or alternative valuations of assets. Capital gains or losses may be included or excluded from income definitions.[9] (d) All estimates of income must decide whether or not to include payments in kind and the "imputed" use of durable consumers' goods.

Turning to possible definitions of "labor's share," at least two

---

[9] Kuznets, for instance, adjusts business savings for the "effects of changing inventory valuations and for the difference between depreciation and depletion at cost prices and at current reproduction prices." *National Income and Capital Formation, 1919–35*, pp. 24 and 61; *National Income and Its Composition, 1919–1938*, II, pp. 410–413.

types of ambiguities arise, the first from types of payments, the second from the classification of individual incomes. (*a*) The return to labor might include only those payments made through markets and arising from services currently rendered. An alternative concept (employee compensation) would include, in addition, direct relief payments, pensions, social security contributions, and accident benefits. (*b*) A second group of variants of labor's share of income emerge from possible boundary lines between individuals classified as "labor" and "nonlabor."

Almost every separation is certain to involve overlapping in individual cases. A distinction might be made according to methods of remuneration. Payment by the piece or hour would separate wage earners from recipients of salaries. But this cleavage is frequently quite arbitrary and reflects few important differences, as is seen in the instance of clerical workers. A line might be drawn between those who receive wages and salaries and all others. But a part of profits would no doubt then be included in labor's share of income. Salaries might be classified separately for clerical and nonsupervisory employees were the data available.

Although many other alternatives are no doubt possible, the availability of material restricts the choice that can be made for statistical manipulation. Wage payments are separately available for certin sectors of the system—agriculture, manufacturing, mining, steam railroads, construction—but only combined wages and salaries for the remaining segments.[10] An indication of the relative components of wages and salaries for manufacturing is provided by the 1937 Census of Manufactures, which reports a wage bill of $10,113 millions against salary payments of $2717 millions, 44 per cent of which went to "clerical and other non-supervisory employees."[11]

The concepts of both labor and total income that have been introduced indicate that any single statement on the movement

[10] The other sectors in Kuznets' classification are: electric light, power, and manufactured gas, other transportation, communications, trade, finance, government, and service.

[11] *Census of Manufactures*, 1937, p. 1624. Wage earners comprise "skilled and un skilled workers of all classes, including piece workers employed at the plant, fore me-and overseers in minor positions who perform work similar to that done by the employees under their supervision. . . . In general, therefore, wage earners may be said to include all manual workers."

CHART I. COMPARISON OF LABOR'S SHARE UNDER VARIOUS DEFINITIONS OF LABOR'S RETURN [12]

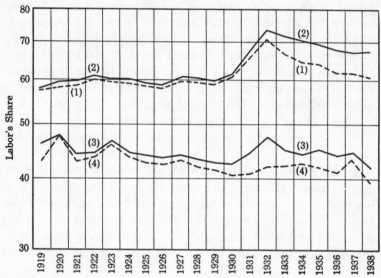

Legend

(1) $\dfrac{\text{Wages and salaries}}{\text{national income}}$, Kuznets [13]

(2) $\dfrac{\text{Employee compensation}}{\text{national income}}$, Kuznets

(3) $\dfrac{\text{Estimated wages}}{\text{national income}}$

(4) $\dfrac{\text{Estimated private wages}}{\text{national income exclusive of government}}$

[12] The first two series are directly from Simon Kuznets, *National Income and Its Composition*, 1919–1938, Table 22 B and C (I, pp. 217–18). Income includes Social Security contributions of employers and is adjusted "for the effects on net savings of corporations and other business firms of gains and losses from sales of capital assets; of inventory revaluations; and of the use of cost rather than reproduction basis for depreciation charges."

The third series estimates wages as per Kalecki's suggestion. (*Loc. cit.*, p. 17.) Wages for agriculture (employee compensation), mining, manufacturing, construction, and steam railroads, Pullman, and express are taken from Kuznets (Table 74). The remaining non-government wages are estimated by assuming that they constitute the same per cent of all wages and salaries as they did in 1925 when King estimated them to be $13 billion. Government wages and salaries (Kuznets, Table 74) are then added to complete the numerator for series 3.

The fourth series simply deducts from series 3 government wages and salaries from the numerator and net income originating in government from the denominator.

[13] The name following the series in this and following charts only indicates the sources of the basic data. Many of the series had to be computed.

in labor's share in income can only be significant when the variations of the many alternatives have been explored and the concepts most relevant to the problem at hand designated. Such a task is not only laborious but rigorously circumscribed by the quality of the statistical information. The absolute size and cyclical pattern of movement of the variants may suggest that some distinctions are of little quantitative importance and may be neglected for empirical purposes.

Three definitions of labor's share are compared in Chart I— wages, wages and salaries, and total employee compensation— where income is specified as net income produced, including the contribution of government. A fourth series indicates private wages as a ratio of net income exclusive of government. The general cyclical pattern of movement of the first three series is very similar; the share increased in periods of marked depression and decreased in prosperity. As would be expected, the employee compensation share is materially higher than wages but only slightly higher than wages and salaries.

The addition of salaries to wages, it should be noted, increases the rate of rise in the share during the depression, 1930–1933. Salary disbursements were evidently curtailed less than the wage bill, a result that could have arisen from a relative stability of salary rates, a relatively greater security of employment in all sectors, or an increase in the relative importance of those sectors where salaried workers predominate. More reliable wage data for specific sectors of the system—mining, manufacturing, construction, and steam railroads—reveal a similar cyclical pattern to the estimated total of all wages.

Chart II compares wage with salary shares for manufacturing; the wage series shows the smaller amplitude of movement.

In contrast to the definitions of labor's return, the cyclical configuration of labor's share is substantially altered by the choice among various national income concepts. Chart III depicts the pattern in the share for variants of the concepts of income paid out and net income, when labor's return is defined as wages and salaries. (a) A most striking contrast in configuration at once emerges between the share in income payments and the two other income definitions. While the share in both variants of net income increased markedly in 1929–1932 and fell sharply in 1932–1934, the share in income paid out or aggregate payments remained virtually constant in comparison. The share in Kuznets'

CHART II. WAGE AND SALARY SHARES IN NET NATIONAL INCOME ORIGINATING IN MANUFACTURING [14]

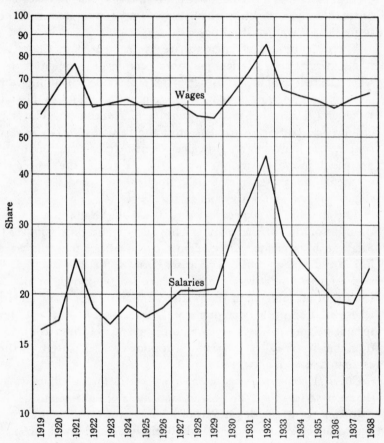

aggregate payments exclusive of entrepreneurial savings fluctuated from a low of 57.9 per cent in 1933 to a high of 63.2 per cent in 1920. Between 1930 and 1935 the maximum range of variation in the Department of Commerce income paid out was

[14] Simon Kuznets, *op. cit.*, Table 74, I, pp. 358–359.

CHART III. COMPARISON OF LABOR'S SHARE UNDER VARIOUS DEFINITIONS OF NATIONAL INCOME [15]

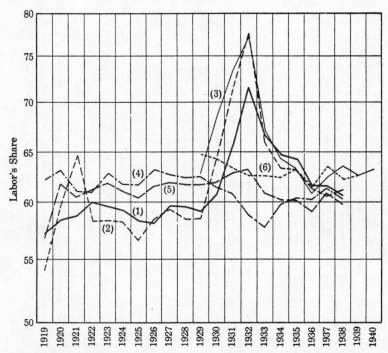

Legend. The numerator of the share is "wages and salaries" in every case. The respective denominators are:

(1) National income with net savings adjusted, Kuznets
(2) National income unadjusted, Kuznets
(3) National income, Department of Commerce
(4) Aggregate payments to individuals, excluding entrepreneurial savings, Kuznets
(5) Aggregate payments to individuals, including entrepreneurial savings, Kuznets
(6) Income paid out, Department of Commerce

[15] The basic sources of the data for the chart are as follows. The numbers correspond to the legend.

(1) Kuznets, *op. cit.*, Table 22 B (I, p. 217).
(2) *Ibid.*, Table 58 (I, p. 322).
(3) Milton Gilbert and Dwight B. Yntema, "National Income Exceeds 76 Billion Dollars in 1940," *Survey of Current Business*, 21 (June 1941) Table 8, p. 17.
(4) *Op. cit.*, Table 1 (I, p. 137).
(5) *Ibid.*, Table 1 (I, p. 137).
(6) Robert R. Nathan, "National Income at Nearly 70 Billion Dollars in 1939," *Survey of Current Business*, 20 (June 1940), Table 2, p. 8.

CHART IV. COMPARISON OF LABOR'S SHARE IN MANUFACTURING UNDER VARIOUS DEFINITIONS OF INCOME [16]

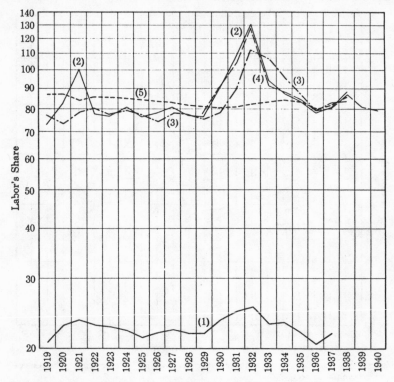

Legend. The numerator of the share is "wages and salaries" in every case. The respective denominators are:

(1) Gross income (value of production adjusted), Kuznets
(2) Net income unadjusted, Kuznets
(3) Net income adjusted, Kuznets
(4) Net income, Department of Commerce
(5) Aggregate payments to individuals, excluding entrepreneurial savings, Kuznets

[16] The basic sources of the data for the chart are as follows. The numbers correspond to the legend.

(1) *Op. cit.*, Table M1, II, p. 576. Also see Division of Economic Research, Department of Commerce, *National Income in the United States*, 1929–35 (Washington Government Printing Office, 1936), p. 107.
(2) *Ibid.*, Table M4, II, p. 578.
(3) *Ibid.*, Table M4, II, p. 578.
(4) Milton Gilbert and Dwight B. Yntema, *op. cit.*, p. 17.
(5) *Op. cit.*, Table M3, II, p. 578.

1.7 percentage points; between no two of these years was the change greater than 0.8 percentage points.

(b) A second contrast may be noted between the share in Kuznets' two variants of net income. Compare series 1 and 2 in Chart III. The adjustment of net income for changing inventory valuations and for the difference between depreciation and depletion at cost prices and current reproduction prices (series 1) shows a smaller rise in the share during depressions than with the unadjusted valuations (series 2). This result is to be expected since the adjustment reduces the amplitude of income fluctuation.

The same data—wages and salaries as a ratio of aggregate payments to individuals and variants of net income—are presented for the manufacturing sector in Chart IV. The two observations made from Chart III apply in this case as well. In addition, the share in gross income (sales) is depicted. The absolute value of labor's share in gross income is naturally much less than the other series. Although the amplitude of variation of this share is smaller than others, the cyclical configurations are similar.

The effect of including or excluding the contribution of government to total employees' compensation, to wages and salaries, and to income is indicated in Chart V. At the outset a serious issue arises in defining the contribution of government to income.[17] Two alternatives have been noted. The Department of Commerce enters government contributions at cost of services rendered, that is, expenditures. Kuznets estimates the contribution on the basis of taxes paid to secure the services of government and then adjusts savings for government debt retirement or increase. Thus in 1929, Kuznets adds an amount of government services at cost (taxes) to the debt repayment (net savings) and obtains the net income originated by government. Under this procedure the rate of participation of labor in income produced by government fluctuates widely depending upon the presence of deficits or debt retirement.

The denominator to the share using the Department of Commerce concept is "government expenditures," while Kuznets'

---

[17] For a discussion of these issues see Simon Kuznets, *loc. cit.*, I, pp. 31–34.

CHART V. THE EFFECT ON LABOR'S SHARE OF INCLUDING GOVERNMENT [18]

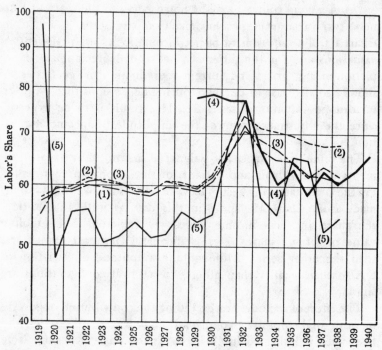

Legend

(1) $\dfrac{\text{Wages and salaries}}{\text{national income}}$, Kuznets

(2) $\dfrac{\text{Employee compensation}}{\text{national income}}$

(3) $\dfrac{\text{Non-government wages and salaries}}{\text{national income excepting government}}$, Kuznets

(4) $\dfrac{\text{Wages and salaries in government}}{\text{government contribution to net national income}}$, Department of Commerce

(5) $\dfrac{\text{Wages and salaries in government}}{\text{net income originating in government}}$, Kuznets

[18] The basic sources of the data for the chart are as follows. The numbers correspond to the legend.

(1) *Op. cit.*, Table 22 B, I, p. 217.
(2) *Ibid.*, Table 22 C, I, p. 218, the first two series in this chart are the same as the first two in Chart I.
(3) *Ibid.*, Table G1, II, p. 811, and Table 22, I, p. 216.
(4) Milton Gilbert and Dwight B. Yntema, *op. cit.*, pp. 17–18.
(5) *Op. cit.*, Table G1, II, p. 811.

concept results in a denominator of "taxes adjusted for government saving or dis-saving." That the Kuznets method results in wider variations of wages and salaries as a ratio to income originating in government is evident from a comparison of series 4 and 5 in Chart V. The Kuznets denominator is relatively increased in 1929 with debt retirement and relatively decreased in 1936 with large net dissaving. The inclusion of government in either Department of Commerce or Kuznets series of wages and salaries and income will tend to increase labor's share because of the relatively high rate of participation of labor in government income compared to other sectors.[19]

A final comparison remains to indicate the effect of various definitions of income and labor's return on the size and pattern of variation in the share. If income for a period is thought of in terms of a pile of goods and services, attention can be centered on the relative share of the heap over which labor has command, that is, labor's real share of real income. Serious difficulties arise in attempting to give such a concept meaning, not to mention the problems of measurement. The national product cannot without difficulty be viewed as a "pile" or even a "stream" of *finished* goods and services; important contributions are made to the productive equipment and process. What can be said, however, is that enterprises, in exchange for services rendered on finished goods, or on the productive plant, give claims which may be used to purchase the finished goods or various types of claims to future income. All claims are in terms of money.

The real share of real income may be statistically approximated by deflating labor's return by the price of goods and services purchased and deflating total money income for variations in the prices in which income is valued. Either a gross or net real-income concept can be used. These computations may be said to specify the way in which labor's real command over goods and services varies relative to the rest of the community. Chart VI shows the comparative variations of the real and money shares in Kuznets' net income in constant prices and two variants of the

---

[19] The problem of shifting weights is considered in the next section. The effect of the relatively greater weight of government in 1933–1938 can be seen by comparing series 1 and 3 in Chart V.

CHART VI. COMPARISON OF LABOR'S REAL AND MONEY SHARE [20]

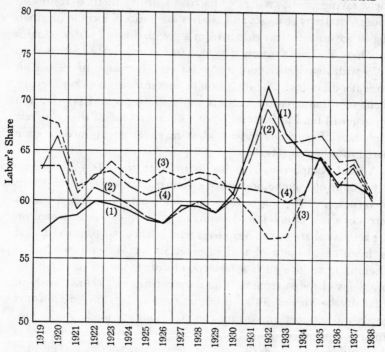

Legend

(1) $\dfrac{\text{Money wages and salaries}}{\text{national income}}$, Kuznets

(2) $\dfrac{\text{Real wages and salaries}}{\text{national income in constant prices}}$, Kuznets

(3) $\dfrac{\text{Real wages and salaries}}{\text{real aggregate payments to individuals excluding entrepreneurial savings}}$, Kuznets

(4) $\dfrac{\text{Real wages and salaries}}{\text{real aggregate payments to individuals including entrepreneurial savings}}$, Kuznets

[20] The sources of the basic data for the chart are as follows. The numbers correspond to the legend.

(1) *Op. cit.*, Table 22 B, I, p. 217.
(2) The money wages and salaries were converted to "real" terms by dividing by the Bureau of Labor Statistics cost of living index. Table 4, I, p. 145. Kuznets data for national income in 1929 prices, Table 5, I, p. 147, were used for the denominator.
(3) The denominator is from Table 5, I, p. 147.
(4) The denominator is from Table 5, I, p. 147.

real share in aggregate payments. The total wages and salaries were simply deflated by the cost of living for industrial wage earners. The translation of labor's share into real terms does not change the relative movements as between net income and aggregate payments to individuals. As in the case of other measures of labor's share, no account is taken of the unemployed. The real share in real aggregate payments excluding entrepreneurial savings declines slightly in deep depression while the series including these savings remains almost exactly constant. The negative savings in 1931–1933 clearly reduce the denominator and hence raise the resultant share relative to series in which the entrepreneurial savings are excluded.

This section has outlined a number of definitions of both "income" and the return to "labor"; the combinations yield a great many concepts of "labor's share." A survey of the size and cyclical pattern of fluctuation of these shares indicated that some of the distinctions are of minor quantitative importance. Although the share of wages and salaries and total employee compensation in net income were both higher than in wages, the cyclical patterns of all three were similar. The share rose sharply in deep depression; in fact only major cyclical swings appear to influence substantially any share estimates. The most striking contrast exists between the share in aggregate payments to individuals or income paid out and the share in net income. The share in income payments remained virtually constant or declined slightly, depending on the precise concepts involved. The addition of government contributions to labor receipts and income raises the problem of the method of valuing government services. Furthermore, as government originating income increases in relative importance, labor's share in the system rises since the participation of labor in government income has been higher than that of most other sectors. The whole problem of changing cyclical importance of various sectors is the subject matter of the next section.

2. *Cyclical Variations in Labor's Share*

The alternative concepts of "income," "labor's return," and the derivative meanings of "share" are applicable to a single enterprise as well as to varying aggregates including the total system.

When more than one enterprise is combined, the share of the aggregate income going to labor will depend upon both the share in each firm and the relative amounts of incomes generated by each concern. A variation in the share in an industry or the total system may arise, therefore, from changes in the share in individual firms and from changes in the relative importance or weight of each sector. If L and Y are the aggregates of labor's return and total income, then:

$$L/Y = \Sigma(l_i/y_i) \cdot (y_i/Y_i) = \Sigma(p_i \cdot w_i)$$

where l_i and y_i refer to sectors and $p_i = l_i/y_i$ and $w_i = y_i/Y$. This section examines recent changes in labor's share, separating these components.

The usage of certain terms will be standardized for the sake of clarity. "Share" will be restricted to the ratio of total labor returns to total income for the whole system, (L/Y), while the "rate of participation" will designate the same ratio for a sector of the system $(p_i = l_i/y_i)$. The ratio of labor income in a single sector to total income of the system may be called the "contribution rate" of labor in the segment $(c = l_i/Y)$. The contribution rate is then clearly the rate of participation multiplied by the weight of the sector in total income $(c_i = l_i/Y = l_i/y_i \cdot y_i/Y = p_i \cdot w_i)$. The sum of all rates of contribution must equal the share of labor returns in total income $(\Sigma c_i = L/Y)$. Any change in the share may, therefore, be reduced to variations in the rates of contribution in the component segments and into changes in the rates of participation and weights.

$$\Delta L/Y = \Sigma\Delta c_i = \Sigma(w_i \cdot \overline{\Delta p_i} + p_i \overline{\Delta w_i} + \overline{\Delta p_i} \cdot \overline{\Delta w_i})$$

A complete statistical study of variation in the share would require weight and rate of participation data for each firm in the system. In lieu of these ideal materials, the largest group of subdivisions or "industries" with available income and labor returns data was selected for detailed analysis. This procedure excludes the possibility of separating the rate of participation change in the smallest available sector into further weight and rate variations. Although this limitation is serious, a division of the system into thirty-two sectors, made possible by Department of Commerce data,[21] will contribute a good deal more to the understanding of fluctuations in the share than is evident from over-all income and labor-returns series. These data define income as the net value of the output of commodities and services (income produced) and labor returns as wages and salaries. The materials refer to the period 1929–1940.

The relative movements of income produced by the thirty sectors of the system (y_i/Y) permits a classification of "industries" according as they gain or lose weight in prosperity and depression. The convention will be adopted of specifying as "weight gaining" those sectors which show an increase of y_i/Y in depression and a decrease in prosperity. The converse will describe "weight-losing industries." Table IX presents the thirty industries with an additional basis of classification, according as the sector appears to be secularly expanding or contracting in income. This factor is denoted by prefixes of (e) and (c).

Chart VII depicts the magnitude of variation in weights of the five groups of "industries" classified in Table IX. These marked shifts in weights underline the necessity for considering the share of labor in smaller segments than the total system. Chart VIII specifies the fluctuation in the rate of labor's participation in income in the same groups. Several observations emerge from a comparison of these charts. (a) Those industries which lost weight most heavily in depressions showed the most marked increase in the rate of participation in the same periods. Contrast Groups I and II (government, insurance, power and gas, communications) with Group V (heavy manufacturing and agriculture). This inverse relation between the magnitude of weight shift and the rate of participation is evident throughout the five groups. The decreased importance in depression of industries whose rate of participation increases most rapidly tends to make for a relatively stable share. (b) The shift in weights through the cycle does not appear to be among sectors of the economy which possess markedly different rates of participation, with the exception of agriculture. While very large shifts in weights did occur, they tended more or

---

[21] Milton Gilbert and Dwight B. Yntema, "National Income Exceeds 76 Billion Dollars in 1940," *Survey of Current Business*, June, 1941, 21, pp. 11–18. Thirty industrial groups ordinarily will be used, as government subdivisions are neglected.

CHART VII. PATTERNS OF WEIGHT SHIFTS BY SUMMARY GROUPS [22]

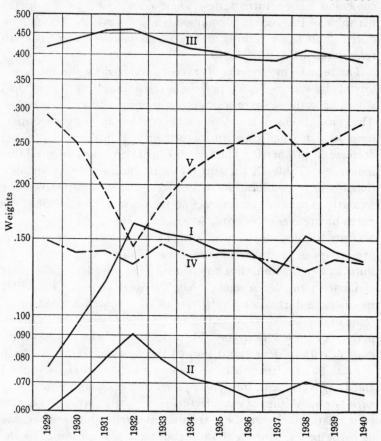

Legend

  I. Government
 II. Heavy weight gaining in contraction
III. Light weight gaining in contraction
 IV. Light weight losing in contraction
  V. Heavy weight losing in contraction

[22] The chart represents the variation in y_i/Y calculated from Department of Commerce data. The industrial groups under each of the five headings are specified in Table IX.

less to cancel themselves out. Groups I and II increased markedly in importance during depression, while Group V declined. But the differences in the initial rates of participation in these groups

CHART VIII. PATTERNS OF RATES OF PARTICIPATION BY SUMMARY GROUPS [23]

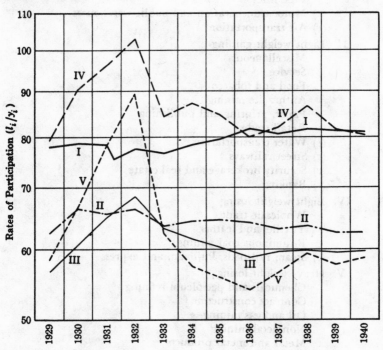

Rates of Participation (l_i/y_i)

Legend
I. Government
II. Heavy weight gaining in contraction
III. Light weight gaining in contraction
IV. Light weight losing in contraction
V. Heavy weight losing in contraction

on balance were not substantial. That is, shifts in weights occurred among sectors of the system which had approximately similar (and high) rates of participation. On balance, therefore, the change in the share had relatively little to do with the chang-

[23] The chart represents the variations in l_i/y_i calculated from Department of Commerce data. The industrial groups under each of the five headings are specified in Table IX.

TABLE IX. CLASSIFICATION OF INDUSTRIES BY WEIGHT SHIFT [24]

I. Extreme weight gaining
   Government

II. Heavy weight gaining
   Insurance
   Power and gas
   Communication
   Pipe lines
   (e) Motor transporation and public warehouses
   (e) Air transportation

III. Light weight gaining
   Miscellaneous
   Service
   Food and tobacco
   Anthracite mining
   Paper, printing and publishing
   Retail trade
   (e) Water transportation
   (c) Street railways
   (c) Security brokerage and real estate
   (c) Banking

IV. Light weight losing
   Wholesale trade
   Textiles and leather
   Bituminous coal mining
   (c) Steam railroads, Pullman, and express

V. Heavy weight losing
   Chemicals and petroleum refining
   Contract construction
   Oil and gas mining
   Nonmetal mining
   Metal and metal products
   Miscellaneous and rubber manufacturing
   Construction materials and furniture
   Metal mining
   (c) Agriculture

[24] The system of classification was drawn up by arraying the thirty industrial groups for several years (1930, 1931, 1932, 1938) in the order of their relative income to 1929. The main break between weight gainers and losers was immediately apparent from gaps in the arrays across which no "industries" moved. The more detailed classification was suggested by other gaps and the secular income position of the "industry." The classification was checked for the entire period 1929–1940. While debate is no doubt possible over the classification of particular series as between "light or heavy," the notion of a hierarchy of weight shifts is fundamental. See Simon Kuznets, *National Income and Capital Formation, 1919–35*, pp. 29–33, and *National Income and Its Composition, 1919–38*, I, pp. 241–250. Kuznets did not examine year-to-year shifts in the cyclical pattern; he deals with five-year periods.

ing importance of various sectors of the system.[25] Variations in the share are fundamentally to be explained in terms of the rates of participation within each sector.

This negative conclusion, eliminating one of the possible explanations for variations in the share, is sufficiently important to warrant further evidence. Following the algebra suggested at the start of this section, calculations were made for w_i, p_i, and c_i $(w_i \cdot p_i)$ for each of the thirty industries for each year, 1929–1940. Consequently, $\Delta L/Y$ could be broken down by calculating (1) $w_i \cdot \overline{\Delta p_i}$, (2) $p_i \cdot \overline{\Delta w_i}$, and (3) $\Delta p_i \cdot \overline{\Delta w_i}$. Table X presents the relative importance of changes in weights and rates of participation for the five groups of industries utilized in Table IX during the years 1930–1934.

The table supports both observations suggested above: (1) the groups which lost most weight during the depression showed the greatest increase in rate of participation, and (2) the net effects of weight shifts are clearly secondary to the change in the rate of participation in determining the variation in the share. Thus $\Sigma w_i \cdot \Delta p_i$ entirely outweighs the much smaller net variations in $\Sigma p_i \cdot \Delta w_i$. The data for the thirty industrial groups indicate similar results. That is, weight shifts were of secondary importance among the most detailed classification available and among sectors when government is included. Weight shifts may be more decisive for the share as among individual enterprises or when national income is defined exclusive of government.

The variation in labor's share in income produced in the period 1929–1940 is conveniently summarized in three charts (IX, X, XI), showing fluctuations in rates of contribution which are resolved into variations in weights and rates of participation. The whole logical framework of the present analysis is evident at a glance. The thirty sectors have been summarized for ease of graphic presentation into twelve industries groups used by the Department of Commerce.

Chart IX indicates the rate of contribution of each sector, that is, the ratio of wages and salaries in each industry to the net value

[25] This statement applies to changes in weights as among the thirty sectors indicated in Table IX. The shifts in weights as among firms within each "industry" may have been more important.

TABLE X. VARIATIONS IN WEIGHTS AND RATES OF PARTICIPATION
BY SUMMARY GROUPS, 1930–1934

Group	$p_i \cdot \Delta w_i$	$w_i \cdot \Delta p_i$
1930		
I	+ 1.364	+ 0.046
II	+ 0.512	+ 0.227
III	+ 1.188	+ 1.821
IV	− 0.697	+ 1.639
V	− 2.336	+ 2.526
Total	+ 0.031	+ 6.259
1931		
I	+ 2.106	− 0.019
II	+ 0.715	− 0.048
III	+ 1.103	+ 1.930
IV	+ 0.036	+ 0.855
V	− 3.741	+ 2.852
Total	+ 0.219	+ 5.570
1932		
I	+ 3.293	− 0.096
II	+ 0.777	+ 0.047
III	+ 0.289	+ 1.508
IV	− 0.876	+ 0.988
V	− 3.847	+ 2.175
Total	− 0.364	+ 4.632
1933		
I	− 0.582	− 0.114
II	− 0.760	− 0.209
III	− 2.145	− 2.403
IV	+ 1.634	− 2.525
V	+ 3.192	− 3.901
Total	+ 1.339	− 9.159
1934		
I	− 0.315	+ 0.217
II	− 0.440	+ 0.032
III	− 0.883	− 0.688
IV	− 0.800	+ 0.427
V	+ 2.219	− 0.951
Total	− 0.219	− 0.970

of all output $(c_i = l_i/Y)$. The sum of the vertical distances in
Chart IX equal labor's share $(L/Y = \Sigma c_i)$. Charts X and XI
separate the variation in c_i into weight changes (w_i) and rate of
participation fluctuations (p_i). (a) The same weight shifts presented in Table X, of course, are evident. The classification here,

CHART IX. CONTRIBUTION RATES IN NET INCOME BY INDUSTRIAL GROUPING

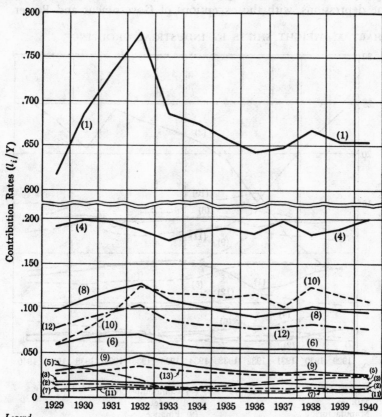

Legend

(1) All industry
(2) Agriculture
(3) Mining
(4) Manufacturing
(5) Construction
(6) Transportation
(7) Communication

(8) Trade
(9) Finance
(10) Government
(11) Power and gas
(12) Service
(13) Miscellaneous

however, is along more conventional lines and thus obscures the full extent of weight variations. "Manufacturing," for instance, includes "food and tobacco," "paper, printing, and publishing," and "textiles and leather," classified previously under Light Weight Gaining or Losing, Groups III or IV. The remainder of the manufacturing series appeared under Heavy Weight Losing, Group V. (*b*) The rate of participation of all sectors rose during the depressions, with the exceptions of Government and Power

CHART X. WEIGHT SHIFTS BY INDUSTRIAL GROUPING

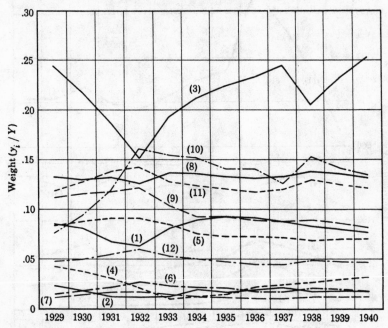

Legend

(1) Agriculture
(2) Mining
(3) Manufacturing
(4) Construction
(5) Transportation
(6) Power and gas

(7) Communication
(8) Trade
(9) Finance
(10) Government
(11) Service
(12) Miscellaneous

and Gas. (*c*) The rate of participation increased most prominently in depression where weights decreased most (manufacturing, construction, and agriculture). That is, wages and salaries increased most as a per cent of net income produced where income contracted most.

CHART XI. PARTICIPATION RATES IN NET INCOME BY INDUSTRIAL GROUPING

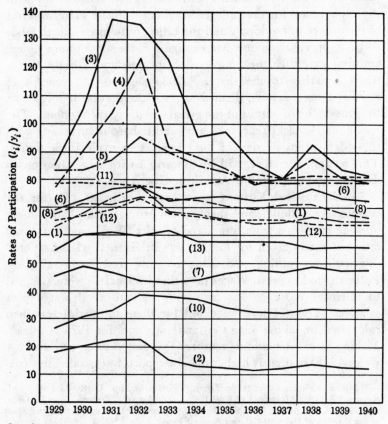

Rates of Participation (l_i/y_i)

Legend

(1) All industry
(2) Agriculture
(3) Mining
(4) Manufacturing
(5) Construction
(6) Transportation
(7) Power and gas

(8) Communication
(9) Trade
(10) Finance
(11) Government
(12) Service
(13) Miscellaneous

3. Kalecki: Wages as a Share in Gross Private Income

Considerable attention has been focused on the issues of labor's share in income as a consequence of Kalecki's writings.[26] At this juncture concern is with his statistical results rather than with the explanation for the "alleged" constancy in the share in terms of the degree of monopoly and the ratio of raw materials to labor costs. A previous section has emphasized the importance of examining carefully the concepts of income and labor's return when referring to the share. Kalecki suggests the concept of manual labor's return, defined as wages, and regards income as the gross value of output of the private sector of the economy. The result that Kalecki reports of a constant share is surprising with these definitions in view of the comparisons made in Section 1. This section, therefore, will be concerned with an analysis of his data as they pertain to the American experience.

Kalecki utilized Kuznets' gross income Variant I [27] (for the private sector alone) and then had to estimate the total volume of wage payments from wages and salaries. Wage payments were only separately given for four sectors in Kuznets' classification [28] —agriculture, mining, and manufacturing, and steam railroads, Pullman, and express. Wages in "other industries" were assumed to fluctuate more or less proportionately to total wages plus salaries.[29] The absolute wage bill for these industries was then calculated by taking King's estimate of wages for 1925 as a base. Making the calculations required by Kalecki's procedure has yielded a share slightly higher than he reports but parallel in varia-

---

[26] Michal Kalecki, *Essays in the Theory of Fluctuations*, pp. 13–41. Also see J. M. Keynes, "Relative Movement of Real Wages and Output," *Economic Journal*, March, 1939, XLIX, pp. 48–50; Michal Kalecki, "A Theory of the Long-Run Distribution of the Product of Industry," *Oxford Economic Papers*, June, 1941, 5, pp. 31–41.

[27] *National Income and Capital Formation, 1919–1935*, pp. 62–67. Kuznets' revised series were not available in 1938; only the older data for the period prior to 1934 are used in this section following Kalecki. Chart I, series 3 and 4, however, shows the share calculated by Kalecki's methods from Kuznets' more recent series.

Variant I adjusts net business saving for gains and losses on the sale of capital assets, that element of revaluation of inventories which is retained in net profit or loss after payment of dividends, and the difference between depreciation and depletion at book value and at reproduction prices.

[28] Separate wage materials were also available for construction from Department of Commerce data, *National Income in the United States, 1929–35*, Government Printing Office, Washington, 1936, p. 121.

[29] *Loc. cit.*, p. 17.

CHART XII.   ESTIMATES OF WAGES AS A SHARE IN NATIONAL INCOME[30]

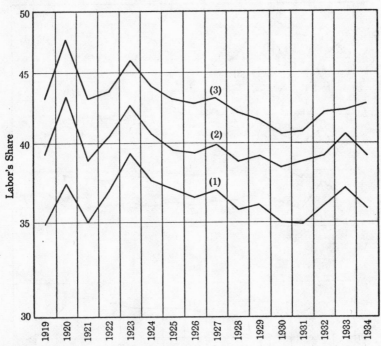

Legend

(1) $\dfrac{\text{Estimated private wages}}{\text{gross private national income}}$, Kalecki

(2) $\dfrac{\text{Estimated private wages}}{\text{gross private national income}}$, calculated by Kalecki's method with his sources

(3) $\dfrac{\text{Estimated private wages}}{\text{net private national income}}$, calculated by Kalecki's method with Kuznets' revised data

tion.[31] Chart XII compares these shares with private wages and salaries as a share in Kuznets' revised estimates of private net income.

What is to account for the relative constancy in the share that Kalecki has chosen to discuss? At first inspection emphasis might

[30] The basic sources of the data for the chart are as follows. The numbers correspond to the legend. (1) Kalecki, *op. cit.*, p. 17. (2) See Chart I, series 4.

[31] The exact reconstruction of Kalecki's results is made difficult because no detailed wage series were published in his work.

CHART XIII. COMPONENT SERIES IN KALECKI'S WAGE SHARE [32]

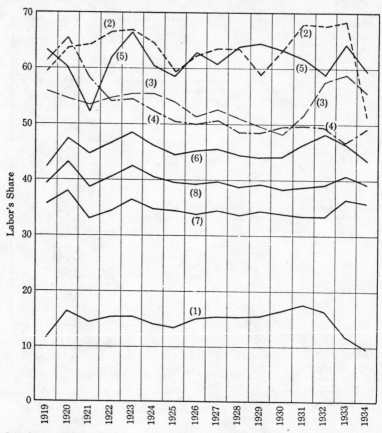

Legend

(1) Agriculture
(2) Mining
(3) Manufacturing
(4) Steam railroads, Pullman and express
(5) Construction
(6) Weighted average of five series
(7) "Other industries"
(8) Total system

[32] Gross income had to be estimated for steam railroads, Pullman and express, as Kuznets' classifications only yielded income originating for this sub-division of "Transportation and other public utilities." Business depreciation and depletion charges were taken from Solomon Fabricant, *Capital Consumption and Adjustment* (New York, National Bureau of Economic Research, 1938), pp. 256–260.

be placed on the character of salaries, but more careful study would seem to emphasize the following issues: (1) Chart IV revealed that the use of gross rather than net income tended to reduce the rate of increase of the share in depressions. Relatively constant dollar allowances for depreciation and obsolescence through the cycle, arising in part from accounting conventions, tend to magnify the fall in net income in the depression and hence raise the share of labor compared to the gross income denominator. (2) A breakdown of Kalecki's over-all share figure (as reconstructed following his procedure) into the five component series [33] for which wage data are available and the "other industry" series, estimated from combined wages and salaries, reveals a pattern with many substantial increases in rates of participation in depression. These data are summarized in Chart XIII. Note the marked fluctuation in rate of participation over the cycle in the five separate series (designated the "selected industries" following Kalecki) for which wage data are available. Certainly the stability that Kalecki finds in the total share does not seem to reside in the individual series.[34] (3) The variation in weights of the series comprising the aggregative share requires examination. Comparison of the "selected" series with Table IX soon reveals that all five can be broadly classified as weight losing. While some of the subgroups of these broad classifications were found to be weight gaining, the preponderant effect was clearly weight losing as Chart X reveals. The industries for which Kalecki had to estimate wages, on the other hand, were weight gaining. These weight shifts might seem unimportant were it not for several additional considerations, made evident in Table XI.

(a) The (selected) industries which lost weight in the depression had a decidedly higher rate of participation than those that gained weight. (b) These weight-losing sectors increased their rate of participation during the depression, while the weight-gaining or "other" industries showed a slight decline in the rate of participation. Thus the over-all movement was largely the re-

---

[33] The five series are the four mentioned above (p. 174) and Construction from Department of Commerce data.

[34] The issue of whether individual series show the same behavior as the total system is important for Kalecki, as his theoretical model is built directly upon the individual firm.

sultant of counteracting rate and weight shifts. (c) The effect of weight shifts on the over-all change in share was much more important in Kalecki's data than for the share examined in the last section (see Table X). There the heavy weight-losing industries also had high rates of participation with the exception in both

TABLE XI. RATE AND WEIGHT SHIFTS IN KALECKI'S DATA [35]

	Weight (w_i)	Rate of Participation (p_iP)	$p_i \Delta w_i$	$w_i \Delta p_i$	$\Delta(p_iw_i)$
1929					
Total		39.05			
Selected	0.4864	43.80			
Other	0.5136	34.56			
1930					
Total		38.43	− 0.256	− 0.343	− 0.625
Selected	0.4587	43.95	− 1.213	+ 0.073	− 1.144
Other	0.5413	33.75	+ 0.957	− 0.416	+ 0.519
1931					
Total		38.78	− 0.457	+ 0.906	+ 0.336
Selected	0.4139	46.22	− 1.969	+ 1.041	− 1.030
Other	0.5861	33.53	+ 1.512	− 0.135	+ 1.366
1932					
Total		38.73	− 0.555	+ 0.563	− 0.059
Selected	0.3701	47.68	− 2.024	+ 0.604	− 1.484
Other	0.6299	33.46	+ 1.469	− 0.041	+ 1.425
1933					
Total		40.62	+ 0.622	+ 1.492	+ 1.891
Selected	0.4139	45.96	+ 2.088	− 0.637	+ 1.376
Other	0.5861	36.84	− 1.466	+ 2.129	+ 0.515
1934					
Total		39.11	+ 0.332	− 1.774	− 1.505
Selected	0.4503	43.19	+ 1.673	− 1.147	+ 0.425
Other	0.5497	35.77	− 1.341	− 0.627	− 1.930

cases of agriculture. These industries also became less important in depression, but government, with a high rate of participation, gained substantially in importance. The net effects of weight shifts were shown in Table X virtually to cancel themselves.

Kalecki, however, considers only the private sector of the system. The aggregative effects of weight shifts on the share of labor are very much more important in Table XI. For instance, in

[35] Values for $\Delta w_i \Delta p_i$ are not included in the table. They can be calculated by subtracting the sum of $p_i \Delta w_i$ and $w_i \Delta p_i$ from $\Delta(p_iw_i)$.

1932 there was almost no change in the share because of offsetting rate and weight shifts. The same point may be made by introducing government income and wages into Kalecki's figures. The aggregative effects of weight shifting are materially reduced.[36] In more common-sense terms, Kalecki's data show little rise in share in 1931 and 1932, because those industries in which labor's relative returns increased became considerably less important, while industries in which labor's returns fell slightly increased substantially in importance. These separate effects tended to counterbalance each other; they would not have balanced had government wages and income been included.

(d) Finally, going behind Kalecki's figures, serious questions must be raised about the method of estimating wages for the "other" industries, that is, those for which data are not directly available.[37] These wages were presumed to vary in proportion to all wages plus salaries. There can be no satisfactory way of checking this assertion in the absence of the data. A great deal depends upon the specific assumption that is made. The best way to proceed—given the undertaking—probably is to array alternative assumptions. Briefly, one might have assumed that "other" wages vary as (a) "selected" wages, (b) "selected" salaries, (c) "selected" wages and salaries, (d) "other" wages and salaries, and (e) all wages and salaries. Care must be taken to avoid smuggling in the notion that one of these alternatives is correct.

Calculations have been made of labor's share in gross private income produced with each of these concepts. Since "selected" wages probably declined relatively more than "others" owing to

[36] The complete tables need not be reproduced, but L/Y and $\Sigma p_i \Delta w_i$ for the recalculation of Kalecki's data may be compared with and without government-produced income and wages.

	GOVERNMENT INCLUDED		GOVERNMENT EXCLUDED	
Year	L/Y	$\Sigma p_i \Delta w_i$	L/Y	$\Sigma p_i \Delta w_i$
1930	40.35	− 0.1113	38.43	− 0.256
1931	42.18	− 0.305	38.78	− 0.457
1932	43.69	+ 0.250	38.72	− 0.555
1933	43.37	+ 1.557	40.61	+ 0.622
1934	41.43	+ 0.070	39.11	+ 0.332

Contrary to other years of increasing activity, the weight of government increased in 1933 using Kalecki's income concept (gross value produced).

[37] Table III shows that in 1930, 54 per cent of all gross income was produced in sectors for which data were unavailable.

greater fluctuations in employment,[38] alternative (a), as expected, reveals a decline in the share in depression. The same applies to (c). Alternative (d) yields a substantially higher share, while (b) and (e) result in little change. While the relative merits of these assumptions may be debated at length, no conclusive evidence is as yet available. Hence Kalecki's wage and share basic material must be viewed with some reserve.

The examination of Kalecki's stimulating statistical study has suggested certain points that may be used to summarize the argument of this section. (1) Legitimate concern with the private sector of the economy resulted in the neglecting of important weight-shifting effects upon labor's share. Instead of a constant share that Kalecki's model seeks to explain,[39] wide variations in the cyclical pattern of the participation rates are found, even using his definitions. Important increases in rates of participation were counteracted by weight shifts to other sectors in which the rate of participation declined very slightly. (2) The estimates of manual labor income, that is, wages, leave much to be desired. (3) The section has underlined the danger of dealing exclusively with aggregates without examining their components wherever possible.[40] Particularly dangerous is the technique of inferring the behavior of single enterprises from over-all data. (4) Finally, the observations of previous sections have been strengthened. Basically, labor's share in total costs and income produced rises markedly in depression in many sectors of the system: characteristically, those sectors in which output falls most. Other segments show a more stable rate of participation; they gain weight. The over-all variation in the share can be viewed as a resultant of these separate changes. Kalecki's preoccupation with labor's share in the private economy *as a whole* neglected the significance of weight shifts.

[38] If "selected" wages had been estimated from all wages and salaries, on the assumption that they varied proportionally, these appraisals would have been over 30 per cent too high in 1932.

[39] Kalecki's analytical model applies to the individual firm; it is logically possible for the share in income produced in each firm to be constant and still have rate of participation variations in the sectors of the system for which data are available as a consequence of weight shifts among firms in the segment.

[40] The use of aggregates is very pervasive in economic and statistical literature. It would be very useful, for instance, to know the extent to which variations in indices of average hourly earnings are a result of weight shifts between low- and high-paid sectors.

4. *Labor's Share in Income Payments*

An earlier section has shown labor's share in income produced and income payments to differ widely in their cyclical patterns. The present section is intended to break down changes in the share in income payments in the same way that Section 2 handled income produced. The argument of the last section reveals the importance of being on guard against offsetting rate and weight variations. Since the techniques have been elaborated previously, there is need to do little more than present results. A much less thorough study was made of income paid out than of income produced. Department of Commerce data [41] on employee compensation and income paid out were utilized for a subdivision of the economy into twelve sectors. The data for "government" excluded work-relief wages. Charts XIV and XV show the fluctuation in participation rates and weights for these twelve groups in the period 1929–1935.

A comparison of the weight changes in Chart XV with those in Chart X for income produced reveals almost identical patterns. The same industrial groups gained or lost weight during the depression. As would be expected, however, the amplitude of weight fluctuations is less with income paid out than with income produced. The most striking contrast, however, is between participation rates. Compare Charts XIV and XI. Participation in the individual series of income paid out remains very much more constant than in income produced. There are no marked peaks in 1931 or 1932 in Chart XIV as in Chart XI. The average participation in income paid out, as was previously noted, remained almost entirely unchanged. The variation was from 64.72 per cent in 1930 to a low of 63.95 per cent in 1932 and a high of 65.40 per cent in 1935. This small decline in 1930–1932 was almost entirely a change in the individual rate of participation; weight shifts were important only in 1932. Calculations of $p_i \Delta w_i$ indicate that the very small weight shifts that did take place in the depression were in the direction of a smaller share. The conclusion must remain that labor's share in income paid out is very constant through the

[41] Department of Commerce, *National Income in the United States, 1929–35*, pp. 37 and 43.

CHART XIV. PARTICIPATION RATES IN INCOME PAID OUT BY INDUSTRIAL GROUPING [42]

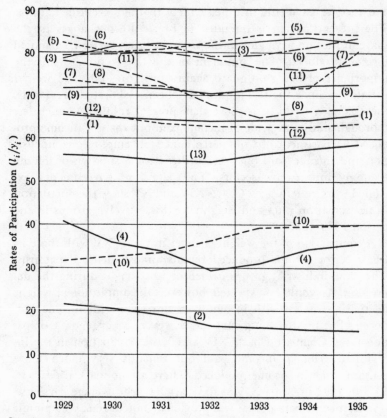

Legend

(1) All industry
(2) Agriculture
(3) Mining
(4) Electric light and power, and gas
(5) Manufacturing
(6) Construction
(7) Transportation

(8) Communication
(9) Trade
(10) Finance
(11) Government, exc. work relief wages
(12) Service
(13) Miscellaneous

[42] Labor's share is compensation of employees in income paid out.

cycle, that is, rates of participation are relatively constant within the individual sectors of the economy for which data are available. The rather large weight shifts do tend to cancel themselves out if government is included as a sector.

CHART XV. WEIGHT SHIFTS BY INDUSTRIAL GROUPING IN IN-COME PAID OUT

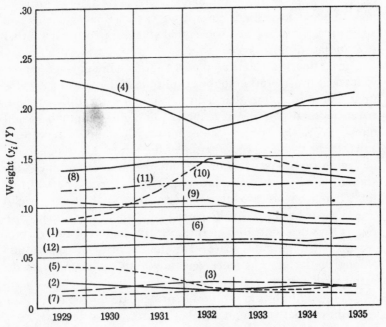

Legend
(1) Agriculture
(2) Mining
(3) Electric light and power, and gas
(4) Manufacturing
(5) Construction
(6) Transportation

(7) Communication
(8) Trade
(9) Finance
(10) Government, exc. work relief wages
(11) Service
(12) Miscellaneous

5. *Theory of Short-run Distributive Shares*

The reader has been led through what may have seemed a jungle of empirical material. The forest that emerges reveals the importance of the various concepts of income and labor's return in determining the share and the necessity of exploring weight and rate of participation shifts in any share variation. But any statistical aggregate over time can always be broken down into rate and weight changes, that is, "explained" in these terms. Furthermore, enterprises can be grouped by an almost infinite range of variables. The purely statistical level of analysis can be revealing but must in no way be mistaken for an analytical explanation of changes in labor's share. The task remains of making some suggestions toward an explanation of changes in labor's share in terms of a conceptual scheme of economics rather than in statistical parlance.

The ordinary theoretical model of the individual enterprise yields a rigorous solution to the magnitude of the rate of participation. The assumption that a firm maximizes the difference between its total cost and revenue requires that output be determined where the marginal contribution of factors to revenue is equal to the marginal cost (price) of the factor. The number and outlay on each type of factor employed is thus determined; the amount of labor hired and the wage bill are specified. Deducting total purchases of parts and supplies from total revenue yields gross income produced by the enterprise. Labor's rate of participation is thus determined. The introductory section of this chapter recalled that this rate varies with the elasticity of substitution among the factors and more generally with the elasticity of demand for the product of the enterprise.

But this equilibrium solution is inadequate for the current interest in cyclical variations in labor's share in two respects. First, the model deals with the single enterprise, while the share refers to the total system, an aggregate of concerns.[43] Second, at least some types of equilibrium are inappropriate to the cyclical pattern. In particular, most plant and equipment is primarily fixed, precluding material adjustment in the cycle to variations in output and prices. While firms may be presumed to minimize losses or to maximize short-run profits, the resultant rate of participa-

---

[43] The marginal product of labor for a total system is ambiguous because the various proportions in which labor is combined through the economy yield outputs that are not readily reducible to a single measure of the increment in product. See R. F. Kahn, "The Elasticity of Substitution and the Relative Share of a Factor," *Review of Economic Studies*, October, 1933, I, p. 78.

tion would no doubt be different if longer run adjustments were permitted. The concept of short-run participation will be adopted as derived from short-run equilibrium. This short-run rate of participation of labor and that of other variable factors may exhaust virtually all of the gross product and more than the net product in periods of markedly reduced demand schedules. Any observed rate of labor's participation cannot be regarded, however, as an exact counterpart of either the short or long-run concepts. Not only are both inseparably involved, but enterprises may not even be in short-run equilibrium.

The model that is suggested in the following pages explains variations in labor's share in familiar terms. Elements in the model will provide the framework for further empirical material in the next chapter. Attention must first be directed toward the single firm and then to the aggregate of the whole system. Individual enterprises are confronted with a fall in demand schedules in depression arising from some decline in investment outlays in the system. The magnitude of the decline will vary from firm to firm, depending upon both the income elasticity of purchasers [44] and the relative competitive position of firms in the immediate sector of the system.

Start with the simplified case of a firm with a total cost function that is linear within the relevant range of output and neglect variations in any factor prices. The continued decrease in demand under these conditions will increase the participation in net or gross receipts going to labor and other variable factors combined. Eventually only variable costs would be covered as price declined and the short-run return to fixed factors was reduced to almost nothing. The decline in labor and material payments would be at a constant rate with respect to output. Receipts would decline even more rapidly in the general case, not alone because revenue functions were shifting downward but also because movement backward along a total revenue function would decrease receipts faster than output. Hence the rate of participation of labor and materials would increase; if labor and purchased

---

[44] Considerations of the acceleration principle and inventories would apply in durable-goods industries where purchasers were ordinarily other enterprises.

supplies do not change in proportions greatly when output declines, labor's participation would clearly increase.

These results will be modified in the light of a number of considerations. (*a*) Cost functions are customarily presumed to involve markedly U-shaped marginal costs. As output contracts in such a firm from very high levels, the initial variation in the rate of participation is uncertain. While the revenue function decreases and movement along the function as output contracts is at an increasing rate of revenue contraction, labor disbursements are also declining at accelerated rates. After demand has ordinarily fallen for some time, the share will rise more rapidly with the inverted ogive cost function than with a linear function. Labor payments will decline at a decreasing rather than at a constant rate with respect to output. The shape of the cost function (technically, the labor cost function) will clearly influence the short-run variation in the rate of participation.

(*b*) Fluctuation in the ratio in which variable factors are employed has so far been neglected. Labor's rate of participation will be influenced by the short-run substitution among these factors which depends upon their relative price variations and the technical possibilities of substitution. The elasticity of substitution between labor and other variable cost components will be significant. The greater the possibilities of short-run substitution and the greater the decline in materials prices relative to labor, the less likely any increase in labor's rate of participation; in fact, a decrease can take place. If materials prices characteristically decline more than wage rates, participation will rise most, the less the possibilities of substitution.

(*c*) The relative variation in prices of variable cost elements, such as labor and materials, will affect labor's participation rate through impacts on product prices and wage payments. Should materials prices decline sharply in depression, wage rates remaining unchanged for instance, product prices would normally be thought to fall depending in amount on the elasticity of product demand. Disbursements to labor can thus be expected to rise as a proportion of the value of output. The greater the share of total costs that are basic raw materials, the larger the increase in labor's participation under these circumstances.

(d) Not only substitution among factors as a result of price variations, but autonomous technical change involving variable factors may shift the labor cost function, and alter its shape, affecting the rate of participation.

(e) As product demand declines in the depression, the direction in which the elasticity for the demand of a single firm varies will affect the rate of participation. The more elastic the demand, the greater will be the rise in labor's participation in income produced as output falls off.

The explanation that is implied for short-run variations in labor's participation in a single firm is simply an application of the usual model of the enterprise. The magnitude of the fluctuation in labor's participation in income produced depends upon (a) extent of fluctuation in output, (b) the shape of the short-run labor cost function, (c) the relative price movements of variable factors and the possibilities of short-run substitution, (d) impact of the absolute fluctuation in variable factor prices on product prices, (e) the magnitude of technical change, and (f) the elasticity of product demand for the enterprise.[45]

These conditions are not inconsistent with Kalecki's stimulating model in which (a) the degree of monopoly [46] and (b) the movement of raw-material prices relative to wage costs are determinants of labor's share. His view that the share was kept constant over past cycles requires the highly tenuous assumption that the two influences just happened to offset each other. The statistical results of previous sections free his model from such narrow interpretation. The six factors that have been here emphasized require much less restrictive assumptions. Technical change is included; the shape of the labor cost function is general, and short-run substitution among variable factors is permissible. The quantitative importance of these factors will be presented in the next chapter. Depending upon the magnitude of these six factors, labor's participation in a single enterprise may increase, remain unchanged,

---

[45] The inverse of the elasticity of demand is equal to the "degree of monopoly power" when the enterprise is in short-run equilibrium.

[46] The degree of monopoly is really identified with the share going to labor since both are defined as the gap between price and marginal labor costs as a ratio to price A rise in the degree of monopoly can hardly, therefore, be said to "cause" a decrease in the relative share, Kalecki, *op. cit.*, p. 31.

or decrease in depressions. While no data for individual firms were examined,[47] the preceding sections indicated that participation (defined as wages and salaries as a ratio of income produced) tended to increase most in sectors of the system in which output declined most. The importance of the other factors is considered in more detail in the next chapter.

An explanation of the movement of labor's share cannot be content with the model of an isolated enterprise. The statistical sections have emphasized the significance of weight shifting among sectors with different levels of participation. Even when these shifts simply cancel out, the explanation cannot alone be built upon a single firm. The cycle clearly involves important weight shifts; in recent years the most violent changes have been in manufacturing and government (Chart X). In fact, the cyclical process might be described as variations in the relative importance of investment-goods expenditures to total income produced. Almost all income may be consumption in periods of low income, while a much larger proportion is net investment when income is high.[48] Weight shifts constitute the cyclical process. The amplitude of variation in net investment and hence income will clearly influence the magnitude of share variation through weight changes.

The share will also be influenced, apart from circumstances already explained within the enterprise, by the magnitude and

[47] The limitations of operating with "sectors" of the system rather than with individual enterprises must be again recognized. Data for the U. S. Steel Corporation, however, reveal that nonconstruction wages and salaries as a ratio (of sales minus goods and services purchased) varied as follows in the period 1927–1938:

Year	Ratio	Year	Ratio
1927	63.1%	1933	77.6%
1928	60.0	1934	73.7
1929	54.2	1935	71.7
1930	60.5	1936	69.6
1931	69.0	1937	61.5
1932	93.9	1938	72.3

For sales and purchases data see *Thirty-Ninth Annual Report for the Fiscal Year Ending December 31, 1940*, p. 10. Wage and salary data are from U. S. Steel Corporation, *An Analysis of Steel Pricing, Volume and Costs*, Pamphlet No. 6, p. 12.

The above data cast some doubt on the claim that the ratio of wages and salaries to net income produced has been importantly influenced by union action. See Clinton S. Golden and Harold J. Ruttenberg, *The Dynamics of Industrial Democracy*, Harper and Brothers, New York, 1942, Chap. VI.

[48] See Alvin H. Hansen, *Fiscal Policy and Business Cycles*, W. W. Norton & Company, Inc., New York, 1941, pp. 225–300.

timing of price variations in basic materials and the speed with which these cost changes are transmitted in product price changes. If large raw-material price reductions are rapidly passed on through the stages of production, labor's share will rise much further and much more rapidly than would otherwise be the case.

Longer run influences can only be mentioned. In the twenties and thirties, the structure of the economy resulted in weight shifts offsetting each other only if government was included as a sector. The growth of more manufacturing at the expense of the agricultural community would be expected to raise the share of wages and salaries as the average participation rate would be materially higher, unless offsetting changes took place. The cyclical pattern apparently would not be materially altered since both manufacturing and agriculture have been weight losers of about the same magnitude. A governmental policy might make agricultural income relatively higher in depressions than it has been; this would lower the share going to labor in depression because a sector with low participation rates would be magnified in importance. Should the secular decline in agriculture be accompanied by the growth of service industries—weight gainers—the share of labor in depression periods may be expected to fall. While the long-run share has been excluded from major consideration, these remarks would suggest that while aggressive labor policy might lower normal profits, affecting participation within each firm, important changes in the share may arise from the long-run variations in the composition of the national product.

Since the preceding sections have shown the cyclical pattern in labor's share to depend upon the definitions adopted—in particular upon the meaning of income and the disposition of government-produced income—the choice among these alternatives must in general depend upon the specific purpose at hand. At least three main areas of concern with labor's share suggest themselves.

(a) Recent economic thinking has emphasized the relation of the level of employment and income to the way in which individuals choose to divide their income between consumption and savings. This consumption function for the whole community must be affected by the relative distribution of income between wage and salary earners and other groups in the community.[49] It might be thought that since wages and salaries on balance go to individuals with lower incomes and presumably with higher marginal propensities to consume, an increase in labor's share in the depression would be a factor tending to increase the level of income. A fall in the share in the boom might be expected to necessitate a still higher level of net investment to maintain income. But do the relevant propensities to consume involve income produced or income payments (the difference being business savings)? This issue hinges on the way in which consumption by individuals with large incomes is affected by capital gains and losses in their assets. While some changes in business savings are undoubtedly regarded as disposable, others are not. The choice among these income concepts for the propensity to consume is thus uncertain.

(b) Labor's share is relevant to problems involving labor costs. A larger share of income going to wages and salaries may mean for the system, although not necessarily, a relative increase in labor costs in single enterprises. Some evidence may be gathered on the issue of labor costs as an impediment to higher volumes of employment, particularly in the thirties, by a study of labor participation rates. The next chapter will analyze this aspect of labor's share, elaborating on the dual character of wages and salaries as income and costs. For these purposes, the concept of income produced would appear to be best suited.

(c) Labor's share in income has been shown to be relevant to the objectives of trade-union wage policy.[50] Once again the concept of income produced is applicable as unions would be con-

---

[49] An unpublished study of Horst Mendershausen shows that the inequality in income increased in depression (1929–1933) among those with incomes below $2000, increased as between these incomes and higher incomes, and decreased for the very highest incomes. Income distributions by individual wage and salary incomes will be available in a few years over a cyclical period from old-age insurance data for incomes below $3000.

[50] When more complete and continuous data are available on the distribution of personal income by size groups, it may be possible to show that the effect of trade union policy has been to influence primarily the distribution of income *within* the brackets below $2500.00. That is, trade union wage policy may have been more instrumental in affecting the distribution of income in the lower income brackets than changing the distribution between low and high income brackets. The influence of trade unions on wage rate differentials is important in this connection.

cerned with their share in the value of goods and services produced; they have been more concerned with earned income of enterprises than with disbursements in dividends.

There are undoubtedly other purposes for which the variation in labor's share is relevant, and these may find income payments more relevant. But certainly for the last two objectives specified above, and perhaps even for the first, the concept of income produced would seem more adequate.

The next chapter is intended to analyze, so far as is possible, labor's participation in individual sectors of the system into statistical counterparts of the six factors indicated in this section as determinating variations in labor's short-run relative return.

CHAPTER IX. LABOR'S RETURN AS A COST

Economic analysis has elaborate models which depict the decision of an enterprise (in a system of markets) directed toward maximizing its present value or the difference between expected revenue and costs. Presuming the firm to know (a) the way total revenue can be expected to vary with the price of the product, (b) technical input-output relations, and (c) the way prices of the factors can be expected to vary with the amounts utilized, pricing and output decisions are determined. The first condition is a revenue function, the last two yield a cost function; the firm is presumed to maximize the difference between these functions by appropriate pricing and output decisions. Save for the determination of factor prices, an elaboration of this model is usually designated the "theory of value and distribution." The precise pricing and output decisions will vary, of course, with the assumed basic conditions, the most common variants being the short and long run and the type of competition envisaged.

The theory of the individual enterprise yields a formal solution to the magnitude of wage payments and hence to wage costs per unit of output and sales that is valid only for equilibrium positions. The last chapter suggested that labor's share in income produced in the total system could be usefully portrayed as depending upon participation rates within individual enterprises and variations in the composition of the economy. A series of factors were listed as analytically affecting the participation rate within the enterprise. Historical movements of costs cannot readily be interpreted, however, from the formalized scheme since movements toward or away from even short-run equilibrium cannot be isolated. A series of logical identities can be developed, none the less, that prove useful in understanding cyclical fluctuations in wage payments and income. Since wages and salaries are at the same time income to labor and costs to enterprises, as a sequel to the last chapter, the present chapter concerns some cost aspects of labor payments.

1. *Fundamental Relationships*

The total revenue from sales, S, of an enterprise is identically equal to wage payments, L, materials and supplies purchased, M, plus a gross margin, E, which includes depreciation, interest charges, taxes, other costs, and profits. Some elements of the gross margin may be negative, although the whole would never be negative except under very special circumstances. This simplification of the accounting of an enterprise is necessarily an abstraction. But more detailed groupings of costs, revenue, and profits could be adopted by subdividing the threefold categories; no loss of generality would follow such substitution.

$$(1) \qquad S_i = L_i + M_i + E_i$$

The revenue as well as each one of the cost components may be broken down into a separate price and quantity component. Thus, sales become output sold, O, times price of the product—average revenue per unit—P; wage payments may be represented by the quantity of labor, H, times the average rate, W, and materials payments are equal to the product of the quantity employed, Q, and their average price, P_m. For a single enterprise, the identity can be written as follows:

$$(2) \qquad OP = HW + QP_m + E$$
$$1 = HW/OP + QP_m/OP + E/OP$$

The expression HW/OP, the rate of participation of labor in sales, is of special interest. Chart IV in the last chapter depicted labor's share in sales for manufacturing. Professor Hansen has contended that "Labor cost per dollar of sales remains remarkably stable."[1] Furthermore, preceding chapters implied that this ratio can be taken to be the focal point of trade-union bargaining. A trade union was envisaged as attempting to maximize the wage bill, HW, which the enterprise must pay out of OP. The bargain was portrayed, however, as taking place in the total context of the claims of other factors. The rate of participation of wage earners in sales is finally of interest for it permits a convenient classification of the influences operating on the labor bargain. Thus the

---

[1] Alvin H. Hansen, *Fiscal Policy and Business Cycles*, W. W. Norton & Company, Inc., New York, 1941, p. 246.

term may be alternatively written in two other forms of signifi cance: $H/O \cdot W/P$ and $HW/O \cdot 1/P$.

$H/O \cdot W/P$ is the product of the "real labor cost" in physical terms and the ratio of the weighted wage rates to weighted prices. H/O is the amount of labor per unit of output or the inverse of output per man-hour, if labor services are measured in hours. Any change in H/O may result from either a movement along a given input-output relation or from a shift of the whole relation. That is, changes in output, substitution among factors involving labor arising from changes in their price ratios, as well as technical change may result in a variation in the man-hour component of output. The second alternative form of labor's share in the sales of an enterprise, $HW/O \cdot 1/P,$ is the product of labor cost per unit of output and the inverse of a weighted product price.

A convenient simplification in notation can be made in equation 2 in which the subscript s denotes sales. Hence

$$(3) = (2) \qquad\qquad 1 = l_s + m_s + e_s$$

A concept of gross income produced by the enterprise is obtained by deducting raw materials and purchases from equation 1; the subscript g will denote shares in gross income.

$$(4) \qquad\qquad 1 = l_g + e_g$$

Finally, by the subtraction of depreciation from equation 1 and treating f as e minus depreciation, shares in net income can be depicted by the subscript y. The terms l_s, l_g, and l_y refer to the

$$(5) \qquad\qquad 1 = l_y + f_y$$

share of labor returns or labor costs in the sales, gross income, and a form of net income of the individual enterprise. These notations are developed in order to emphasize the interdependence of labor's return in various concepts of the receipts of the enterprise, to stress the dual character of wages and salaries as costs and income, and to clarify the locus of collective bargaining.

2. The Locus of Collective Bargaining

Equation 2 provides a convenient way of relating the discussion of wage policies of trade unions to the study of costs and income, particularly in the course of the cycle. The bargain between a trade union and an enterprise concerns the average level of W in HW/OP. If the union is again presumed to be preoccupied with securing the largest possible wage bill,[2] the bargaining will determine how much of expected receipts (anticipated OP) will have to be expended in wage bill HW. In the course of bargaining, the magnitude of OP anticipated by the enterprise may be quite different from that which the union anticipates for the enterprise. The wage bargain is placed in the context of total sales rather than net or gross income in accordance with the earlier discussion of wage policy (Chap. IV). The time pattern of influences on wage determination are more clearly emphasized when the wage bill is greater than net income produced; the inclusion of materials purchased in OP emphasizes the dependence of wage rates upon allied factor markets that was underlined earlier.

Both the magnitude and timing[3] of downward pressures on average wage rates with a fall in effective demand[4] will vary among enterprises according to the same factors that were listed in the last chapter as affecting the share—decline in output and shape of cost function, short-run substitution, technical change, magnitude of other variable-factor price changes, and the elasticity of product demand. Since these conditions are not all directly measurable by available statistics, transformation into the terms of equation 2 is necessary for empirical inquiry. The conditions directly impinging on the wage bill and rate will be first considered one at a time; later an attempt will be made to bring them together in typical patterns in connection with empirical material.

(a) Clearly the size of HW/OP itself will be an approximate index of the concern of the enterprise with the wage bill and wage rate. When wages are a small fraction of receipts, that is, when materials and overhead are large, less downward pressure

[2] The largest wage bill for the union does not necessarily imply maximizing HW from each enterprise considered separately. See the discussion in Chap. IV of the element of wage policy concerned with wage levels among competing enterprises. A differentiated wage structure among enterprises might yield the largest wage bill for the union but create impossible political conditions within a union extending over many enterprises.

[3] See Chap. VII.

[4] The converse will apply to increases in effective demand during periods of upswing.

in depressions and less resistance to increases in prosperity may be expected as compared to situations in which HW/OP is large. The importance of this idea has long been recognized; it is explicit, for instance, in Marshall's discussion [5] of derived demand. The size of HW/OP is largely dependent upon the degree of vertical integration, the scale of plant and hence the importance of fixed charges, and the related characteristics of the products or services produced. That highly integrated enterprises have been strongly opposed to trade unions in the past seems attributable to more than monopsonistic position in the labor market and opposition on principle. Since wage changes within an enterprise can be confined to a limited group of workers only with extreme difficulty, a highly integrated enterprise would be particularly vulnerable to labor cost changes. Not only are there more local markets from which changes may be initiated, but any change in rates means a much larger increase in wage bill and total costs.

(b) The impact of changes in demand for the product of an enterprise upon the wage structure will also be significantly influenced by variations in H/O. "Man-hours per unit of output" is not a simple analytical category and so may be influenced by variations in output, substitution from factor price variations, technical change, and alterations in the scale of plant. The wide use of the inverse, O/H, as a measure for the rate of technical change is thus open to serious limitations,[6] particularly as applied to the course of the cycle. During periods of reduced demand, technical change and reduction of output can usually be expected to affect H/O in opposite directions. In some sectors the technical change effect will offset the impact of reduced output, while in others cost functions may be so shaped that the decline in output raises H/O on balance. The greater the decline in real labor input per unit of output, the less the downward pressure on wage rates in depression. The greater the rate of technical change and the less the decline in output, the less intense the downward pressure on the wage structure.

---

[5] *Principles of Economics*, 8th ed., Macmillan & Company, Ltd., London, p. 385.
[6] Conference on Price Research, National Bureau of Economic Research, Inc., *Cost Behavior and Price Policy*, Chap. VII. New York, 1943.

(c) The behavior of raw-material prices must be specified as an important determinant of the probable course of wage rates. The more severe the decline in materials costs QP_m/OP influenced by both materials prices and the relative importance of purchases in total cost, the more successful trade unions may be in resisting declines in wage rates. If market structures are such that declines in firm revenue are absorbed by price reductions to elementary producers, domestic or foreign, wage rates may be confronted by less pressure. The size of QP_m/OP is of significance in considering the effects of any decline in the price of raw materials.

Logically, mention should also be made of changes in Q/O, materials content per unit of output, which might affect materials costs in the same way as materials price declines. The evidence marshaled in the next section would suggest that this possibility has probably not been very important on balance in recent years. Substitution no doubt takes place among various types of materials. But the over-all effect has apparently been significant only in isolated cases. For this reason no separate listing has been made of this channel of absorbing the shock of decreases in demand.

(d) The size of E/OP is of importance in estimating the impact of declines in output on wage rates and the wage bill. If that part of E which constitutes fixed costs is large, then it may be possible for trade unions to force the absorption of a large proportion of the decline in revenue on the enterprise for the short run. The plight of office buildings in periods of depression may be enlightening in this regard since a very high proportion of all costs are fixed with respect to rentals. Wage earners may be able to secure virtually all cash receipts. Where almost no fixed costs exist, on the other hand, a decline in revenue may either force immediate wage-rate concessions or result in the enterprise closing entirely.

(e) The variation in product prices, particularly as affected through competitive conditions in product markets, will be crucial in its impact on wage structures. Sharp declines in prices are apt to put very strong pressure on the wage structure in an enterprise. Aside from the pure bargaining power that arises from a comparison of changes in wage rates and product prices, the decline in *OP* is likely to result in strong insistence by the enterprise for wage concessions. Since the amount of labor hired declines more or less proportionally to output (depending upon the input-output relations), the reduction in product prices requires some cost reduction, and the enterprise may well attempt to secure wage reductions.

The elaboration of the setting of the wage bargain that has been provided applies logically in the short run to any variable factor in a market cluster. Materials suppliers must recognize that their receipts come out of the sales of other enterprises. Yet materials purchasers cannot be presumed to be attempting to secure so large a materials bill or so large a share of sales as possible; they are alleged to be maximizing profits. Under conditions of perfect competition in the long run, sales would be exhausted as among all factors according to their prices and marginal productivities. But in the cyclical context with more complex market structures, the payments and shares are determined by shorter run conditions set forth in the last chapter.

The five conditions that have just been regarded as conditioning the wage bargain have been derived from equation 2 above and are seen to have analytical counterparts, although not in unique correspondence. These magnitudes—the relative size of HW/OP, QP_m/OP, and E/OP and the variations in H/O, P_m, and P—have been adopted since they admit of statistical manipulation for a wide range of industrial groups. The values involved are related in a way made clear by the identity in equation 2. Care should be taken in asserting that any observed wage pattern is "explained" by these magnitudes. Actually they are necessarily related. The following empirical work is intended to explore typical patterns of cyclical variation as among industrial groups rather than to attempt to deduce explanations that are logically necessary anyway. For instance, if P_m alone declines, then HW/OP will increase. One development does not explain the other in any important sense. The objective of the next section is rather to attempt to discover typical patterns, if any, for recent cyclical periods in the related variations of these measurable magnitudes.

3. Cost Variation by Industrial Grouping

Once again data are not available for individual enterprises, and it is necessary to resort to aggregates of firms grouped by convention. The limitations of this method, which in effect presumes the industrial group to be 'an enterprise or regards the relative importance of the different firms to be unaltered, have been recognized previously. The data are from three sources, the Census of Manufactures, the National Research Project study of productivity,[7] and the National Bureau of Economic Research.[8] For present purposes, the census data yield value of product, OP; total wages and salaries, HW; cost of materials QP_m; overhead expenses plus profit, E; and value added by manufacturing, a gross income produced, Y_g. The separation of profits and fixed costs would permit the measurement of net income, but labor's share in such a concept was explored in the last chapter. The National Bureau computations, largely from census data, yield indices of physical output, O. Thus labor costs and materials costs per unit of output, HW/O and QP_m/O, in addition to labor's participation in sales, HW/OP or l_s and in gross income, HW/Y_g or l_g, can be calculated. Finally, the National Research Project data on output per man-hour were utilized to compute H/O.

Special care had been taken by the National Bureau of Economic Research to ensure comparability of the industrial classification between the output indices and census data. The National Research Project presented more serious difficulties.[9] The fifty-nine industrial groups presented by this investigation were examined with some care as to comparability of definition, and finally thirty-seven industrial groups were selected for which reasonably comparable definitions seemed assured. This problem, it must be emphasized, arises only with respect to the measurement

[7] National Research Project, Works Progress Administration, Production, *Employment and Productivity in 59 Manufacturing Industries*, Works Progress Administration, National Research Project, Report S-1, 1939, 3 vols.

[8] The National Bureau of Economic Research very kindly permitted the use of work sheets which contained indices as well as raw data from the census. The indices of output have been a part of the published works of F. C. Mills and Solomon Fabricant. See Solomon Fabricant, *The Output of Manufacturing Industries, 1899–1937*, National Bureau of Economic Research, Inc., New York, 1940, Appendices A and B.

[9] For a comparison of census classification and that of the National Research Project, see *loc. cit.*, I, p. 23.

of man-hours per unit of output. These thirty-seven groups are clearly but a sample of the total system. The basis of selection, moreover, depended purely upon the availability of the data. A study of these series suggests that they contain a picture representative of large areas of manufacturing activity; they do not apply to other sectors of the system. Since the present concern is with patterns of cyclical movement rather than with a single over-all picture, the matter of sampling need not be pressed.

The biannual values for the primary and derived magnitudes in equation 2 were plotted for each industrial grouping, usually for the period 1919–1937. Since it is impossible here to reproduce all these charts and the data that lie behind them, samples from the petroleum-refining and clay-products industries are illustrated in Tables XII and XIII. Labor's participation in sales of petroleum refining showed a substantial percentage increase in depression

TABLE XII. ANALYSIS OF LABOR BARGAIN IN PETROLEUM REFINING

	1919	1921	1923	1925	1927	1929	1931	1933	1935	1937
H/O	189.0	171.4	131.8	101.1	100.0	92.4	78.7	70.0	62.1	54.8
HW/O	181.9	174.4	130.5	102.3	100.0	92.8	84.5	74.6	79.1	83.9
HW/OP	103.6	111.6	109.1	83.0	100.0	93.6	132.8	122.7	112.3	103.9
HW/OY_g	80.0	101.7	96.5	73.7	100.0	73.9	117.8	97.8	104.2	98.3
MP_m/OP	93.4	97.8	97.1	97.2	100.0	94.1	97.1	94.4	98.3	98.7
MP_m/O	164.1	152.8	116.2	119.8	100.0	93.2	61.7	57.3	69.2	79.7

TABLE XIII. ANALYSIS OF LABOR BARGAIN IN CLAY PRODUCTS

	1919	1921	1923	1925	1927	1929	1931	1933	1935	1937
H/O	134.6	128.4	110.3	106.2	100.0	95.8	92.6	90.8	90.4	86.4
HW/O	113.2	112.2	108.7	104.5	100.0	93.3	81.2	61.8	75.5	86.3
HW/OP	98.2	99.5	97.4	99.1	100.0	94.9	91.7	77.3	81.9	88.1
HW/OY_g	100.5	105.9	97.4	98.4	100.0	99.2	88.9	77.0	85.5	90.4
MP_m/OP	103.7	112.5	99.3	96.0	100.0	88.8	92.9	99.0	109.2	105.7
MP_m/O	119.6	126.9	110.8	100.4	100.0	87.4	82.2	79.1	100.6	103.5

despite the fact that the absolute share in 1933 was only 6.51 per cent, having risen from 4.96 per cent in 1929. The ratio of wages and salaries to gross income (value added) varied in similar pattern. Table XII also shows real labor costs to have decreased materially throughout the period. The 15.0 per cent decline in output between 1929 and 1933, combined with the shape of the cost function, was not great enough to result in a rise in H/O. Materials costs per unit of output showed very sharp reductions in the period, particularly from 1929 to 1933, but materials costs as a percentage of sales remained relatively unchanged. These results must be attributed to the tremendous decline in materials prices with product prices following fairly closely. Labor costs per unit of output fell during 1929–1933 with the sharp decline in H/O despite even an increase in average wage rates. As a ratio to price, wage rates had to increase materially in order for H/O to fall and yet have HW/OP rise. The percentage variations between 1929 and 1933 for each of the terms in HW/OP were calculated to be: H, -35.6; W, $+6.0$; O, -15.0; P, -38.5, so that the total expression increased 30.9 per cent.[10] In accordance with the analysis of the last section, little downward pressure on wage rates should have been expected in this case. Not only are labor costs a very small proportion of total costs, but output declined considerably less than the average for all industries. Furthermore, both H/O and QP_m/O declined very sharply.

The case of clay products (Table XIII) provides a second and contrasting illustration. Participation in sales showed small variation, with a decline in the depression period 1929–1933, in contrast to most other industrial groups. Labor costs were almost as high a proportion of sales as among any of the other thirty-seven groups, being 36.02 per cent in 1929 and 29.37 per cent in 1933. Labor's participation in value added showed a fairly similar pattern of variation. Real labor costs again declined throughout the period but by a much smaller extent than in the case of petroleum refining. It is indeed remarkable that H/O did not rise in the depression of 1929–1933 in the face of a fall in output of 73.4 per cent.[11] Materials costs per unit of output were reduced, but as a ratio to revenue they increased. This latter development

[10] The values for the percentage changes of each term in HW/OP are calculable because H/O, HW/O, and HW/OP are known in addition to the percentage changes in O. The percentage change in H, W, and P can then be calculated in sequence. The values for changes in wage rates (strictly, average hourly earnings) is consistent with usual measures for the period when they are available. Thus calculations for cotton textiles and automobiles yield wage changes comparable with National Industrial Conference Board series for the period.

[11] Among other considerations at work undoubtedly was the concentration of output in fewer firms with somewhat more favorable cost conditions. The number of establishments actually was cut by half. The assumption of treating a sector of the economy as an enterprise, in the absence of firm data, has been recognized as a serious limitation.

is probably related to the fact that materials prices may have fallen less than product prices. Labor costs fell materially more than the per unit of output costs of materials. The percentage variations between 1929 and 1933 for each of the terms in HW/OP were calculated to be: $H, -$ 69.5; $W, -$ 29.6; $O, -$ 73.4; $P, -$ 20.0; so that the total expression decreased 18.5 per cent. In the face of the large reduction in output, the relatively small change in H/O, the relatively large importance of wage costs, and the rise of QP_m/OP, average hourly earnings must have faced very strong downward pressure. This pressure was effective for HW/O and HW/OP to have decreased so much. The fall in product prices tended to magnify the strain on the wage structure. The actual wage decline was more than that of product price, almost 30 per cent from 1929 to 1933.

The examination of similar tables for all thirty-seven industrial groups indicates certain uniformities. (*a*) The participation of labor in sales tended to rise during the depression periods of 1921 and 1929–1933; a few showed almost no variations, while only one or two indicated the pattern of clay products. These results are in accordance with the over-all data for manufacturing presented in Chart IV of the last chapter. (*b*) The magnitude of the decline in H/O through the period 1919–1937 is of considerable importance. Typically, this decrease continued through depression periods and showed no rise in periods of high prosperity. In some industrial groups, such as coke, iron and steel (blast furnaces), agricultural implements, motor vehicles, and tobacco manufactures (for some reason), H/O increased sharply in the period 1929–1933 under the impact of very low levels of output. (*c*) Materials costs per unit of output characteristically declined by large amounts, and there can be no doubt that additional pressure on the wage structure was avoided by the large reductions in materials prices. In almost every case (clay products and fertilizers being exceptions), materials costs consequently declined more than wage costs per unit of product. (*d*) Finally, the observation is important that labor's participation in sales in 1935 was in most industrial groups of about the same magnitude as in 1927 and 1929. Certainly the participation rates were not materially higher in manufacturing industries in the late thirties than they were in the late twenties. Thus wages alone constituted 16.8 and 16.1 per cent of the gross value of manufacturing in 1927 and 1929 compared to 16.3 and 16.6 per cent for 1935 and 1937.[12] These overall results are substantiated in the individual series that were charted. The relevance of this observation to the issue of the extent to which unemployment in the thirties was related to wage-rate structures is considered in a final section of this chapter.

These observations do not constitute an entirely rigorous or exhaustive summary of the data required for equation 2 and compiled for thirty-seven industrial groups. Logically it might be possible to regard the variations in labor's participation in sales as an independent variable to be statistically explained (approximated) by some derived relation from the absolute size of labor's share, the variation in materials prices, the change in man-hours per unit of output, and product price movements. While the logical identity in equation 2 must always hold, some indication of the relative importance of the various factors just mentioned might be found. But the hazards of partial correlation have dictated a less ambitious course, although bunch map techniques might have provided illuminating answers as to which of these variables could have been omitted or which others might possibly have been added.

Table XIV arrays the industrial groups according to the absolute magnitude of their labor cost ratios to sales in 1929. A somewhat arbitrary division is made indicating "light" and "heavy" labor using industrial categories. The average for all manufacturing industries, as calculated from the Census of Manufactures, falls between these groups. The use of 1933 instead of 1929 does not fundamentally alter the general pattern and only changes the classification of several sectors near the dividing line.

Table XV arrays the variation in output, O between 1929 and 1933 in comparison with changes in real labor cost per unit of output, H/O.

Table XVI specifies for the same industries during the same period the change in labor and materials cost per unit of sales as well as the variation in the ratio of average hourly earnings to product prices.

[12] *Census of Manufactures.*

TABLE XIV. ARRAY OF LABOR COST RATIOS TO SALES (*HW/OP*), 1929 AND 1933

Industrial Group	1929	1933
Flour and other grain-mill products	3.31	3.98
Cane-sugar refining	3.51	3.63
Smelting and refining nonferrous metals	3.66	4.96
Meat packing	4.83	7.54
Petroleum refining	4.96	6.51
Smelting and refining, not from ore	5.26	6.07
Paints and varnish	7.42	8.22
Tobacco manufactures	7.59	5.60
Fertilizers	7.69	7.66
Coke	8.02	9.37
Beet sugar	9.23	8.56
Canning and preserving, fruits and vegetables	9.99	10.28
Ice cream	10.27	10.20
Canning and preserving, fish, etc.	10.88	11.03
Chemicals	12.83	12.43
Nonferrous metal alloys and products	12.85	18.28
Leather	13.17	18.16
Pulp	13.7	13.5
Confectionery	14.35	15.58
Paper	14.52	14.45
Rubber tires and tubes	16.50	18.29
Bread and bakery products	18.00	21.30
Cement	18.26	15.95
Worsted goods	18.31	20.53
Motor vehicles	19.76	22.98
Ice manufactured	20.09	16.40
Iron and steel, steel works, rolling	20.47	22.62
Rubber goods other than tires and shoes	20.55	22.79
Independent planing mills	21.02	21.03
Agricultural implements	21.21	32.19
Cotton goods	21.28	25.12
Woolen goods	22.69	25.78
Boots and shoes	23.03	25.68
Knit goods	23.42	26.49
Rayon	29.90	24.61
Lumber	33.12	32.30
Clay products	36.02	29.37

These statistical data [13] have been presented not in order to draw a regression between any two terms, but rather to illustrate that taken together a useful explanation can be presented of the circumstances underlying the wage bargain. Enterprises and industrial groups vary widely in (*a*) the amount of labor they use relative to materials and fixed capital, (*b*) the magnitude of their

[13] The years of 1929–1933 that have been presented in the preceding tables are taken to illustrate the issues under discussion.

TABLE XV. LINK RELATIVES OF OUTPUT AND REAL LABOR COST
1933; 1929 BASE

Industrial Group	Output Link	(H/O) Link	Heavy or Light Labor Using
Rayon	209.2	45.4	H
Beet sugar	155.0	77.1	L
Knit goods	99.4	64.0	H
Pulp	98.5	81.1	L
Meat packing	96.7	85.0	L
Boots and shoes	94.1	88.5	H
Cotton goods	87.8	88.9	H
Canning and preserving, fruits and vegetables	87.8	69.6	L
Tobacco manufactures	86.2	95.6	L
Leather	86.0	89.0	L
Petroleum refining	85.0	75.8	L
Chemicals	81.6	81.0	L
Paper	81.6	86.3	L
Flour and other grain mill products	81.1	93.5	L
Confectionery	79.2	73.8	L
Cane Sugar	77.0	83.2	L
Bread and bakery products	75.2	105.1	H
Ice manufactured	74.3	77.2	H
Canning and preserving, fish	71.5	74.8	L
Smelting and refining, not from ore	68.3	75.1	L
Paints and varnish	62.4	98.3	L
Rubber tires and tubes	60.8	71.5	H
Ice cream	60.5	91.4	L
Fertilizers	60.0	86.7	L
Nonferrous metal alloys and products	45.0	97.1	— —
Iron and steel, steel works, rolling	42.4	100.3	H
Coke	42.4	138.2	L
Lumber	40.1	90.0	H
Smelting and refining nonferrous metals	38.5	94.6	L
Motor vehicles	38.2	107.2	H
Cement	36.6	86.3	— —
Independent planing mills	32.4	96.1	H
Clay products	26.6	94.8	H
Agricultural implements	11.8	154.8	H

variation in output in the cycle, related to income elasticities of households, inventories, and the acceleration principle, (c) the variation in real labor input per unit of output, (d) the pattern of materials prices, and (e) the product price fluctuation. Nothing should imply that wage levels are in any sense independent variables here; they are more appropriately another variable. Despite the wide diversity of industrial characteristics with respect to these variables, certain relationships must logically hold among

TABLE XVI. LINK RELATIVES OF LABOR AND MATERIALS COST PER UNIT OF OUTPUT AND RATIO OF HOURLY EARNINGS TO PRICES, 1933; 1929 BASE

Industrial Group	Link Labor costs per unit of sales	Link Materials cost per unit of sales	Link Ratio of A.H.E. to Prices
	HW/OP	QP_m/OP	(W/P)
Tobacco manufactures	68.7	82.4	71.9
Clay products	81.4	111.4	85.8
Ice manufactured	81.5	102.6	105.6
Rayon	82.1	125.8	181.0
Cement	91.4	87.4	106.0
Beet sugar	92.7	91.6	120.2
Lumber	96.3	106.8	105.9
Chemicals	96.9	94.4	119.5
Pulp	98.5	87.6	121.5
Ice cream	99.0	88.2	108.5
Paper	99.7	98.2	115.2
Fertilizers	99.8	105.8	115.0
Independent planing mills	100.0	102.2	104.1
Canning and preserving, fish	101.2	98.3	135.2
Canning and preserving, fruits	103.0	99.1	148.0
Cane sugar	103.0	96.6	123.6
Confectionery	108.5	98.5	147.0
Iron and steel, steel works, etc.	110.0	106.9	109.7
Paints and varnishes	110.8	90.0	112.5
Rubber tires and tubes	110.9	83.5	155.1
Boots and shoes	111.7	97.0	126.2
Knit goods	113.1	94.0	176.9
Smelting and refining, not from ore	115.0	96.9	153.4
Coke	117.0	110.0	84.7
Motor vehicles	117.5	88.9	109.6
Cotton goods	118.0	94.0	132.6
Bread and bakery products	119.0	96.2	113.2
Flour and grain mill products	124.0	93.1	132.7
Petroleum refining	131.0	103.1	172.8
Smelting and refining, nonferrous metals	135.0	94.4	143.0
Leather	139.8	83.1	154.9
Nonferrous metal alloys and products	142.2	81.3	146.7
Agricultural implements	151.5	95.6	97.9
Meat packing	156.0	93.2	183.7

some of them as summarized in equation 2. Furthermore, certain common patterns for recent years were noted earlier in this section.

Additional observations are evident from the preceding tables. (a) Extreme contractions of output are likely to result in increased H/O that are not offset by technical change in contraction. Instances in which high levels of output force increases in H/O that are not offset by technical change were not noted in the yearly data. (*b*) Labor participation in sales increased most in depression in those industries which fall into one of the following categories: (1) Output declined so much that H/O increased sharply owing to the technical conditions of production reflected in the shape of the cost function. Agricultural implements is clearly an example. (2) Conditions of competition in the product market are of such a nature as to force a reduction in product prices of a considerable magnitude. Bread and bakery products seem to be an illustration of this case. (3) Conditions of competition in the materials markets may force such a tremendous reduction in materials prices and costs that product prices fall, increasing the participation of labor in sales. The meat-packing and leather industries would seem to fit this description. A careful study of the data behind Table XVI implies that this third channel through which labor's participation typically increases may be quantitatively the most important. The influence of allied factor markets on wage rates can only be appreciated in the framework of market clusters. (*c*) Those instances in which labor's participation in sales decline in the depression are of two general types. (1) Technical change and substitution may. so reduce H/O that participation rates fall. (2) Very strong adverse pressure on the wage structure may lead to reductions that are more than proportional to product prices. The weakest in the system of related markets may be the labor market. Again participation rates would fall. Rayon and beet sugar are clearly illustrations of the first mechanism, while clay products has been shown to fit the second. These several channels of impact may, of course, be operative at the same time.

4. *Some Implications for Wage Policy*

A great deal of popular and technical discussion has ranged over the issue of the extent to which the high volume of unemployment in the thirties is to be attributed to unduly high wage structures. Most students seem agreed that wage levels in some sectors, such as construction, along with certain materials prices, may have proved serious bars to expansion. But the more fundamental issue concerns the whole wage structure. Some have contended that all one need do is look at the rapid rate of increase in wage levels in the thirties to know that they were "too high." [14] In a similar vein, the analogy of the grocer's shelf has been insisted upon. "General unemployment appears when asking too much is a general phenomenon." [15] Inspired by Hansen and Keynes, the opposing position can be taken that the level of investment was not sufficient to maintain employment, and more importantly, net investment tends to move in waves, within wide limits rather independent of the wage structure. The prospects of net investment hinge largely on the capital requirement character of technical change, defined in broadest terms. Now, these issues are not the direct and primary concern of this study. But the findings of the last section do have relevance to these problems that may be briefly indicated.

At first impression it would seem that wage levels could hardly be said to be too high in the mid-thirties if the labor participation in sales was no higher than in the twenties. Data for particular industrial groups, as well as for manufacturing as an aggregate, constitute the findings of fact. If no larger share on the whole of the receipts of enterprises went to labor, the offhand conclusion would appear that labor's price could not be primarily responsible for the differences in the volume of unemployment. But the matter is not quite so simple. (a) Both the level and composition of output were so different in the two periods (say, 1927–1929 and 1935–1937) that it could be argued that comparable levels of production relative to capacity in the thirties would have yielded higher participation rates in sales. The logical possibility must be recognized, but there is little evidence to support the view that high levels of manufacturing output—except under the pressure of wartime—have characteristically been produced under conditions of markedly increased marginal costs. It seems highly doubtful if considerably higher levels of output in the thirties would have resulted in much higher real labor inputs per unit of output. [16] (b) Wage rates may have been so high in the

---

[14] Average hourly earnings according to National Industrial Conference Board series in 1939 were 22 per cent higher than in 1929 and 47 per cent higher than in 1933.

[15] Edwin Cannan, "The Demand for Labor," *Economic Journal*, 1932, XLII, p. 367.

[16] Reference is made to the expanding literature on the shape of the cost function. See in particular Joel Dean, *The Relation of Cost to Output for a Leather Belt Shop*, National Bureau of Economic Research, Inc., New York, 1941. See also the critical appraisal of these studies, Hans Staehle, "Statistical Cost Functions: Appraisal of Recent Contributions," *American Economic Review*, June, 1942, XXXII, pp. 321–333.

thirties that substitution of other factors for labor decreased employment so much that the participation in sales remained unchanged. There can be little doubt that this factor was operative in the period in many guises. Raw materials as well as fixed capital may be substituted for labor services. But few have contended that the differences in unemployment in the periods can be attributed in any important degree to substitution that would have been avoided had wage levels remained unchanged relative to the prices of these other factors. (c) Returns to labor may be in other forms than those indicated by the statistics of wages and salaries. Thus increases in taxes to be used in governmental programs of relief, social insurance, and public works may have constituted an important bar to expanded employment. Real return to labor in these forms might constitute a modification of the statistical evidence. The relative importance of this magnitude is not readily measurable. (d) It can be alleged that the expectations in the thirties of wage rates of the future were the important bar to expansion in employment. Even though labor's participation in sales was unchanged, the fear that all profits might be taken away by future trade-union action may have constituted the important deterrent. In a period of profound social unrest like 1935–1937, this factor may have been of some importance, even though the fear probably represents a misunderstanding of the character of American trade unions.

There are no doubt other objections that can be raised with the contention that since the share in sales going to labor was unchanged, the general level of wage rates could not have been primarily responsible for unemployment. But the preceding points have seemed the most cogent. How far these considerations modify the crude inference is clearly a matter of judgment. Those who have pressed the view that the wage level contributed importantly to unemployment in the thirties have not chosen to examine the evidence here under review. There can be little doubt that the preceding findings on balance make their task considerably more difficult.[17]

[17] A further implication of the preceding analysis is a criticism of numerous recent studies of labor productivity and labor costs. They have failed to recognize that the labor bargain must be placed in the context of a cluster of related product and factor markets. The mere comparison of H/O, or even HW/O, with wage rates neglects the total view.

CHAPTER X. THE PRICE MECHANISM AND COLLECTIVE BARGAINING

The growth of trade unions to a position of real importance in the American labor market and the widening area of governmental decisions directly affecting the pricing process—not to mention more familiar changes in business enterprises [1]—compel a review of the functioning of the price mechanism. It was the genius of Adam Smith to see so lucidly the fact of spontaneous exchange in the absence of "any human wisdom, which foresees and intends that general opulence."

But shall this pricing process be continued fundamentally as semiautomatic, disassociated from centralized public directive and human wisdom that foresees and intends the general opulence? That is, shall the results as to the distribution of earned income, the volume of output each year, the allocation of particular goods, and the kind of commodities and services produced be accepted without serious alterations? Such phraseology is not intended to formulate issues for useful theoretical discussion or for political debate. But attention is focused on the cluster of issues that seems to loom pivotal to the next several generations. The war experience cannot but suggest that since the uncontrolled price mechanism is admittedly inadequate for military objectives, the automatic operation in peace may likewise be open to serious re-examination.

There are at least four versions of the price mechanism: (1) the formalized construction of value and distribution portrayed in strict economic theory, (2) the admonitions for public policy from treatise or pamphlet, (3) the institutional forms through which pricing decisions are formulated, (4) and the actual course

---

[1] For example, A. A. Berle and Gardner C. Means, *The Modern Corporation and Private Property*, The Macmillan Company, New York, 1933; Ruth P. Mack, *The Flow of Business Funds and Consumer Purchasing Power*, Columbia University Press, New York, 1941, and the hearings, monographs and reports of the Temporary National Economic Committee.

of price and output fluctuations as reported in statistically convenient pigeonholes. The linguistic trap of shifting unwittingly from one meaning to another is certain to catch the unwary. The first two perspectives are alike the creation of men's minds and sentiments; neither analytical models nor exhortations to governments constitute the pricing process. Both of these groups of ideas have changed over time as have the market institutions and the resultant prices and outputs.[2] The relations among these four meanings of price mechanism in the process of their mutual change is a field that awaits a classic.[3] There can be little question, however, that exceedingly rapid changes have been taking place on all four levels; in fact, they constitute one phase of the twentieth-century revolution.

Economic theory has been buzzing with fundamental issues of the operation of the price mechanism. Central to the whole discussion evoked by the *General Theory* has been the issue of the ability of market institutions to achieve and to maintain full employment. Mr. Keynes has divorced equilibrium and full utilization of resources. Individuals may make decisions and maintain positions that are internally inconsistent with full employment. In particular, the disposition of income between consumption and savings may be incompatible with full employment in the light of the allocation the same group of individuals and organizations make of their assets among cash, securities, consumer goods, and capital goods. While such inconsistencies cannot be denied, judgments differ as to whether the incompatible propensities arise from the policies of pricing institutions (rigid wages and prices which decrease the attractiveness of durable assets), from short-run time horizons (an inordinate desire to hold cash), or from more fundamental characteristics of the system. Furthermore, judgments will differ as to the length of time, if ever, that the pricing mechanism will take to alter the decisions that are incompatible with full employment.[4]

[2] There have also been changes in the proportion of goods and services produced that flow through the market mechanism.

[3] Among the most stimulating investigations must be mentioned: Elie Halévy, *The Growth of Philosophical Radicalism*, translated by Mary Morris, Faber and Gwyn, Ltd., London, 1928.

[4] Recent analytical discussion has also examined the path of variation in output in a single market that arises from a lag in the adjustment of supply and demand (the cobweb problem).

Even more intense debates have featured the public policy version of the price mechanism. The last three-quarters of the nineteenth century for western Europe (and the first quarter of the twentieth for the United States) are designated with increasing frequency *the interlude of laissez faire*. The interlude of the *idea* of laissez faire is even more appropriate. The triumph of the ideas of reliance upon automatic market forces applied to international markets, domestic commodity, capital, and labor markets alike. In fact, the rationale for self-operation in any single market was contingent upon the interdependence of the total price mechanism.[5] The recent accelerated governmental participation in pricing is illustrated by minimum wage laws, policies designed to affect the prices of agricultural products, electric-power rates, and interest charges to certain types of borrowers. War brings rationing and direct price-fixing. These changes in institutions have been associated with significant shifts in the ideas of appropriate public policy vis-à-vis the automatic price mechanism.

But changes have not alone taken place in governmental institutions affecting pricing. Sources and channels of information relevant to decisions have expanded; decisions have become institutionalized in departments within larger enterprises rather than being the fiat of a single individual.[6] Codes of standard practices have developed in many sectors of the system; nonprice competition has received increased attention, and the professional manager has assumed greater importance. These considerations have undoubtedly altered the bargaining power of enterprises in product and factor markets. In this context the emergence of the trade union is of the first importance. Institutional changes of these types are illustrative of innovations in that version of the pricing mechanism that is conceived in terms of specific agencies.

This final chapter is intended to place the broad problems of wage control by governmental agency or collective bargaining in the context of wide and general alterations in all four versions of the pricing mechanism. Consideration will be given in succes-

[5] Lionel Robbins, *Economic Planning and International Order*, Macmillan & Company, Ltd., London, 1937, pp. 13–96.

[6] Temporary National Economic Committee, *Industrial Wage Rates, Labor Costs and Price Policies*, Government Printing Office, Washington, 1940, Monograph No. 5, pp. 80–85.

sive sections to: (1) the function and purposes of wage rates and wage income under automatic pricing, (2) the reliance upon this pricing system to fulfill these functions in peace and war, and (3) the impact of collective bargaining institutions upon the mechanism.

1. Wages and the "Automatic Mechanism"

The structure of wage rates is a crucial cluster of prices in the operation of the market mechanism. Even the common-sense observer readily sees that the level of wage rates in money terms will significantly influence the level of money prices. Mr. Keynes' choice of the "wage unit" as a *numeraire* is an interesting example of this same truth, although the relation he posits between changes in money wage rates and prices is undoubtedly an oversimplification for many problems. The role of wage rates in pricing is best viewed in the perspective of a threefold impact on the automatic mechanism.

(a) Both the level of money (real) wage rates and differentials in the structure have powerful impacts on the total *supply of labor* available and the relative amounts of labor effort as among types of operations (occupations), regions, and enterprises. (b) The wage-rate structure is an important determinant of *costs* in enterprises. The types of goods produced, the methods of production, locations, the determination of successful firms, and the relative employment of the various productive factors are significantly influenced. In more indirect ways the total level of output will also be affected. (c) A final category of impacts is that on the magnitude of the *income stream* going to wage earners and appearing, in part, on the market as consumers' effective demand. Wage income and expenditure (by enterprises) is, of course, the product of both rates and employment. Clearly, the second and third of these factors indicate merely that the wage structure is one significant dimension that influences the income expenditure flow.[7] The price of labor thus performs at least three functions: calls forth labor services of specific qualities, provides the rate of command of wage earners over goods and services, and constitutes a barrier for the use of labor in certain firms,

[7] See Chaps. VII to IX.

methods, and locations in order to release these services for alternative uses that prove more profitable to enterprises.[8]

The price mechanism as idea or institution can be appraised from at least two vantage points. Attention may be directed toward the technical or mechanical [9] operation of the system as a means of performing the functions designated under conditions of fixed or varying tastes, technology, and asset distribution. Appraisal can also be made of the operation of the system in terms of a system of values. That is, the mechanism as analytical model, institutions, or policies may be held to be technically inadequate in certain respects. Difficulties and defects arise in the course of operation; the theory of monopoly and monopolistic competition is an example of one type of difficulty. In contrast, the pricing process may also be charged with yielding results that are inconsistent with larger normative postulates. The argument of this section will now be directed toward examining technical difficulties in the operation of the labor-market mechanism.

Discussions of analytical models of market operations are apt to contend that technical or mechanical defects spring entirely from the absence of assumed conditions of mobility, homogeneity, divisibility, and perfect knowledge.[10] While such statements may be valid, they seem largely sterile if the argument proceeds no further. An attempt is made to identify problems in the labor market ordinarily shrouded in the term "frictions."

(a) Economic thinking about the labor market has always recognized that wage determination must refer to a specific quality of labor training and skill. A price is determined for each kind of service. Analysts have thought this a sufficient concession to the complexities of the labor market for they envisage a series of discrete occupations. But actually there are very fine gradations among operations in modern mass-production industry, and rigorous occupational lines are limited to a minority of tasks. While the market mechanism might be able to determine the rates for

[8] Austin Robinson, "The Problems of Wage-Policy in War Time," *Economic Journal,* December, 1939, XLIX, pp. 640–655.

[9] Frank H. Knight, "The Business Cycle, Interest, and Money: A Methodological Approach," *The Review of Economic Statistics,* May, 1941, XXIII, p. 53.

[10] See the stimulating article of Fritz Machlup, "Competition, Pliopoly and Profit," *Economica,* February, 1942, IX (New Series), pp. 1–23.

a limited number of key tasks, the thousands of different rates that may exist in even a single large establishment present serious doubts and difficulties to those who would put complete reliance in the market mechanism. Some operations are just too "thin" for a continuing and effective market; further, enterprises may exhibit a great variety of minor methods in the organization of a single operation. The emergence of job evaluation [11] and rate setting, particularly in the last decade, are testimony to the necessity for some means of interpolation between rates determined by the market.

This first difficulty with the pricing mechanism may be expressed in other terms. The market process is too rough a tool to make the distinctions that the enterprise and wage earners have found useful. The caprice of a foreman or supervisor is a mutually unsatisfactory means of settling differentials. Some rules of thumb must be devised, particularly when frequent style and engineering changes would otherwise create added opportunity for bickering and debate. The job-evaluation plans require a rigorous definition of the elements of a task. Certain job factors are then selected, such as training, intelligence, experience, responsibility, and physical application, and a system of weights assigns a relative importance to each factor. Then each job is appraised in terms of these job factors and a hierarchy of tasks results. Differentials in points can then be translated into dollars and cents as interpolations between market-determined rates. The economist must recognize that these schemes fulfill the important function of providing a definite, well-known, and relatively impersonal mechanism for settling differentials within rather wide ranges in an area where the pricing mechanism in any conceivable institutional form would prove utterly inadequate. The observation is important that administrative procedure within the enterprise has developed to fulfill functions the pricing mechanism could not perform.

(*b*) An area of particularly inadequate operation of the pricing system is suggested by a study of longshoremen, seamen, and other

[11] National Industrial Conference Board, *Job Evaluation: Formal Plans for Determining Basic Pay Differentials*, Studies in Personnel Policy No. 25, National Industrial Conference Board, Inc., New York, 1940.

casual labor markets. In the absence of rationalization through unions or governments, an inordinate supply of labor seems to be attached to these markets unless one thinks that wage earners in these markets prefer casual employment. The buyers of labor are not disposed to discourage the amount of services available, and the learned cliché, "immobility," can only be intellectually frustrating. More detailed explanation in economic terms is possible without being guilty of economic "imperialism" in the sense of claiming jurisdiction over all aspects of conduct. Other analytical models of this immobility in terms of social and even biological determinants are not precluded.

The analysis of the timing of adjustments to market changes presented in Chap. II can be applied here. There is probably little doubt that movement out of casual labor markets in the past would have yielded larger individual incomes eventually. But the negative impact effects are very serious because of the immediate loss of earnings, and the possible costs of movement and retraining are large. Variations from the earnings expected in the casual occupation can be graphically represented by Fig. 1 (Chap. II). An individual wage earner would be less likely to move the longer and deeper the impact effect. The shape and position of the (net) expectations curve will be clearly influenced by retraining and transfer costs, the presence and earnings of supplementary wage earners in the household, and present and future occupational life-expectancies. Most wage earners in casual occupations would seem to remain because the short-run impact losses of transfer cannot be borne. Technically, one might prefer to say the rate of discount within the household is prohibitive.

The market mechanism under these circumstances has failed to allocate labor services in a fashion that would yield the largest product over time. Trade unions entering a casual labor market are faced with the alternatives of maintaining the existing excess supply or reducing the number of wage earners. An organization interested in maximizing its dues collections will no doubt elect the first alternative, for the smaller the individual dues rate absolutely, the easier the collection in all probability. (The larger the number of members, the larger the collections with the same wage bill for the industry.) If the second alternative is adopted independently, or with the aid of government, the imperfection of the market mechanism will be reduced.[12] In addition, decasualization with the aid of the hiring hall has served the purpose of rectifying gross injustices in the individual distribution of available work. The casual labor case may be generalized so that large and prolonged impact effects of contemplated transfers anywhere may prevent the labor market from performing satisfactorily. Administrative decisions by unions or government may mitigate the ineffectiveness of the market apparatus by such measures as temporary exclusion of new entrants, payment of transportation costs, maintenance of unemployed,[13] and improved labor-market information.

(c) A technical difficulty with institutional labor markets emerges from the lags in reaction to changes in data. Instantaneous adjustments are not to be expected in any mechanism, Professor Knight is wont to remind us. In terms of Fig. 1, the preceding problem concerned the rate of net personal costs of mobility while the present emphasis is upon the length of time required for the impact effect to be completed. An increase in the demand for a particular kind of specialized labor, for example, may increase substantially the wage rates to levels that cannot be maintained after the training of additional workers. The rapid expansion of the full-fashioned hosiery industry in the twenties created such a short-run distortion in the knitters' rates. The decline in employment in the early thirties similarly was overcompensated in the skilled trades by what proved to be by 1936 an inordinate reduction in new entrants. Careful administrative decisions through collective bargaining could no doubt have materially reduced the magnitude of both distortions.

The demand for labor services has fluctuated typically in short periods over a much wider range than variations in the amount of labor offered for sale. Changes in product demand reflected in the labor market is the volatile factor. The price of labor does not typically adjust itself to each such variation in product demand.

---

[12] For a discussion of waterfront casual labor markets, see Boris Stern, *Cargo Handling and Longshore Labor Conditions*, Bureau of Labor Statistics Bulletin No. 550, Government Printing Office, Washington, 1932.

[13] It is ordinarily assumed that maintenance of the unemployed will reduce mobility.

While the presence of inventories and elastic supply curves of labor to the single enterprise may leap to the mind as explanations, more fundamental considerations emerge from the earlier chapters. Both buyers and sellers soon recognize that the price of labor is incapable of rapid and successful adjustments to every change in the orders received or products sold by the firm. To expect to change wage rates in textile machinery every time the rate of sale of suits altered would be to neglect important relations. Lags in adjustment arise because directions of change are not immediately and unequivocally evident, the parties differ in their willingness and capacity to bear short-run losses or forego temporary advantages, as well as a host of personal and so-called institutional factors. In the light of the very many adjustments that would be constantly required of an exactly compensating system and the cumulative uncertainties of the lags, the tendency for all parties in the labor market (organized or unorganized) to prefer rates that are definitely and assuredly settled, save for infrequent (longer run) changes, is not difficult to understand. Imagine the labor market in which price quotations changed each day for each type of labor; imagine the production manager greeted with a new set of quotations each morning. The labor market is not that delicate an instrument; it has adjusted slowly to more basic and long-run currents. The lags in the reactions to the shorter run changes are so large that automatic adjustments would be impossible. The apparatus may even prove too crude for smoothing adjustments of rather fundamental changes like the expansion of the full-fashioned hosiery industry.

(d) Another technical difficulty with the price mechanism, regarded as a set of institutions, arises from the tendency of corrective price movements to set in motion others that may be non-equilibrating. Consider, for example, a substantial increase in the demand for labor by one industry in a community. Wages may rise for the firms affected under the pressure from wage earners (organized or unorganized). Instead of attracting workmen from other establishments at the higher rates, the immediate result on many occasions will be to initiate demands for wage increases in the other industries, quite regardless of any substantial increase in product demand. "The other fellows are getting a raise; why shouldn't we?" is a very common reaction, union or no union. Since the parties to collective bargaining seldom exact the limit of short-run bargaining power, a union may well secure some increase. In this fashion, wage changes serving a useful function in one sector may spill over and dislocate others; in fact a substantial upward movement could be initiated if the "other" industries had some material control over product prices. In much the same way, a decrease in wage rates, entirely required in one sector, may initiate a downward spiral elsewhere. An earlier chapter (IX), examining wage patterns in the cycle, discovered the tendency for decreases to come first where they probably do the least good.

To explain these and similar difficulties with the price apparatus as "frictions" is formally permissible but beautifully irrelevant and even vicious. Truly, wage rates in a local industry might not be expected to increase at all with greater demand if any unemployment existed, and a slight increase in rates would attract the whole market supply. But if rates had been cut previously, an early consensus for restoration will often arise among both employers and workers with increasing activity. Seniority and other attachments to particular firms will be operative. The length of time the increase in demand may be expected to maintain itself will importantly influence the ability of a wage increase to attract workers from other establishments.[14] Since actual labor markets are difficult to envisage without these and other complicating factors, a single equilibrating movement in the labor market may result in other distortions. More direct interventions with collective bargaining may be able to transfer wage earners from one industry to another without wage distortions.

(e) The most serious charge that can be brought against the price mechanism is the inability to provide a continuously high level of employment. The possibility of mutually inconsistent decisions within the system resulting in less than full utilization of resources has been noted. The way the community divides income between consumption and savings may be inconsistent with full

---

[14] For a discussion of other considerations which influence wage earners' designation of a preferable job, see E. Wight Bakke, *The Unemployed Worker*, Yale University Press, New Haven, 1940, pp. 3–34.

employment and other decisions as to the distribution of assets among cash, securities, consumers' goods, and real capital. Whether these conflicts are regarded as short run, as persistent features of the pricing process, or as the result of "interferences" with an idealized mechanism is here of secondary moment. Few writers would seriously insist today that the price mechanism in any institutional form could bring about, or has ever brought about, sufficiently rapid adjustments to mitigate pronounced fluctuations in output and employment. The cumulative effects of the preceding four technical difficulties with the pricing mechanism make this certain.

A decrease in the investment demand for durable goods in one sector is not likely to be immediately and directly compensated for by the price mechanism. A boom built largely on housing, for instance, would require the emergence of other investment expenditures as housing declined. To argue that more housing alone would result if construction prices were adjusted is to overlook the cumulative downward impact of suitable wage and price adjustments in housing that would spread to other sectors. Furthermore, great difficulty would be encountered typically in securing the necessary downward price adjustments in prosperity to sustain the boom. The possibilities of fairly uniform levels of output under "automatic" pricing processes seem rather remote.[15]

2. *The Price Mechanism and Modern War*

The problems of the automatic pricing process that have just been elaborated are nowhere so clearly evidenced as against the backdrop of war. Modern wars are large-scale undertakings. The development of the technology of war widens the scope of economic mobilization. The transition from small weapons to highly complicated machines (First World War) is followed by the application of methods of mass production to the manufacture of these implements of war (Second World War). Total war, involving mobilization of all military and economic resources, often treated as a Nazi invention, is in reality warfare conducted on the

[15] All the technical difficulties with the pricing process are not exhausted by this discussion. See E. F. M. Durbin, "The Social Significance of the Theory of Value," *Economic Journal*, December, 1935, XLV, pp. 700–710.

level imposed by the modern military technique. Over-all planning and husbandry of resources becomes unavoidable in order to achieve the maximum military effort.

It is of particular interest to observe how rationality (choice of most effective means) in the management of social and economic affairs seems to break through only if necessitated by the utmost "irrational" motivations. The waste and mechanical defects in the national organization of the economy in peacetime are compatible with highly rationalized individual units. Just so "irrationality" in the international field (war) is based on the highest possible organization and rationalization of the national units. While planning and rational allocation of resources (to maximize welfare) meet passionate resistance in peacetime, regulation and governmental control are regarded as justified if necessitated by military considerations. The inference is suggested that the structure of the peacetime economy has fitted certain interests best and is defended by their spokesmen because it maximizes the benefits accruing to those interests. The opposition to planning in wartime is based less on the conviction that "rationalization" may be detrimental to successful prosecution of the war than on the fear that the measures adopted will become irreversible and make the return to peacetime forms of private-profit maximization impossible.

An automatic mechanism for allocating resources might be expected to be just the answer to the central transition problem of shifting men and equipment to conform to military purposes. But the pricing apparatus has been reduced to a minor role, if not almost completely abandoned, as a regulator in modern warfare. Some of the reasons for this displacement can be briefly surveyed, particularly as they pertain to the labor market. These mechanical difficulties have their counterpart in the last section.

(a) The imperative of speedy production precludes the *slower* process of bidding resources away from consumption. Only if "nonessential" production is shut off by fiat will military output be maximized, at least such is the inference of recent experience. The pricing system also involves the well-known dangers of cumulative dislocation. Even when the major transition has been made, minor adjustments, such as attracting more women into industry, increasing some output, and shifting the type of agricultural production, are more speedily and thoroughly accomplished within the general framework of administrative direction.

(b) The various segments of the market apparatus may be ill coordinated. The demand for increased labor services of a specified type in a local market may be alternatively impeded by lack of housing facilities, poor transportation arrangements, lack of training agencies, and low wage rates. There is no evidence that the market mechanism in a short period would fix upon the real difficulty. In fact, the simple answer of higher rates dictated by the mechanism may result only in higher rents to householders, transportation companies, or wage earners without very much increase in labor services. Administrative processes may be much more effective in locating the precise difficulty and eliminating many unnecessary changes.

(c) When the limits of short-run supply are approximated in a labor market, the pricing apparatus may lead to excessive movement that theoretically could approach a situation in which each wage earner continually shifted as enterprises bid against each other. It is no accident that modern war economies require a worker to show good cause before allowing a transfer to another enterprise. "A 'freezing' of essential workers in critical war industries to their present jobs was decided upon today by the War Manpower Commission to stop 'labor pirating.' " [16] Under boom conditions the price mechanism yields too much movement, while speeds of reaction were observed to be extremely slow in other situations.

(d) The same degree of rationalization achieved within firms may not exist throughout the system as a whole. Mr. Robertson's delightful analogy of a sea of buttermilk with floating lumps of butter to denote administrative units has already been noted. The relative areas of resource allocation covered by the market and by nonpricing controls are constantly undergoing some change. At any one time there are undoubtedly many changes in the division of function among firms, or among firms and the market, that can be made to the advantage of increased output. An ex-

[16] *The New York Times*, Thursday, May 28, 1942, XCI, p. 1.

ample is suggested by a recent news item: "After newspaper trucks in some of the smaller midwestern cities deliver their editions outside their respective 15-mile areas, they come back on return trips carrying farm produce and other goods they collect by pre-arrangement—and save a lot of gas and tires." The dovetailing of part-time or seasonal occupations, without any change in the relative preferences for leisure and income, provides an illustration from the labor market. A great many such areas of social waste are forced to the surface in wartime. Whether the market mechanism would ever bring about these rationalizations, given inertia and existing lines of firm demarcation, is dubious though debatable. There is little doubt that extending the area of butter may make for many over-all economies, just as reversing the process may yield similar results in other cases.

(e) The pricing mechanism in wartime is particularly vulnerable to the difficulty of achieving long-term commitments because of the uncertainties of the length of the war. The outlays in fixed plant by the enterprise or the costs of movement by the wage earner may be recouped only over a period. Large impact effects may keep resources out of wartime uses just as casual labor was observed to remain in overcrowded markets (section 1). A wage earner will be interested not only in costs of transportation, rents, temporary idleness, retraining costs, but also in his chances of getting an old job back again if he moves. Where seniority clauses exist in contracts, much can be done to facilitate transfer by continuing the relative seniority position if a worker takes a job in a war industry.

Aside from these mechanical difficulties with the pricing process, others involving value judgments are probably central to policy formation. One of these concerns the distribution of the reduced volume of consumers' goods. The automatic pricing mechanism might allocate many goods so that only a few individuals received a large share of the goods available. Although there is nothing unusual in unequal distributions, successful prosecution of a war requires that individuals most essential for the war receive at least certain minimum standards. Thus the pricing mechanism could result in all tires and scarcer foods going to those with highest incomes. Rationing is intended to replace the price apparatus as a method of distributing many commodities. Theoretically, the pricing process could be left unmolested and these equal rationings achieved by taxation. But to put goods of certain types into the hands of particular individuals without primary respect to their income could hardly be achieved by fiscal measures. Modern warfare boldly focuses attention on the distribution of real income; political and social judgments of the community under the impact of war require more equal distributions. In this respect, as in others, modern war serves as a magnifying glass, amplifying the blemishes and difficulties of the automatic price mechanism.

3. *Pricing under Collective Bargaining*

Since trade unions have grown to a position of first-rank importance, the automatic mechanism in any institutional form in the labor market must be relegated to history. Not that every wage earner is organized today. But ten to twelve million workers under contract cannot but make vast differences in the operation of the labor market as compared to two or three millions organized in the late twenties, particularly when this number now includes the bulk of the strategic heavy industries. Neither let it be said that the pricing apparatus is abolished in the labor market; services are bought and sold at a bargained rate structure within the framework of associations of wage earners and employers.

An over-all picture of the trade union must be kept in mind if its operation in the labor market is to be understood. The model of an organization maximizing the wage bill of its members (Chap. III) is only a convenient abstraction to parallel the rigorous partiality of all economic theory. A trade union is at once a social system and a part of a larger one. As a social system it is amenable to careful study from the perspective of all disciplines concerned with human behavior. The marshaling of the diverse techniques and insights on the single subject of the trade union would no doubt yield substantial results. The trade union constitutes, at least, a system of industrial jurisprudence, a means of political action in the sense of affecting power relations within the community, an avenue of social mobility, a focus for personal loyalties and emotions, as well as a mechanism for pricing labor services. For even an understanding of pricing, abstraction from these other features of a trade union can only be a first step. Not only do the market and the political process represent alternative means of affecting prices—and the market conditions which in turn must influence the price of labor services, but the bargaining process may overlap jurisprudence and wage structure. An earlier chapter (III) elaborated the possibilities of substitution between the nonpecuniary and the wage-structure terms of a contract.

Perhaps the most important conclusion that emerges from a comparison of the "automatic" and the "administered" labor market is that collective bargaining is a much more powerful and effective tool, much more potent for good or for evil. Many of the limitations and difficulties with the automatic apparatus can be mitigated, although a new order of problems admittedly arises. Resources may be reallocated more rapidly, information is rapidly diffused, more resources are devoted to a study of the effects of contemplated actions, changes can be made more regular and less erratic, radical short-run distortions in rates can be largely eliminated, and the resources to be transferred more specially and delicately treated. The longer run implications of all actions in the labor market can receive more careful attention and weight. In these terms, collective bargaining can be a more powerful and precise instrument for allocating resources in the labor market. Comparison is not being made between models of the automatic mechanism and actual collective-bargaining institutions, rather are the corresponding levels paired.

If the administrative tool can be more powerful and effective, the issue then arises whether collective bargaining has been, or is likely to be, used to achieve a distribution and utilization of resources that yields a relatively higher level of national dividend over time. Any categorical resolution of the problem is presumptive on the evidence yet available. There has been little experience with mature trade unions as stable organizations with widespread influence. A more useful conclusion would be an examination of some of the more central problems whose resolution will largely condition the future efficacy of collective bargaining as an instrument of resource allocation and income creation.

(a) The area of the bargaining unit is of pivotal importance for the results of collective bargaining. The larger the area of the system under consideration at the time wage decisions are formulated, in general, the more completely the total effects of proposed policies are likely to be seen. The narrower the union "splinter," the more inelastic the demand for labor will appear and the more likely a small group will be able to push up rates to the detriment of the total working force. The institutional structure of unions and bargaining units, therefore, is of first-rank economic significance.

The attitude engendered by a narrow unit is "we make the wage demand; the problem of raising the funds is up to the company." Larger units compel the union or unions to become intimately familiar with the technology of the industry, competitive conditions in product markets, the capital structure of the enterprises, and other management problems in formulating and rationalizing wage demands. But large units are not without difficulties; the position of minority unions, the dangers of industrial gerrymandering, issues of differentials among firms and wage earners, and the dangers of joint action of unions and enterprises against the rest of the community are problems of the first importance. On balance, the judgment of this study must be that larger units will result in wage policies that are conducive to larger outputs and better allocations.

(b) The way in which collective bargaining works will be significantly affected by the degree and character of organization among enterprises. Just as a weak spot in the labor market may spread, so a single employer may force a series of increases. The recent instance of the "Weir cycle" is a case in point. It is virtually certain that a considerably smaller increase than 10 cents would have carried through manufacturing industries in 1941 had not Mr. Weir for strategic reasons of his own granted 10 cents. As trade unions grow in strength and bargaining power, the future of collective bargaining as a means of maintaining a high level of utilization and distribution of resources must depend considerably on organized employers. Their policies in this field will significantly condition the size of profits and consequently investment expenditures; the relative shares in increased productivity as between the consuming public and the particular wage earners will be related to employer collective action.

(c) A crucial area of the operation of collective bargaining is in expanding industries. Increasing demands for a product may be translated into increased demand for employment or into increased wage rates for the existing work force. Wage rates in other industries and the possibilities of employer organization naturally set some limits to the possible curtailment of employment. None the less, it is important that the spearheads of expansion be not dissipated to any marked degree by the peculiar position of a narrow union. The problem that is raised is particularly acute since unions in expanding areas are apt to be without considerable experience and in the midst of organizing drives in which wage increases may yield large dividends.

(d) The kind of participation and interest trade unions take in the product markets most closely influencing their wage rates is central to the future of collective bargaining. "Mad syndicalism" is not an impossibility with employers and unions combining to raise product prices and wage rates in turn. Such combinations would be particularly apt to press for tariff arrangements which would reduce foreign competition. Knowledge of product markets, and probably certain types of policies under monopsonistic conditions, is required of a trade union for fruitful (socially) collective bargaining. But the dangers of combination against weaker markets cannot be entirely ignored.

(e) The position taken by trade unions on the role of government in the pricing process is an issue whose resolution will be crucial for the future of collective bargaining. General governmental wage and price determination in the absence of a labor government is probably certain to be opposed by trade unions. Even small increases in wage-setting activity by government run the danger of detracting from the prestige and strength of trade unions. The resort to governmental agencies for pricing by a trade union (legalizing of collective agreements, minimum wage rates, rates on government contracts) is likely to represent only small tactical moves. Trade unions are likely to find agencies to fix product prices just as useful as direct wage action, with the added advantage of leaving the union prestige unchallenged.

These measures may prove particularly powerful for a union when they prescribe prices in terms of costs, including union wage rates.

The automatic pricing mechanism as *model* or *institution* in the labor market is dead. Whether this more powerful pricing tool leads to a better allocation of resources and a higher degree of utilization over time or results in the disaster of more restrictive monopolies depends in large measure upon how the preceding problems are handled. The economic future of the country will in no small way depend upon the kind of collective bargaining that emerges. These problems are of such importance as to command continuous and careful study for the next generation.

INDEX

American Federation of Labor, 37, 48, 51, 52, 53, 103
Andrews, J. B., 75
Anti-trust, 107, 115–116
Average Hourly Earnings,
 Contrasted with Wage Rates, 19–26, 118
 Influence of Employment Shifts, 21
 Influence of Overtime, 21–22, 25–26
 Straight Time Hourly Earnings, 25

Bakke, E. Wight, 45, 58, 219
Barbers, 110
Bargaining Power, 74–94, 116, 145–146
 Defined and Measured, 76–82
 Pure, 77
Barkin, Solomon, 110
Berle, A. A., 210
Bissell, Richard M., Jr., 116
Blum, Solomon, 75–76
Bowden, Witt, 21
Bowley, A. L., 23
Brewery Workers, 101
Bricklayers, 107

Cannan, Edwin, 208
Carpenters, 102
Chamberlin, E. H., 16
Cigar Makers, 102, 113
Clothing Workers, 72
Cluster Analysis, 7, 75, 94, 95–97, 116, 145–146
Collective Bargaining,
 Future of Collective Bargaining, 7, 224–228
 Locus of Bargaining, 194–198
Commons, John R., 51, 75
Congress of Industrial Organizations, 53–54, 149
Consumption Function, 189–190

Daugherty, Carroll R., 75–76
Dean, Joel, 208
Dickson, William J., 30
Dunlop, John T., 51, 54, 126, 140
Durbin, E. F. M., 220

Edgeworth, F. Y., 80
Electrical Workers, 107

Fabricant, Solomon, 176, 199
Feldman, H., 66
Fisher, Waldo E., 23
Frey, John P., 52

Garment Workers, 98
Gilbert, Milton, 157–158, 160, 165
Glass Bottle Blowers, 48–49, 97, 101
Golden, Clinton S., 188
Gompers, Samuel, 51, 54
Gordon, Melvin Joy, 24
Gray, E. M., 25
Green, William, 53

Halevy, Elie, 211
Hall, W. Scott, 110
Hansen, Alvin H., 3, 151, 188, 193
Hart, Albert G., 14
Hat, Cap, and Millinery, 47, 99–100, 111
Hicks, John R., 28, 150
Higgins, Benjamin, 74, 83, 92
Hockman, Julius, 98
Hosiery, 47, 58, 64, 66, 72, 101, 103, 113
Humphrey, Don D., 30

Jewkes, John, 25

Kahn, R. F., 184
Kalecki, Michal, 151, 154, 174–180, 187
Keynes, J. M., 125, 151, 174, 211
Knight, Frank H., 28, 214
Kuznets, Simon, 151–162, 168, 174, 176

Labor Costs, 71–72, 131–132, 144–145, 186, 190, 191–209, 213
Labor Market,
 Distinctive Features, 11–12, 15, 74, 118
 Free and Automatic, 4, 213–220
 Speeds of Reaction, 68–70
 Technical Difficulties, 213–220
Labor's Share in Income, 149–191
 Cyclical Variation, 163–183
 Meaning, 151–163
 Theory, 183–191, 209
Lerner, A. P., 78–79
Lester, Richard A., 150–151

Machinists, 48, 65–67, 69
Machlup, Fritz, 8, 214
Mack, Ruth P., 210

229